Material Culture

Aspects of contemporary Australian craft and design

Robert Bell

■ national gallery of **australia**

First published in Australia in 2002
by the National Gallery of Australia,
Parkes Place, Canberra, ACT 2601
nga.gov.au

© National Gallery of Australia, 2002.
All rights reserved. No part of this publication may be
reproduced or transmitted in any form or by any means,
electronic or mechanical (including photocopying, recording
or any information storage and retrieval system), without
permission from the publisher.

Produced by the Publications Department,
National Gallery of Australia
Designer: Carla Da Silva Pastrello
Editor: Alistair McGhie
Photographers: Bruce Moore, Steve Nebauer
and Eleni Kypridis (unless noted otherwise)
Printed in Australia by National Capital Printing

Cataloguing-in-Publication data
Bell, Robert, 1946– .
Material culture : aspects of contemporary Australian craft
and design.

Bibliography.
ISBN 0 642 54118 3.

1. National Gallery of Australia - Exhibitions.
2.Handicraft - Australia - Exhibitions. 3. Design -
Australia - Exhibitions. I. National Gallery of Australia.
II. Title.

745.0994

Distributed in Australia by
Thames and Hudson
11 Central Boulevard Business Park
Port Melbourne, Victoria 3207

Distributed in the United Kingdom by
Thames and Hudson
181A High Holborn
London WC1V 7QX, UK

Distributed in the United States of America by
University of Washington Press
1326 Fifth Avenue, Ste 555
Seattle, WA 98101-2604

This catalogue accompanies the exhibition *Material Culture:
Aspects of contemporary Australian craft and design* at the
National Gallery of Australia, Canberra, from 9 February to
30 June 2002.

Front cover:
Klaus Moje *Fragments 1–2001* 2001
fused and ground mosaic glass
Photography by Klaus Moje

Acknowledgements

The exhibition, *Material Culture: Aspects of
contemporary Australian craft and design*, is
the first exhibition from the National Gallery
of Australia's Department of Decorative Arts
and Design, created in 2000. I would like to
thank the National Gallery Council and the
Director, Dr Brian Kennedy, for their support
for the Department and the acquisitions that
comprise this exhibition. I wish to thank the
artists for their enthusiasm for the project and
for welcoming me to their homes and studios
to discuss their work. I value the assistance of
their dealers and agents in the acquisition of
many of the works in the exhibition.

The exhibition and catalogue are the result of
careful and committed work by my
colleagues at the National Gallery of
Australia, particularly those in the
departments of Registration, Exhibition
Design, Installation, Conservation, Imaging
Resources and Public Programs. I thank them
for their collective enthusiasm and interest in
the documentation, preparation and
installation of the works for the exhibition
and the catalogue. In particular, I thank
Project Manager, Jude Savage, for her
assistance with the administration of the
exhibition; Objects Conservator, Benita
Johnson, and Senior Textile Conservator,
Debbie Ward and their teams for the
preparation of the works for display and
Exhibition Designer, Patrice Riboust and his
design team for the exhibition presentation.

In the preparation of the catalogue, I thank
Editor, Alistair McGhie and Graphic Designer,
Carla Da Silva Pastrello, for her sensitive
design of the publication. Finally, I thank
Assistant Director, Australian Art, Dr Anna
Gray, for her encouragement and
departmental support for the project and
Eugenie Keefer Bell for her personal support
during its development.

Robert Bell

Contents

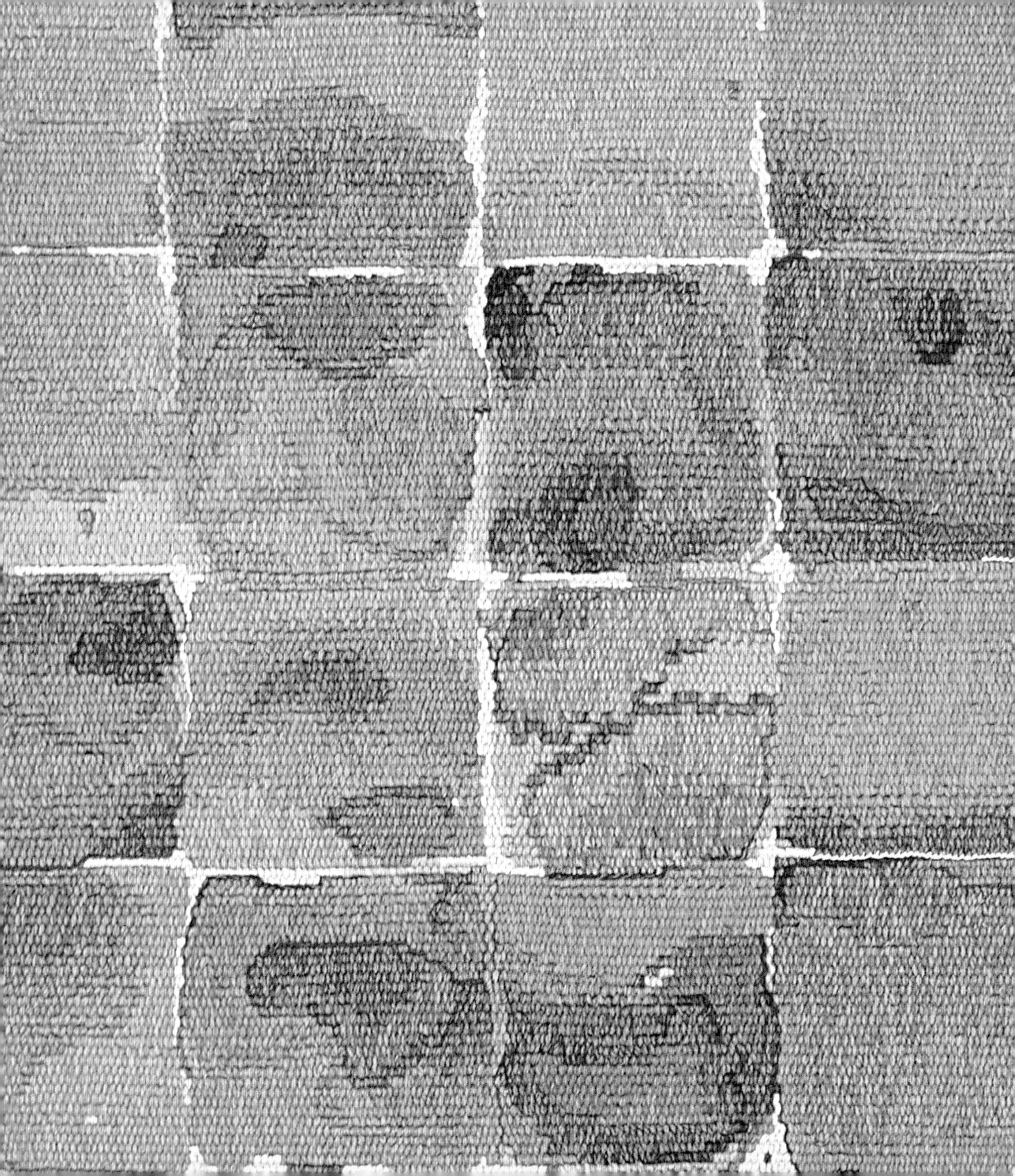

Foreword

The National Gallery of Australia has collected the best of Australian craft and design for several decades and, in recent years, in line with a review of all its collecting areas, a department of Decorative Arts and Design was established. The Gallery was delighted when Robert Bell accepted the post of curator. He is widely regarded as one of the most expert and experienced in his field. In the exhibition, *Material Culture: Aspects of contemporary Australian craft and design*, the Gallery presents many recent acquisitions. Together in an exhibition, they offer an excellent overview of the range and quality of contemporary Australian craft and design.

Material Culture focuses on recent works in ceramics, glass, textiles, furniture, jewellery and metal. It illustrates, through themes of structure, narrative and transformation, the ways that some of Australia's most highly regarded object designers and craft practitioners are expressing and giving meaning to our material culture.

We hope that the exhibition and this catalogue will challenge perceptions about the nature of objects and their place in the Australian cultural landscape. There can be no doubt that Australia has benefited hugely from the diversity of its practitioners and their broad range of backgrounds, many being immigrants to Australia from around the world.

The National Gallery of Australia is committed to the display of the best of the visual arts across all media. Our displays seek to integrate many different kinds of objects, and to link the best of Australian art with that of the wider world. I congratulate Robert Bell, and all involved, on an important and timely contribution celebrating contemporary Australian material culture.

Dr Brian Kennedy
Director, National Gallery of Australia

Introduction

Australian craft and design has been collected by the National Gallery of Australia since its establishment in 1973 and forms an important part of its historical and contemporary Australian art collection.[1] The earliest works in the Gallery's collection are from the period of first European settlement in Australia and illustrate how the European design styles of the late 18th century were interpreted through the learned or acquired skills of the settlers. The objects that they produced reflect their new environment and show their responses to the unfamiliar raw materials at their disposal. Standard techniques and working methods for European woods did not readily translate to Australian native timbers or achieve the same design results, and this led to regional variations on fashionable English and European styles, and eventually to a strong vernacular tradition.

Such adaptations continued to influence the design of Australian objects through the 19th century, culminating in the adoption of the principles and stylistic language of the Arts and Crafts Movement, a style that would serve the burgeoning nationalism of the Federation period of around 1900 to 1910.[2] Craft training, within the growing field of technical education, began to offer a more professional approach to the production of functional and decorative objects and advance the use of an Australian idiom in design. The 20th century saw various craft skills brought to edge of extinction through disuse or irrelevancy, while others, often debased, served as a foundation for rehabilitation and to educate several generations of students in the applied arts.

Material culture gathers from the planned as much as from the spontaneous, the banal as much as the enlightened, the local and the global. It can translate into poetry or dross, the mawkish or the transcendent and its progress is as much about timing as it is about technical or artistic achievement. The flowering of Australian studio crafts in the period from about 1965 to 1985 was not planned, but it progressed with committed and timely support from Government funding agencies and craft organisations.[3] It has left a unique material legacy of extraordinary innovation that remains undervalued, lightly assessed and somewhat in eclipse at the beginning of the 21st century, even though it has spawned a new generation of craft artists. It is possible to examine work of that period and gain insights into a material culture that reflected the Australian environment, yet acknowledged the achievements of overseas craft practitioners and designers as they too interpreted their own traditions in the spirit of modernism.

Today, a blind adherence to tradition is seldom part of the practice of an Australian craft artist or designer. The artists whose work engages us have not subsumed their values to those of another time or culture, but sought to give form to the realities of this time and place. However, searching for an identifiable Australian style in contemporary craft can be futile. What unites the works illustrated in this catalogue is a sure and confident sense of inquiry into the nature of materials, the observation of structure, the inherited and indigenous traditions of design and manufacture, the natural environment and the human body itself.

The objects in *Material Culture* demonstrate an easy physicality, a sense of lightness, a confidence, a precision and their makers' pleasure in controlling and manipulating materials. Each object is a theatre for experimentation and interaction where intuition, design and the mastery of skills are a cause for celebration. This is an art that communicates through the head, the heart and the hand.

In a world that seems to be increasingly volatile and unpredictable, crafts operate in an environment of control and discipline over materials and form. Their uniqueness contradicts globalisation and the corporatisation of the world of commodities.[4] Their makers eschew mass production and work to avoid compromises that can come from designing and building to cost, material availability and production schedules. The values implicit in a slower, more intuitive creative process are transmitted through the finished object; its complexities of surface, form and texture invite intimacy and the inquiring gaze. The shifting relationship of an object with light and its interaction with its surrounding space and environment is shown in the work of many contemporary makers, who are increasingly at ease collaborating with other professionals such as architects and interior designers.

Objects that are the result of a long process of design decisions, compromises on materials and manufacturing, marketing analysis and merchandising imperatives can often fail to engage us emotionally. Their appeal can appear as manufactured as their marketing strategies and the short-term thrill of fashion fails to sustain them beyond a season of coordinated marketing and promotion. Cutting across the mainstream can be misunderstood in an environment that encourages planning, five-year strategies, measurable outputs and outcomes. The handmade comes with a nervous uncertainty that allows it to transcend the merely fashionable, to posit a set of values that must be encountered, if not embraced before hidden subtleties can be contemplated.

The celebration of the local, the regional, the private and the personal, and the value of experience and memory, is territory that many contemporary designers and makers seek to articulate and make real. For them, the interpretation of the achievements of the past is both a technical and aesthetic challenge and a statement about the loss of values in mainstream culture.

The growing anxiety at the ease by which systems can be corrupted by such things as viruses or terrorism gives us cause to question the processes, the use of resources and the consequences of any form of production.[5] In designing and making objects, craft artists are perhaps more aware than others of the value of materials and labour. For example, jewellers have had to consider the politics of precious metal and gem production and distribution; textile and fashion designers, the implications of using cheap offshore labour and environmentally damaging production processes, and furniture designers, the depletion of indigenous timber resources. The natural environment of Australia has been a source of pleasure and compelling subject matter for artists for thousands of years. Indigenous craft practices used scarce animal and plant resources for the refined, minimal kit of tools necessary for survival as well as for expressing myriad regional cultures.

In a world that is simultaneously widened by globalism and narrowed by local and regional issues, the dilemma for craft artists and designers is finding supportive and appreciative audiences and clients. A growing number is increasingly defined by the images of their work on websites, in specialist design and craft journals as well as in the popular fashion and lifestyle press, yet they are still limited in their ability to deliver it in reality. We may be global in our reach, but the long distances between Australia's cities and overseas markets remain, presenting artists with the continual problems of the cost and logistics of freight and supply. The importance of collecting contemporary craft and developing knowledgeable audiences has been recognised nationally, regionally and locally through the acquisition and exhibition policies of public and institutional museums and art galleries.[6] The resulting collections reveal a rich and diverse interpretation of contemporary Australian material culture and the viability and relevance of craft practice as part of both visual art and design.

Works by 34 Australian craft artists and designers, recently acquired by the National Gallery of Australia, are included in this catalogue. They are grouped in this publication as they are in the exhibition, to illustrate themes of structure and material expression, narrative and history, and the transformation of materials and meaning. Collectively, they show aspects of the eloquence and diversity of contemporary Australian craft practice as it engages with the currents, issues and contradictions of urban life. Individually, each invites us into the world of makers as they articulate materials in the service of imagination.

Robert Bell
Senior Curator, Decorative Arts and Design,
National Gallery of Australia

1 See John McPhee, *Australian Decorative Arts in the Australian National Gallery*, Canberra: Australian National Gallery, 1982, p. 7.
2 See Robert Bell, 'Designing the Australian experience' in John McDonald, *Federation: Australian Art and Society 1901–2001*, Canberra: National Gallery of Australia, 2000, pp. 226–51.
3 See Grace Cochrane, *The Crafts Movement in Australia – A history*, Sydney: New South Wales University Press, 1992, pp. 113–18, pp. 248–54.
4 See Noris Ioannou, 'Old paradigms for new: designer makers' models and the dilemma of globalism versus regionalism' in Robert Crocker (ed.) *Designing Minds – Contemporary issues in craft, design and industry* (Proceedings of the Designing Minds Symposium), Adelaide: University of South Australia, 2000, pp. 23–28.
5 See Helmut Lueckenhausen and Valerie Austin, 'A new suit – craft in contemporary design and production' in Crocker, op cit, pp. 49–52.
6 For commentary on the development of collections of Australian craft and design in three Australian state art museums, see *Decorative Arts and Design From the Powerhouse Museum*, Sydney: Powerhouse Publishing, 1991; Robert Bell, 'Craft and design' in *State Art Collection – Art Gallery of Western Australia, Perth*: Art Gallery of Western Australia, 1997; Christopher Menz, *Australian Decorative Arts – 1820s–1990s: Art Gallery of South Australia*, Adelaide: Art Gallery of South Australia, 1996.

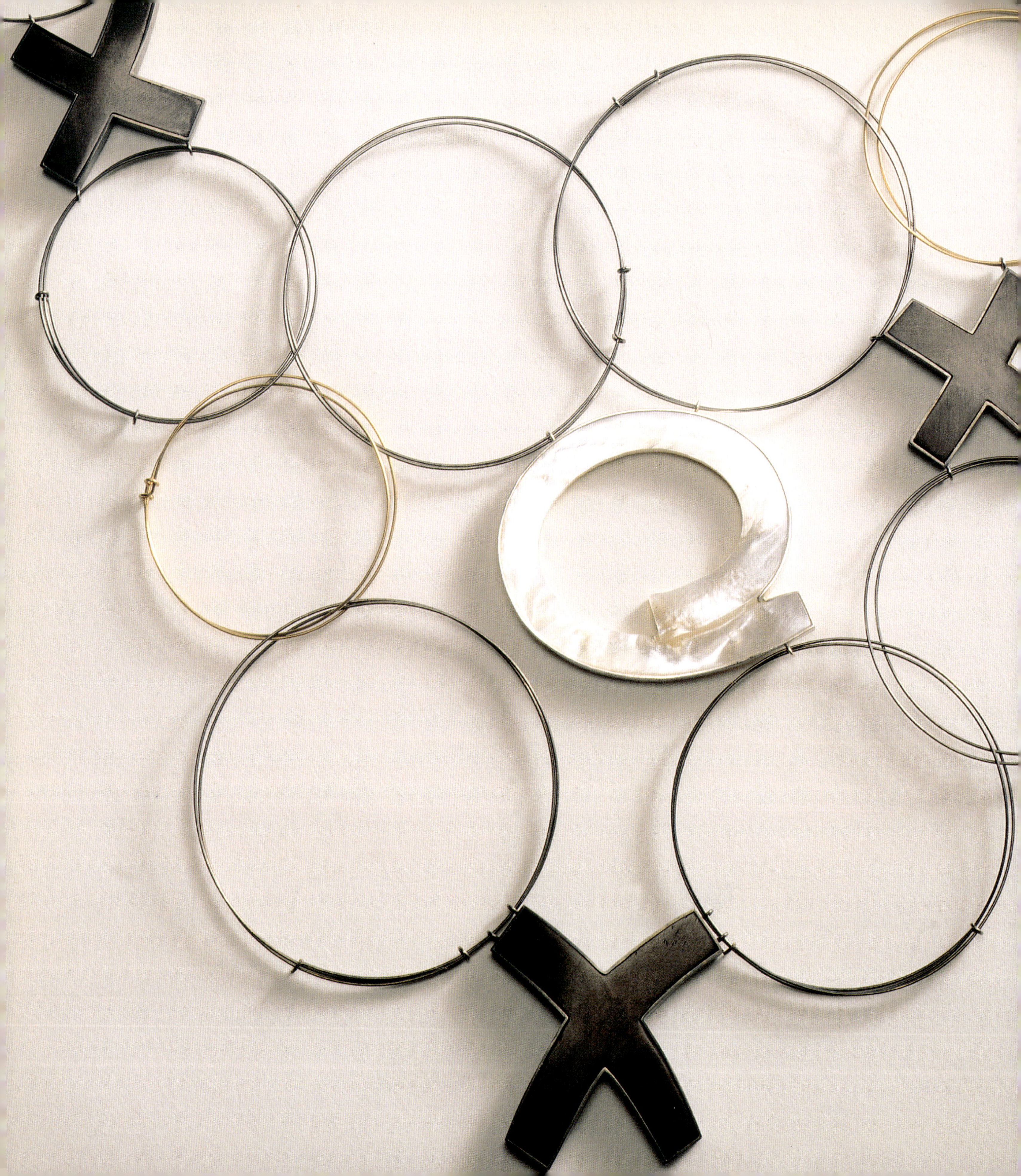

Structure

The doctrine of the Arts and Crafts Movement of the late 19th century focused on the revelation of structure and the natural qualities of materials as central to the design and decoration of objects. These tenets were incorporated into the early phases of Modernism and created an awareness of the expressive possibilities of functional design. We now have a world in which advanced materials and technologies reach into the most intimate spheres of our lives through a plethora of functional and decorative objects. The delivery systems of this technology have made us aware of the electronic structure that lies unseen within many objects and upon which we are increasingly dependent. The ubiquity of transparent and translucent materials in current design reflects our desire to see into objects, as if to verify the actuality of the systems in which we place so much trust.

The orchestration of the structure, and the performance and physical attributes of materials, lie at the centre of craft practice. The artists in this section are linked by an understanding of these qualities, allied with refined design and technical skills. Each displays technical bravura, in materials as diverse as titanium and wood or glass and wool, but moves beyond it to suggest that such materials hold for us a resonance of a world not quite within our grasp. In these works, neither structure nor material is subservient to function, rather they act as poetic interventions in the chaotic structure of contemporary urban life.

Robert **Baines** Frank **Bauer** Matthew **Curtis** Mark **Edgoose** Villiama **Grakalic** Johannes **Kuhnen** Sue **Lorraine** Klaus **Moje** Catherine **Truman** Jenny **Turner** Richard **Whiteley**

Robert **Baines**
Melbourne, Victoria
Born Melbourne, Victoria 1949

Training
Diploma of Art (Gold and Silversmithing), Royal Melbourne Institute of Technology, Melbourne, Vic., 1969.

Related professional experience
Lecturer in Goldsmithing at RMIT University, Melbourne, Vic., since 1980. Research on ancient goldsmithing techniques since 1979.

Selected solo exhibitions
Sculpture, Jewellery and Other Objects, Realities Gallery, Melbourne, Vic., 1977; *Sculpture to be Worn*, David Jones Art Gallery, Sydney, NSW, 1978; Bonython Galley, Adelaide, SA, 1979; *A Visible Likeness*, Robin Gibson Gallery, Sydney, NSW and Georges Gallery, Melbourne, Vic., 1981; *Antipodean Forms*, Bonython Gallery, Adelaide, SA, 1982; *Misteri Antipodei*, Via Veneto 50, Rome, Italy, 1982; *A Journey to the Plenitude*, Realities Gallery, Melbourne, Vic., 1985; *The Plenitude*, Bonython-Meadmore Gallery, Adelaide, SA, 1985; *Travel*, travelling exhibition to Victorian regional art galleries, 1988–89; *From the Plenitude*, City of Horsham Regional Art Gallery, Horsham, Vic., 1989; *The Plenitude*, Solander Gallery, Canberra, ACT, 1989; *The Waikato Pieces*, Waikato Museum for Art and History, Hamilton, Fluxus, Dunedin, and Fingers, Auckland, New Zealand, 1989; *Adventures of the Archegos*, Lauraine Diggins Fine Art, Melbourne, Vic., 1992; *The Art of the Goldsmith*, travelling exhibition in New Zealand, 1992–93; *Adornments form the Waikato and Beyond*, Lauraine Diggins Fine Art, Melbourne, Vic., 1993; *WORD Action Artifact: Worship*, Celebration Arts, St Johns, Melbourne, Vic., 1995; *Redline, Part 2 of AAA......REDEVENT*, Lauraine Diggins Fine Arts, Melbourne, Vic., 1996; *The Intervention of Red, Part 3 of AAA......REDEVENT*, Galerie Biró, Munich, Germany, 1997; *AAA,AA......REDEVENT: Survey*, Brisbane City Gallery, Brisbane, Qld, 1997; *REDEVENT: Bloodier than black*, Helen Drutt Gallery, Philadelphia, PA, USA, 2000; *Bloodier Than Black*, Galerie Biró, Munich, Germany, 2000.

Selected group exhibitions since 1992
Design Visions: Australian International Crafts Triennial, Art Gallery of Western Australia, Perth, WA, 1992; *Australian Modernism: The complexity and the diversity*, Lauraine Diggins Fine Art, Melbourne, Vic., 1992; *Directions: Glass jewellery 1993*, Canberra School of Art Gallery, Canberra, ACT, 1993; *The Changing Face of Melbourne 1841–1993*, Lauraine Diggins Fine Art, Melbourne, Vic., 1993; *Armed*, The Door Exhibition Space, Fremantle, WA, 1994; *25: Craft Victoria Artists*, Arts Victoria, Melbourne, Vic., 1995; *Australian Decorative Arts Survey 1995: The object all sublime*, Lauraine Diggins Fine Art, Melbourne, Vic., 1995; *VicHealth National Craft Award*, National Gallery of Victoria, Melbourne, Vic., 1995; *Granulation 1996: Internationaler Schmuckwettbewerb*, travelling in Germany 1996; *Collecting Today for Tomorrow*, Powerhouse Museum, Sydney, NSW, 1996; *In Praise of Make-Up*, Plimsoll Gallery, University of Tasmania, Hobart, Tas., 1997; *Contemporary Vessels and Jewels: Australian fine metalwork*, Shanghai Museum, Shanghai, China, 1997; *Cicely and Colin Rigg Craft Award*, National Gallery of Victoria, Melbourne, Vic., 1997; *Art of Gold*, Ballarat Fine Art Gallery, Ballarat, Vic., 1997; *Schmuck '98: Sonderschau der 50*, Internationaler Handwerksmesse, Munich, Germany, 1998; *Contemporary Jewellery: Value added*, National Gallery of Victoria, Melbourne, Vic., 1998; *The Deacons, Graham and James Arts 21 Award*, The Ian Potter Museum of Art, Melbourne, Vic., 1998; *Jewellery Moves*, National Museum of Scotland, Edinburgh, Scotland, 1998; *Brooching it Diplomatically; A tribute to Madeleine K. Albright*, Helen Drutt Gallery, Philadelphia, PA, USA, 1998, travelling in Europe 1998–99; *RMIT Fine Art*, Hong Kong Arts Centre, Wanchai, Hong Kong, 1998; *Seppelt Contemporary Art Award*, Museum of Contemporary Art, Sydney, NSW, 1999; *Skill*, Craft Victoria Gallery, Melbourne, Vic., 1999; *Contemporary Australian Craft*, Hokkaido Museum of Modern Art, Sapporo, Japan, 1999; *Water Medicine*, John Curtin Gallery, Curtin University, Perth, WA, 1999 and national tour 1999–2000; *Handmade: Shifting paradigms*, Singapore Art Museum, Singapore, 1999; *Trace*, Museum of Art Craft, Itami and Gallery Yu, Tokyo, Japan, 1999; *Imagining: Art of the twentieth century*, Art Gallery of Western Australia, Perth, WA, 1999; *Be Jewelled*, Monash University, Melbourne, 2000; *Commemorative Medals and Trophies: The politics of history*, Helen Drutt Gallery, Philadelphia, PA, USA, 2000; *Craft from Scratch: 8th Trienniale - Form and Matters - Australia and Germany*, Museum für Angewandte Kunst, Frankfurt, Germany, travelling exhibition, 2000; *Spectaculum*, Tarbekunstimuseumis, Tallinn, Estonia, 2000; *Hermanns Art Award*, Sherman Galleries, Sydney, NSW, 2001; *Micromegas*, Galerie für Angewande Kunst, Bayerischer Kunstgewerbe-Verein, Munich, Germany; *Nocturnos*, International Jewellery Colloquium, Estonia, 2001; *The Tactile Art Exhibition*, Object Galleries, Sydney, NSW, 2001.

Public collections (Australia)
Art Gallery of South Australia, Adelaide, SA; Art Gallery of Western Australia, Perth, WA; National Gallery of Australia, Canberra, ACT; National Gallery of Victoria, Melbourne, Vic.; Powerhouse Museum, Sydney, NSW; Queensland Art Gallery, Brisbane, Qld; RMIT University, Melbourne, Vic.; Victorian State Craft Collection, Melbourne, Vic.

Public collections (international)
Victoria and Albert Museum, London, UK; Waikato Polytechnic, Hamilton, New Zealand

Robert **Baines**
La Columbella tea and coffee set, titanium and sterling silver,

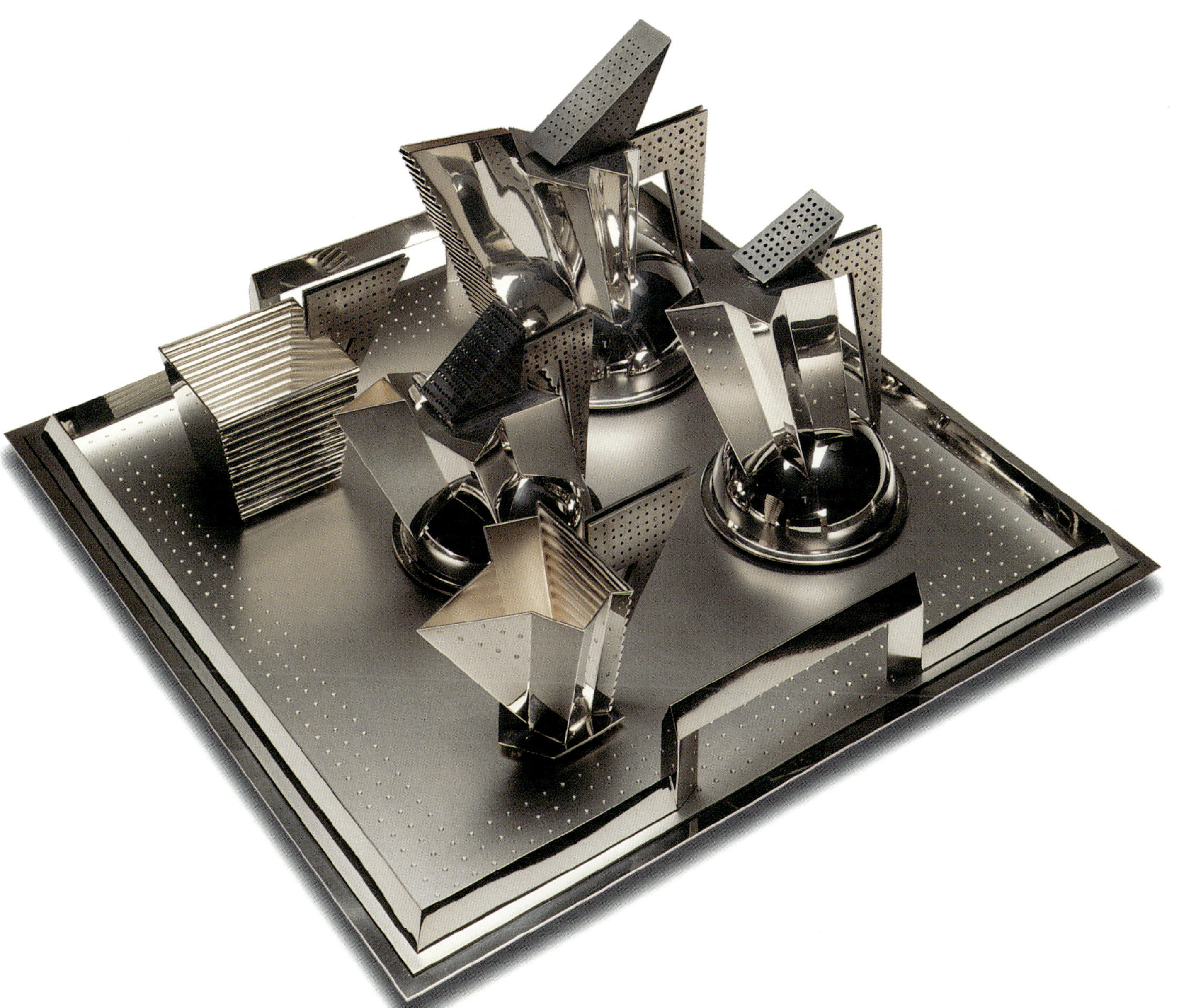

Robert **Baines**

Robert Baines is known for work in jewellery and for larger, complex hollow ware, which often combines precious materials such as gold with high-technology materials such as titanium. This set of vessels and a tray, in the format of the traditional tea and coffee service, uses function as a starting point for a complex assemblage of forms and interactions of material, light and volume. Its title, *La Columbella*, derives from the important Etruscan archaeological site of Columbella at Palestrina and refers to Baines' research into the techniques of ancient goldsmithing.[1] Its exaggerated, multi-angled forms and geometric contrasts also satirise the exuberant Italian interpretation of Post-Modernism in the 1980s. The qualities of each part of this set are enhanced through the complex polished and corrugated surfaces of the silver. The intricate series of fine drill holes on the black lids are an abstraction of the ancient goldsmithing technique of granulation, contrasting with the handles, made from the space age material of titanium, with their repetitive pattern of dots and thermally-treated multiple colouration.

1 Baines was awarded a Winston Churchill Fellowship in 1979 to study the metalwork of Greek and Etruscan goldsmiths. His most recent support for this research was in 1997, when he received a Senior Fulbright Award to conduct a research project on Etruscan goldworks at the Sherman Fairchild Center for Object Conservation in the Metropolitan Museum of Art, New York.

Frank **Bauer**
Adelaide, South Australia
Born Hannover, Germany 1942,
arrived Australia 1971

Training

Praktikum in architectural Drawing, Hannover, Germany, 1958; Music studies, Musik Konservatorium Hannover, 1959; Praktikum in blacksmithing and welding, Hannover, 1962; Apprenticeships in gold and silversmithing with Carl van Dornick and Reinhard Rischke, Hildesheim, Germany, 1962; Industrial design and architecture studies, Artschool Kassel, Kassel, Germany, 1967; Architecture studies, Hochschule für Bildende Künste, Hamburg, Germany, 1969.

Selected solo exhibitions

Bonython Gallery, Sydney, NSW, 1973; David Jones Art Gallery, Sydney, 1973; *Frank Bauer: Jewellery and Objects*, Jam Factory Gallery, Adelaide, SA, 1976; Bonython Gallery, Adelaide, SA, 1978; Studio Gallery, London, UK, 1979; Electrum Gallery, London, UK, 1980; Arnolfini Gallery, Bristol, UK, 1981 (with Elizabeth Holder); Orfevre Galerie, Düsseldorf, Germany, 1981 (with Helen Aitken); Spectrum Gallery, Munich, Germany, 1982; Gallery Marzee, Nijmegen, The Netherlands, 1983; Victoria and Albert Museum, London, UK, 1985; Galerie am Graben, Vienna, Austria, 1985; *Frank Bauer Design Collection*, BMG Fine Art, Adelaide, SA, 1990; Helen Drutt Gallery, Philadelphia, PA, USA, 1995; *Frank Bauer: Designer – jewellery, metalwork, lighting 1975–2000*, JamFactory Galleries, Adelaide, SA and Powerhouse Museum, Sydney, NSW, 2000.

Selected group exhibitions since 1980

Tendenzen, Schmuckmuseum, Pforzheim, Germany, 1982; *9 x London*, Handwerksform, Hannover, Germany, 1982; *The Maker's Eye*, Crafts Council Gallery, London, UK, 1982; *Jewellery Redefined*, British Craft Centre, London, UK, 1982; *Australian Jewellery*, Goldsmiths Hall, London, UK, 1982; *A Child's View*, Australian National Gallery, Canberra, ACT, 1988; *Australian Decorative Arts 1788–1988*, Australian National Gallery, Canberra, ACT, 1988; *Concept and Realisation in Hollow Ware*, Canberra School of Art Gallery, Canberra, ACT, 1988; *A Free Hand*, Powerhouse Museum, Sydney, NSW, 1988; *Contemporary Australian Hollow Ware*, Hamilton Art Gallery, Hamilton, Vic. and national and international tour, 1991–93; *Recent Acquisitions*, Art Gallery of South Australia, Adelaide, SA, 1992; *Celebrate*, Jam Factory Gallery, Adelaide, SA, 1994; *South Australia: Emerging crucible of contemporary design*, Jam Factory Gallery, Adelaide, SA, 1996; *SOFA*, Navy Pier, Chicago, IL, USA, 1996; *Spectacles: A Recent history*, Crafts Council, London, UK, 1997.

Public collections (Australia)

Art Gallery of South Australia, Adelaide, SA; Art Gallery of Western Australia, Perth, WA; National Gallery of Australia, Canberra, ACT; National Gallery of Victoria, Melbourne, Vic.; Powerhouse Museum, Sydney, NSW.

Public collections (international)

Bauhaus Archiv, Museum für Gestaltung, Berlin, Germany; Schmuckmuseum, Pforzheim, Germany; Stadtmuseum Munchen, Munich, Germany; Victoria and Albert Museum, London, UK.

Frank **Bauer**
Light sculpture
perforated, anodised aluminium;
21 x 12-volt Xenon lamps

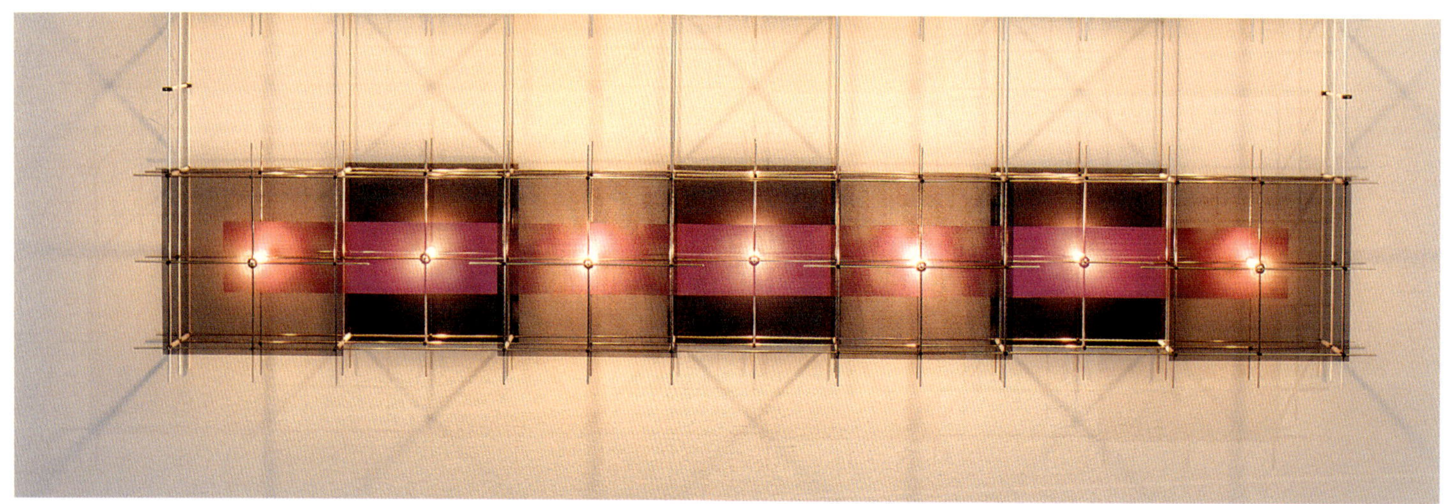

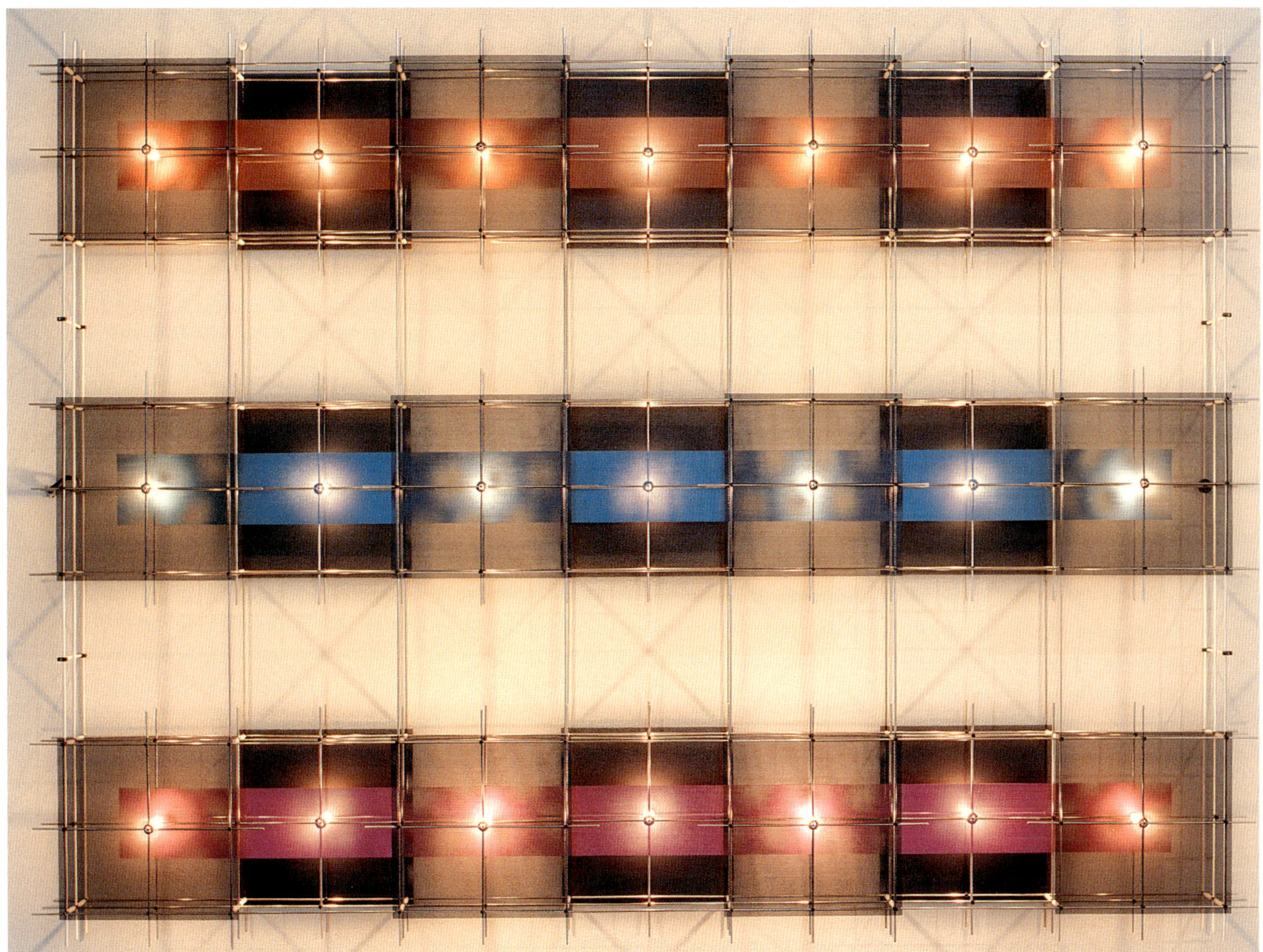

Frank **Bauer**

Frank Bauer works as a goldsmith, lighting designer and kinetic sculptor. He brings a contemporary expression to the aesthetic language of early Modernism that influenced his craft and design training in Germany.[1] The precise engineering and craftsmanship that characterises his geometric and reductive jewellery is reflected in a larger scale in this wall-mounted light sculpture. Using his patented system of small, low-voltage lamps as visual connectors through a complex and rhythmical structure of perforated anodised aluminium sheets, Bauer orchestrates reflected, coloured light in an abstraction of the technical systems of the contemporary built environment.

1 See Frank Bauer, 'Frank Bauer: Designer – Bauhaus inheritance' in *Frank Bauer: Designer – jewellery, metalwork, lighting, 1975–2000*, Adelaide: Frank Bauer, 2000, pp. 6–7.

13

Matthew **Curtis**
Sydney, New South Wales
Born Luton, Great Britain 1964,
arrived Australia 1981

Training
Assistant to Robert Wynne, Denizen Glass
Studio, Sydney, NSW, 1991–98;
Fellowship, Creative Glass Center of
America, Wheaton, NJ, USA, 1999.

Related professional experience
Hot glass tutor, Sydney College of the
Arts, Sydney, NSW, 1998–2000

Selected solo exhibitions
Explorations in Glass, Glass Artists' Gallery,
Sydney, NSW, 1997; *Symmetry x 2* (with
Richard Whiteley), Axia Modern Art,
Melbourne, Vic., 2001

Selected group exhibitions
Just One of a Kind, Glass Artists' Gallery,
Sydney, NSW, 1994; *Year of the Pig*,
Tanjana, Sydney, NSW, 1995; *RFC Glass
Prize*, Glass Artists' Gallery, Sydney, NSW,
1996; *Australian Glass*, Art Forum,
Singapore, 1997; *Past Tense, Future
Perfect*, Craftwest, Perth and The Moores
Building, Fremantle, WA and travelling in
Australia, 1999; *SOFA Chicago*, Chicago,
IL, USA (Glass Artists' Gallery), 1998; *SOFA
New York*, New York, USA (Glass Artists'
Gallery), 1998; *Translucence*, Quadrivium
Gallery, Sydney NSW, 1998; *Metallica*,
Glass Artists' Gallery, Sydney, NSW, 1999;
RFC Glass Prize, Volvo Gallery, Sydney,
NSW, 1999; *SOFA Chicago*, Chicago, IL,
USA (Glass Artists' Gallery), 1999;
3 Perspectives in Glass, Axia Modern Art,
Melbourne, Vic., 1999;

Quadrivium's Finest, Quadrivium Gallery,
Sydney, NSW, 2000; *RFC Glass Prize*,
Volvo Gallery, Sydney, NSW, 2000;
Transparent Things: Expressions in glass,
National Gallery of Australia Travelling
Exhibition, Wagga Wagga Regional Art
Gallery, Wagga Wagga, NSW, 2001.

Public collections
National Gallery of Australia, Canberra,
ACT.

Matthew **Curtis**
Constructed bowl (Ruby)
glass and stainless steel

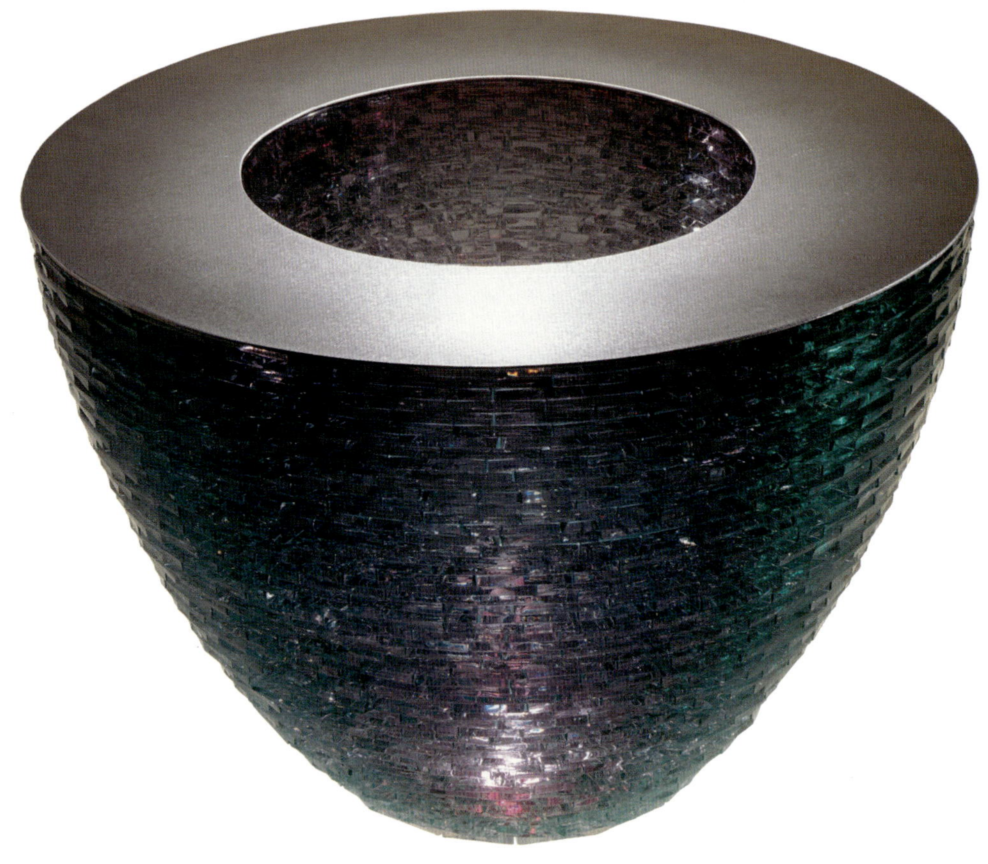

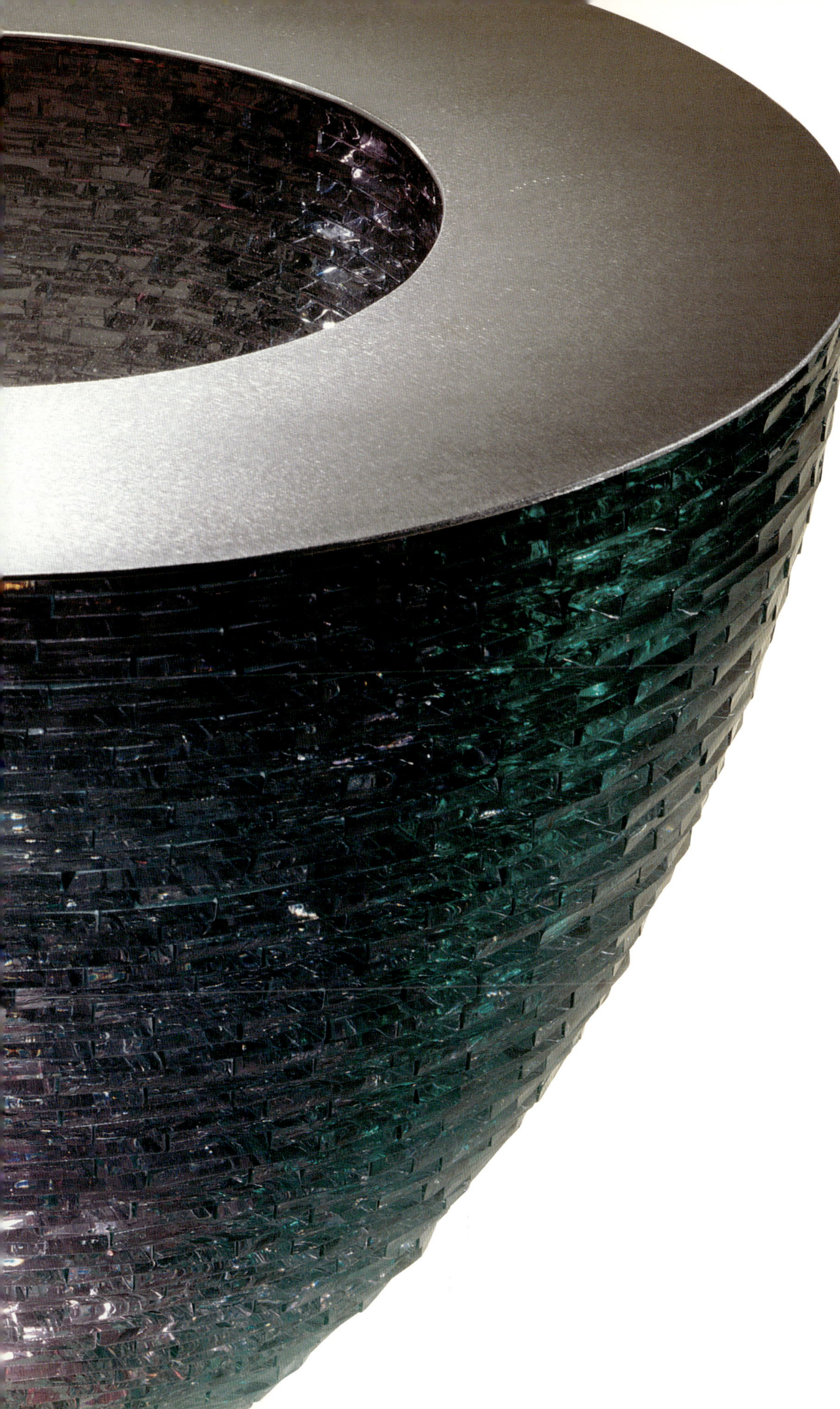

Matthew **Curtis**

Matthew Curtis usually works with the technique of cased glass, in which overlays of coloured glass are blown together then carved away to reveal contrasting layers. This interplay between the internal and external 'skins' of his blown vessels is suggested in this large bowl. Differing qualities and forms of glass are used to articulate the tension between the inner volume and outer form of the work. One thousand three hundred tiles of cut plate glass with ground edges have been constructed around an internal blown form of ruby-purple glass, with a stainless steel rim circling the top of the vase. This complex construction exploits the relationship between glass and light to give physical form to refracted colour.

Mark **Edgoose**

Sydney, New South Wales

Born Warragul, Victoria 1960

Training

Diploma and Post-Graduate Diploma in Gold and Silversmithing, Royal Melbourne Institute of Technology, Melbourne, Vic., 1984, 1988; Master of Arts, RMIT University, Melbourne, Vic., 1997.

Related professional experience

Coordinator Metal Studies, Peninsula School of Art, Monash University, Melbourne, Vic., 1990–97; Lecturer, Jewellery and Object Design (since 1998), Coordinator, Object Art and Design (1999–2000) and Coordinator, Foundation (since 2001), Sydney College of the Arts, University of Sydney, Sydney, NSW.

Solo exhibitions

Makers Mark, Melbourne, Vic., 1994; Melbourne Contemporary Art Gallery, Melbourne, Vic., 1994; RMIT University Masters Gallery, Melbourne, 1997; Smyrnios Gallery, Melbourne, Vic., 2000; Object Galleries, Sydney, NSW, 2001.

Selected group exhibitions since 1992

Australia Gold, travelling to SE Asia and Japan, 1993; *The Art of the Object*, Craft Australia travelling exhibition, Salon Municipal de Exposiciones, Montevideo, Uruguay and Instituto Cultural de Las Condes, Santiago, Chile, 1994; *VicHealth National Craft Award*, National Gallery of Victoria, Melbourne, Vic., 1994; *Class of '95* Royal College of Art, London, UK, 1995; *Production/Reproduction*, Gallery 101, Melbourne, Vic., 1995; *Australian Decorative Arts Survey: The object all sublime*, Lauraine Diggins Fine Art, Melbourne, Vic., 1995; *The Deacons, Graham and James Arts 21 Award*, The Ian Potter Museum of Art, Melbourne, Vic., 1998; *Box*, Craft Victoria Gallery, Melbourne, Vic., 1996; *See the Light*, Craftspace, Sydney, NSW, 1996; *Cecily and Colin Rigg Craft Award*, National Gallery of Victoria, Melbourne, Vic., 1997; Contemporary Gallery Chika, Tokyo, Japan, 1997; *City of Hobart Award*, Hobart, Tas., 1997; *The Japan Inspiration: Influence in crafts and design*, Art Gallery of Western Australia, Perth, WA, 1997; *St Etienne Design Biennale*, St Etienne, France, 1998, 2000; *Imagining: Art of the twentieth century*, Art Gallery of Western Australia, Perth, WA, 1999; *Contemporary Australian Craft*, Hokkaido Museum of Modern Art, Sapporo, Japan, 1999; *Blessed be the Work: Australian contemporary design in Jewish ceremony II*, The Jewish Museum of Australia, Melbourne, 1999 and national tour 1999–2001; *Defining the Object*, Quadrivium, Sydney, NSW, 1999; *Australia 2000*, Lesley Craze Gallery, London, UK, 2000; *Australian Metalwork*, Victoria and Albert Museum, London, UK, 2000; *Makers Mark* Sydney, NSW, 2001.

Public collections

Art Gallery of Western Australia, Perth, WA; Eltham Shire Art Collection, Eltham, VIC; Hamilton Art Gallery, Hamilton, Vic.; National Gallery of Australia, Canberra, ACT; National Gallery of Victoria, Melbourne, Vic.; Queensland Art Gallery, Brisbane, Qld; Powerhouse Museum, Sydney, NSW; The Jewish Museum of Australia, Melbourne, Vic.; Victorian State Craft Collection, Melbourne, Vic.

Mark **Edgoose**

Circle

titanium, aluminium and nylon brush

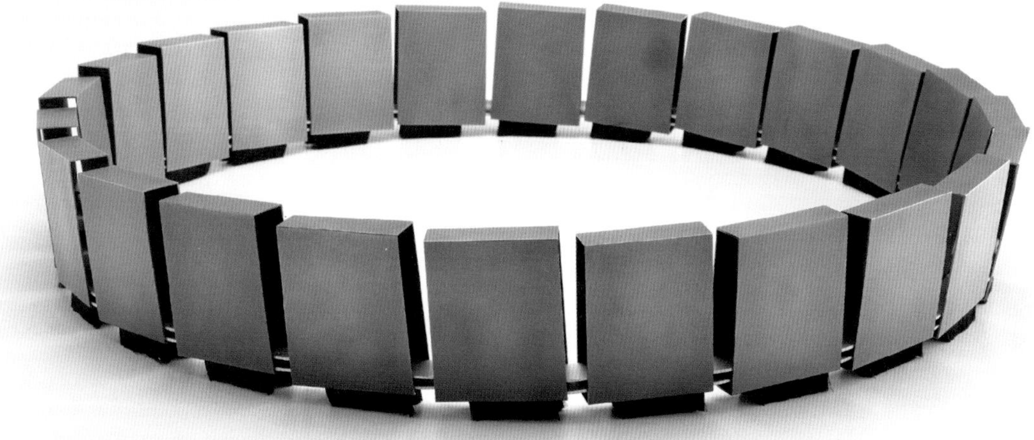

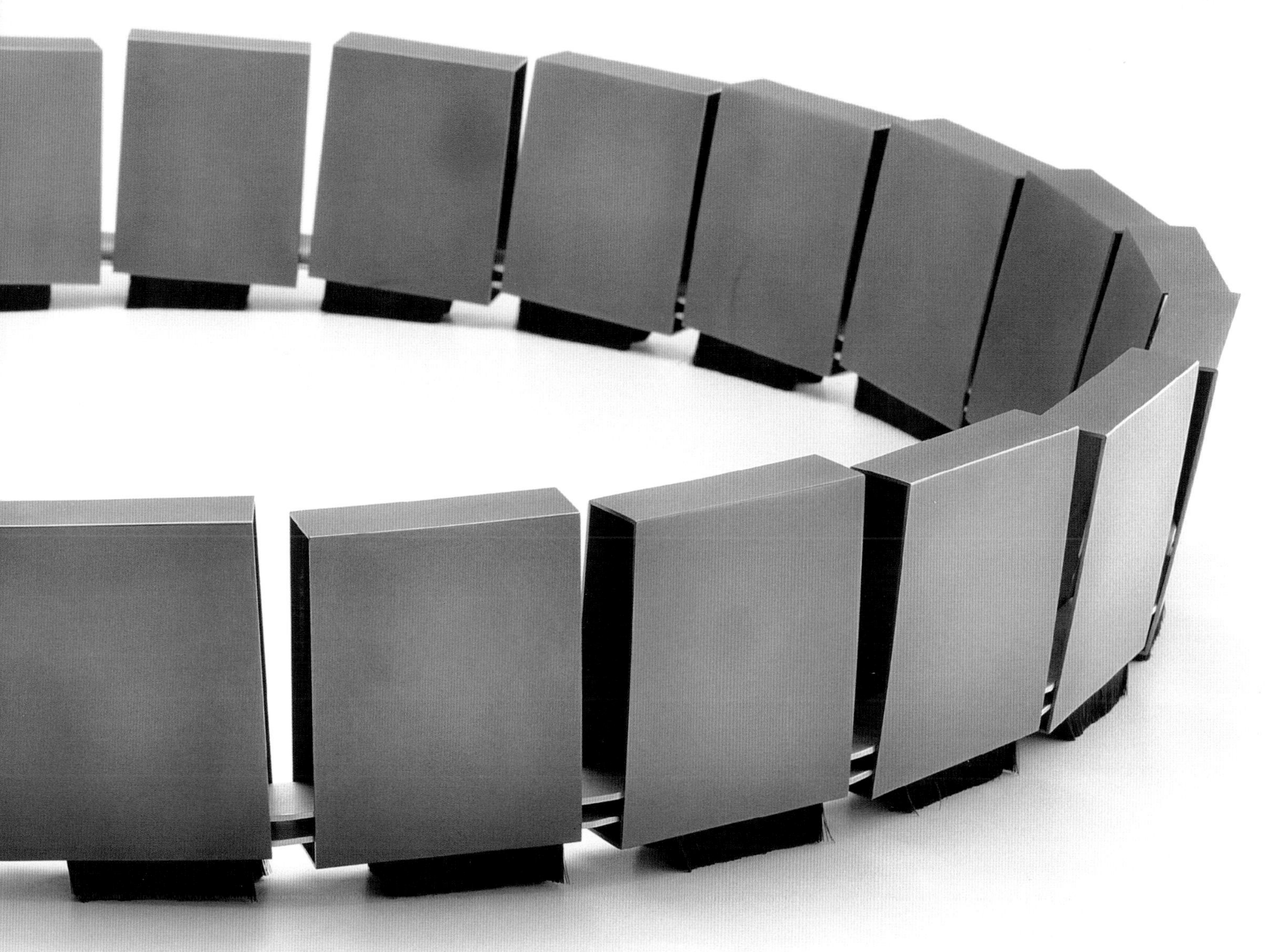

Mark **Edgoose**

Mark Edgoose's work is distinguished by his precise and adventurous use of advanced metals to make complex and ambiguous containers. This circle of interlinked titanium boxes delineates contained space, which remains empty but charged with possibility. The ordered procession of unopenable containers, each resting caterpillar-like on a flexible brush, invites speculation about its function. While its repetitive shapes and ingenious linkages reprise the pleasure and satisfaction of early mechanical toys such as Meccano or model trains, its visual and physical impregnability hints at unalterable systems and a darker, more controlled purpose.

Viliama **Grakalic**

Elsternwick, Victoria

Born Zagreb, Yugoslavia 1942,
arrived Australia 1963

Training

Graduate Diploma in Gold and
Silversmithing, RMIT University, Melbourne,
Vic., 1987; Bachelor of Arts (Sculpture),
RMIT University, Melbourne, VIC, 1988;
Master of Visual Arts, University of Sydney,
Sydney, NSW, 1998.

Selected solo exhibitions

The Dream of Flight, Makers Mark Gallery,
Melbourne, Vic., 1983; *Clouds*, Gallery
Gold and Silver, Melbourne, Vic., 1993;
Clouds II, Jam Factory Craft and Design
Centre, Adelaide, SA, 1994; *Deleterious
Vessels*, Gallery One, Sydney College of
the Arts, Sydney, NSW, 1998; *Lesser
Vessels*, Sydney College of the Arts,
Sydney, NSW, 1999 and Shepparton Art
Gallery, Shepparton, Vic., 2001.

Selected group exhibitions

Objects to Human Scale, Crafts Board of
the Australia Council travelling exhibition
to Japan and SE Asia, 1980; *Australian
Jewellery*, Crafts Board of the Australia
Council travelling exhibition to Europe,
1982; *Imagination and Metaphor*, Griffith
Regional Art Gallery, Griffith, NSW, 1988;
New Generation Gold and Silversmithing,
RMIT Gallery, Melbourne, Vic., 1989;
*Art of Adornment: Australian
contemporary jewellery*, Travelling
exhibition to Japan, 1989; *VicHealth
National Craft Award*, National Gallery of
Victoria, Melbourne, Vic., 1995; *National
Craft Acquisition Award*, Museum and Art
Gallery of the Northern Territory, Darwin,
NT, 1998; *Contemporary Wearables 99*,
Toowoomba Art Gallery, Toowoomba, Qld,
1999; *Australia 2000*, Lesley Craze
Gallery, London, UK, 2000; *Metal Element
III*, Quadrivium, Sydney, NSW, 2000;
Contemporary Wearables '01, Toowoomba
Art Gallery, Toowoomba, Qld, 2001.

Public collections (Australia)

Art Gallery of Western Australia, Perth,
WA; Griffith Regional Art Gallery, Griffith,
NSW; Museum and Art Gallery of the
Northern Territory, Darwin, NT; National
Gallery of Australia, Canberra, ACT;
National Gallery of Victoria, Melbourne,
Vic.; Queen Victoria Museum and Art
Gallery, Launceston, Tas.; Powerhouse
Museum, Sydney, NSW; Queensland Art
Gallery, Brisbane, Qld.; W.E. McMillan
Collection, RMIT University, Melbourne,
VIC; Shire of Diamond Valley, Diamond
Valley, Vic.; Toowoomba Art Gallery,
Toowoomba, Qld; Victorian State Craft
Collection, Melbourne, Vic.

Public collections (international)

Schmuckmuseum, Pforzheim, Germany.

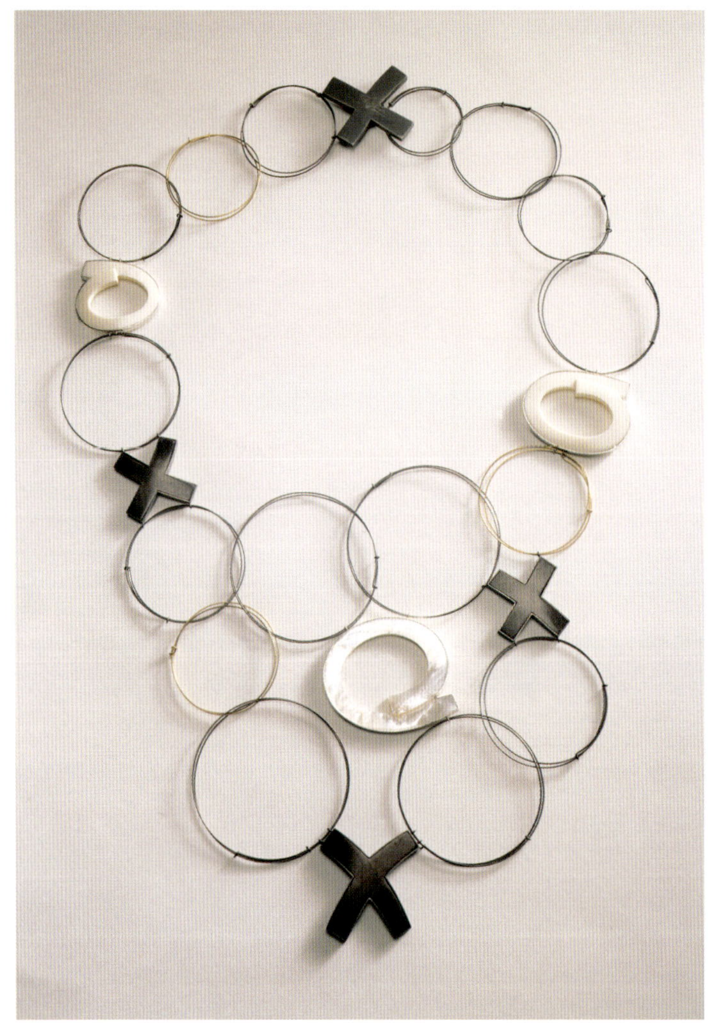

Viliama **Grakalic**
Noughts and crosses
925 silver, bone, mother-of-pearl,
18 carat gold, magnet and epoxy

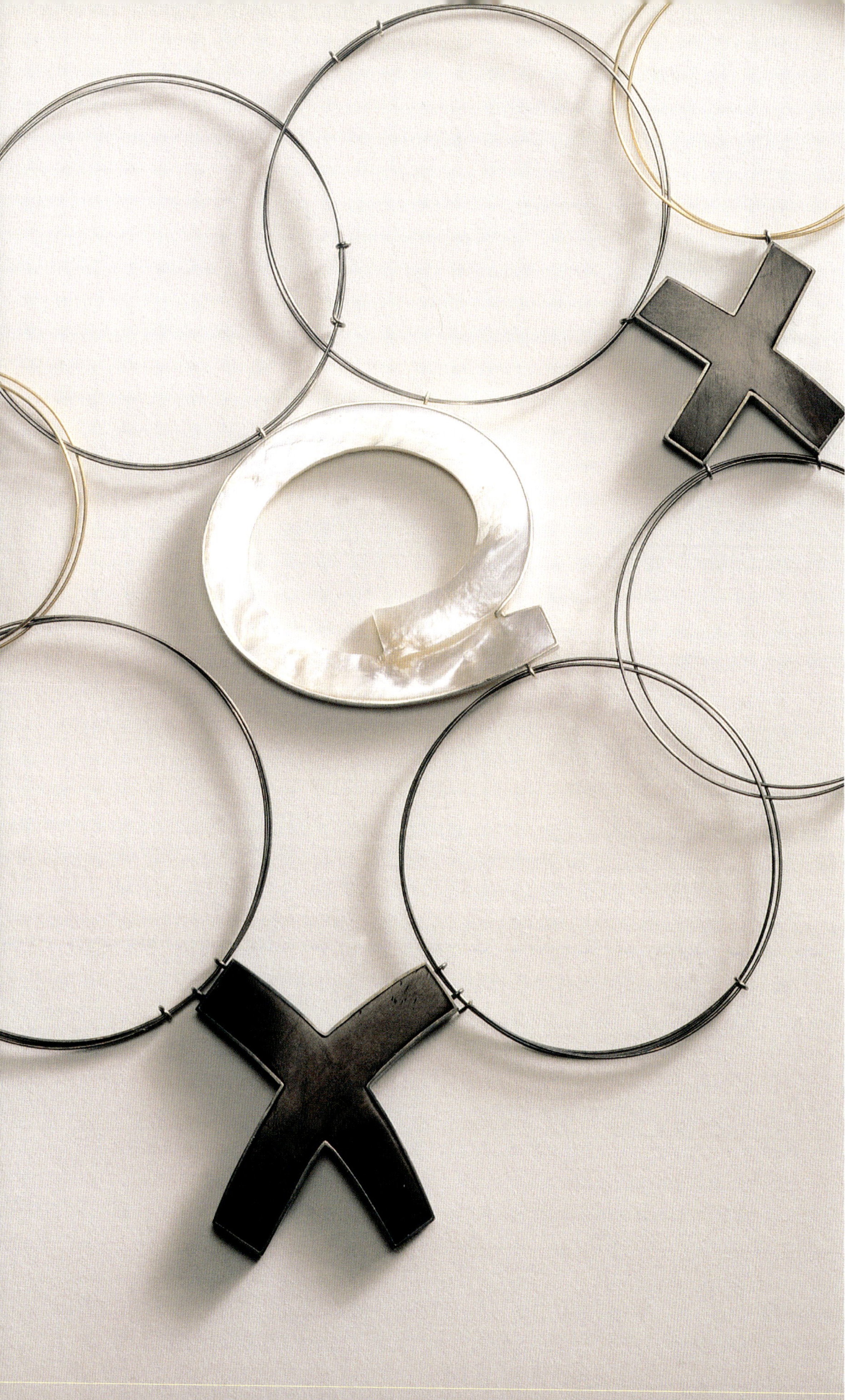

Viliama **Grakalic**

Viliama Grakalic's jewellery
is characterised by her use of
symbols and graphic imagery.
In this large necklace, with its
loose construction of circles
and the noughts and crosses
of the popular game, she turns
the body into a site for the
random distribution of marks
and gestures. While the game is
associated with killing time,
Grakalic's construction of these
shapes in mother-of-pearl
reminds us of the slow growth
of this precious material and the
equally painstaking way it was
cut for use in commemorative
jewellery and souvenirs in the
past.

Johannes **Kuhnen**
Queanbeyan, New South Wales
Born Essen, Germany 1952,
arrived Australia 1981

Training
Apprenticeship with Prof. Friedrich Becker,
Düsseldorf, Germany, 1969–73;
Fachoberschule für Gestaltung, Düsseldorf,
Germany, 1973–74; Product Design,
Fachhochschule Düsseldorf, Germany,
1974–78.

Related professional experience
Lecturer, Fachhochschule Düsseldorf,
Germany, 1980; Lecturer Silversmithing,
Royal Melbourne Institute of Technology,
Melbourne, Vic., 1982; Lecturer Gold and
Silversmithing, 1984–2001, and Head of
Gold and Silversmithing Workshop from
2001, Canberra School of Art, Australian
National University, Canberra, ACT.

Selected solo exhibitions
Gallery Neon, Brussels, Belgium, 1979,
1990; Galerie RA, Amsterdam, The
Netherlands, 1980; Gallery Decus,
Nürnberg, West Germany, 1980;
Contemporary Jewellery Gallery, Sydney,
NSW, 1987, 1989; Gallery Fluxus,
Dunedin, New Zealand, 1988; Fingers,
Auckland, New Zealand, 1998; Solander
Gallery, Canberra, ACT, 1988; Gallery
Pavè, Düsseldorf, Germany, 1990;
Gallery Gold and Silver, Melbourne, Vic.,
1993; Electrum Gallery, London, UK and
Schmuckform, Zurich, Switzerland, 1994;
Gallery Brodhag & Worn, Berlin and
Gallery Knauth & Hagen, Bonn, Germany,
1995; Gallery Funaki, Melbourne, Vic,
1996; *Glasses*, Quadrivium, Sydney, NSW,
1999; *Corresponding Colour: Jewellery
1999*, Gallery Funaki, Melbourne,
Vic., 1999.

Selected group exhibitions since 1992
Besteck [cutlery], Gallery Knauth und
Hagen, Bonn, Germany, 1992;
Internationale Silvertriennale, Deutsches
Goldschmiedehaus, Hanau, Germany,
1992; *National Craft Award*, National
Gallery of Victoria, Melbourne, Vic., 1992;
*Design Visions: Australian International
Crafts Triennial*, Art Gallery of Western
Australia, Perth, WA, 1992; *Australian
Craft*, Gallery L, Hamburg, Germany, 1992;
Visuelle Spiele, Handwerksmesse, Munich,
Germany, 1993; *Art of Adornment*,
travelling exhibition in Japan, Korea and
Indonesia, 1993; *20th Century Silver*,
Crafts Council, London, UK, 1993; *The Art
of the Object*, Craft Australia travelling
exhibition, Salon Municipal de
Exposiciones, Montevideo, Uruguay and
Instituto Cultural de Las Condes, Santiago,
Chile, 1994; *Production/Reproduction*,
Gallery 101, Melbourne, Vic., 1995; *Made
to Matter*, Crafts ACT Gallery, Canberra,
ACT, 1996; *Contemporary Vessels*,
Queensland Art Gallery travelling
exhibition to Shanghai Museum ,
Shanghai, China, 1997; *Defining the
Object*, Quadrivium, Sydney, NSW, 1999;
Contemporary Australian Craft, Hokkaido
Museum of Modern Art, Sapporo, Japan,
1999; *Imagining: Art of the twentieth
century*, Art Gallery of Western Australia,
Perth, WA, 1999; *Defining the Object 2*,
Quadrivium, Sydney, NSW, 2000;
Schmuck, International Crafts Fair, Munich,
Germany, 2001; *31@20: An exhibition
from the Gold and Silversmithing
Workshop of the Canberra School of Art*,
Deutsche Goldschmiedehaus, Hanau,
Germany and travelling to Taiwan and in
Australia, 2001–02.

Public collections (Australia)
Art Gallery of South Australia, Adelaide,
SA; Art Gallery of Western Australia, Perth,
WA; Hamilton Art Gallery, Hamilton, Vic.;
Melbourne University, Melbourne, Vic.;
National Gallery of Australia, Canberra,
ACT; National Gallery of Victoria,
Melbourne, Vic.; Parliament House,
Canberra, ACT; Powerhouse Museum,
Sydney, NSW; Queen Victoria Museum and
Art Gallery, Launceston, Tas.; Queensland
Art Gallery, Brisbane, Qld; Victorian State
Craft Collection, Melbourne, Vic.

Public collections (international)
Badisches Landesmuseum, Karlsruhe,
Germany; Galerie Orfévre, Düsseldorf,
Germany; Kunstgewerbemuseum, Berlin,
Germany; Museum Boymans van
Beuningen, Rotterdam, The Netherlands;
Museum für Kunst und Gewerbe,
Hamburg, Germany; National Museum of
Scotland, Edinburgh, UK; Victoria and
Albert Museum, London, UK.

Johannes **Kuhnen**
Centrepiece/Tray
anodised aluminium, silver and monel

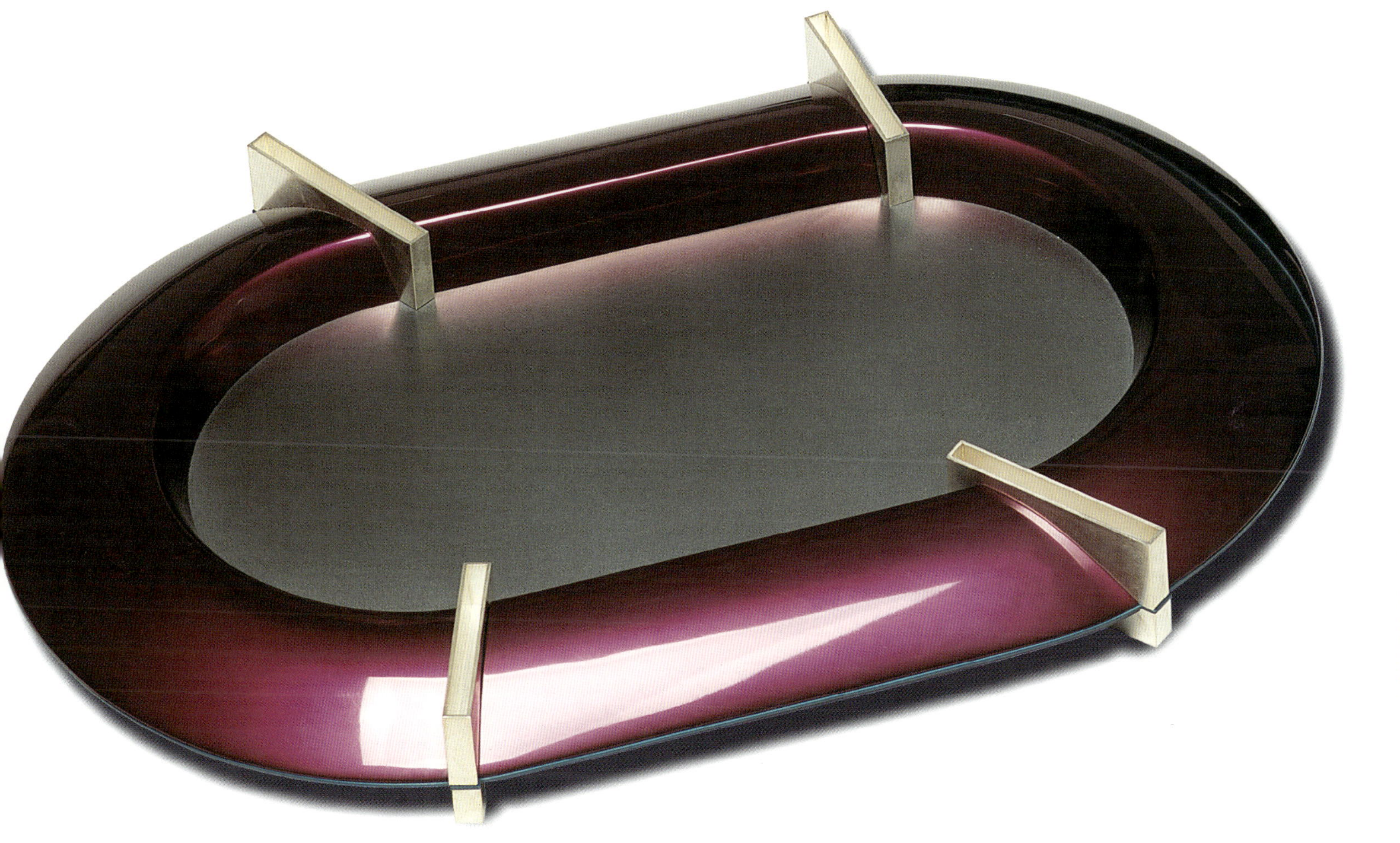

Johannes **Kuhnen**

In his work as a jeweller, object maker and photographer, Johannes Kuhnen is engaged with the interpretation and manipulation of a precise visual language of forms. The dramatic curvilinear shape of this centrepiece has been designed to emphasise the particular visual qualities of its materials and to fulfil its role as a low, but commanding central presence on a table. The vivid, iridescent colour of its anodised aluminium rim is designed to interact with differing light conditions, while the technical and precious qualities of its monel and silver elements play against each other. This orchestration of metals is underpinned with an unseen but precise and ingenious inner structure, giving this object weight and functional strength.

Sue **Lorraine**

Adelaide, South Australia
Born Melbourne, Victoria 1955

Training

Gold and Silversmithing, Royal Melbourne
Institute of Technology, Melbourne, Vic,,
1975–76; Diploma of Art and Design,
Preston Institute of Technology,
Melbourne, Vic., 1979–89; Architectural
studies, University of Adelaide, Adelaide,
SA, 1989–90.

Related professional experience

Founded Gray Street Workshop, Norwood,
SA, with Catherine Truman and Anne
Brennan, 1985; Studio Head, Metal
Design, JamFactory Contemporary Craft
and Design, Adelaide, SA, 1999 – present.

Selected solo exhibitions

Kitsch Lorraine, Distelfink Gallery,
Melbourne, Vic., 1981; *Rads, Rods and
Rays*, Makers Mark, Melbourne, Vic.,
1984; Editions Gallery, Fremantle, WA,
1984; *Lorraine 3*, Switchback Gallery,
Churchill, Vic., 1985; *Sticks and Stones*,
Contemporary Jewellery Gallery, Sydney,
NSW, 1987; *em/body*, Artspace, Festival
Centre, Adelaide, SA and Craft Victoria
Gallery, Melbourne, Vic., 1994 and
Craftspace, Sydney, NSW, 1995;
disembody, Craft ACT Gallery, Canberra,
ACT, 1998 and JamFactory Galleries,
Adelaide, SA and Craftwest Gallery, Perth,
WA, 1999; *Sensuous Interiors Under
Scrutiny* (with Catherine Truman), Gallery
Funaki, Melbourne, Vic., 2001.

Selected group exhibitions since 1992

Neckworks, Fremantle Arts centre,
Fremantle, WA, 1992; *Gray Street
Workshop at Fluxus*, Fluxus Contemporary
Jewellery, Dunedin, NZ, 1992; *Home is
Where the Art Is*, Artspace, Festival Centre,
Adelaide, SA, 1992; *Limited Editions*,
Festival Centre, Adelaide, SA, 1993;
Turning Ten, The Women's Gallery,
Melbourne, VIC and The Dowse Art
Museum, Wellington, NZ, 1995; *SOFA*
(Jam Factory Craft and Design Centre),
Chicago, Il, USA, 1995; *Jam Factory a
Vicenza*, Vicenza Oro, Vicenza, Italy, 1996;
A Matter of Weight, Wollongong City Art
Gallery, Wollongong, NSW, 1996; *Tags*,
Craft ACT Gallery, Canberra, ACT, 1996;
SOFA (Despard Gallery), Chicago, Il, USA,
1996; *artCoop*, Salamanca Arts Centre,
Hobart, Tas., 1996; *City of Hobart Art
Prize*, Carnegie Gallery, Hobart, Tas., 1997;
18th Biennial Craft Event, Mornington
Peninsula Regional Gallery, Mornington,
Vic., 1997; *Circles About the Body*,
University Gallery, Launceston, Tas., 1997;
Australian Jewellery, Galerie Tiller, Vienna,
Austria, 1998; *Ra-expositie: New jewellery
by Australian artists*, Galerie Ra,
Amsterdam, The Netherlands, 1998; Jam
Factory Biennial, JamFactory Galleries,
Adelaide, SA, 1999, 2001; *Magnetic:
Contemporary steel*, Brisbane City Gallery,
Brisbane, Qld, 1999; *Metallic*, Newland
Gallery, Adelaide, SA, 1999; *Gray Street
Production*, JamFactory Galleries, Adelaide,
SA, 2000; *Circling the Square*, Gray Street
Workshop, Adelaide, SA and Australian
and SE Asian tour, 2000–02; *Gray Street
Workshop 15 years*, Art Gallery of South
Australia, Adelaide, SA, 2000, and national
and international tour 2001; *Jam Packed*,
Customs House Art Gallery, Brisbane, Qld.,
2000; *Craft Feast*, Adelaide Central Gallery,
Adelaide, SA, 2000; *Chemistry, Art in
South Australia 1990–2000*, Art Gallery of
South Australia, Adelaide, SA, 2000.

Public collections

Art Gallery of South Australia, Adelaide,
SA; Art Gallery of Western Australia, Perth,
WA; National Gallery of Australia,
Canberra, ACT; National Gallery of
Victoria, Melbourne, Vic.; Powerhouse
Museum, Sydney, NSW; Queen Victoria
Museum and Art Gallery, Launceston, Tas.;
Queensland Art Gallery, Brisbane, Qld.

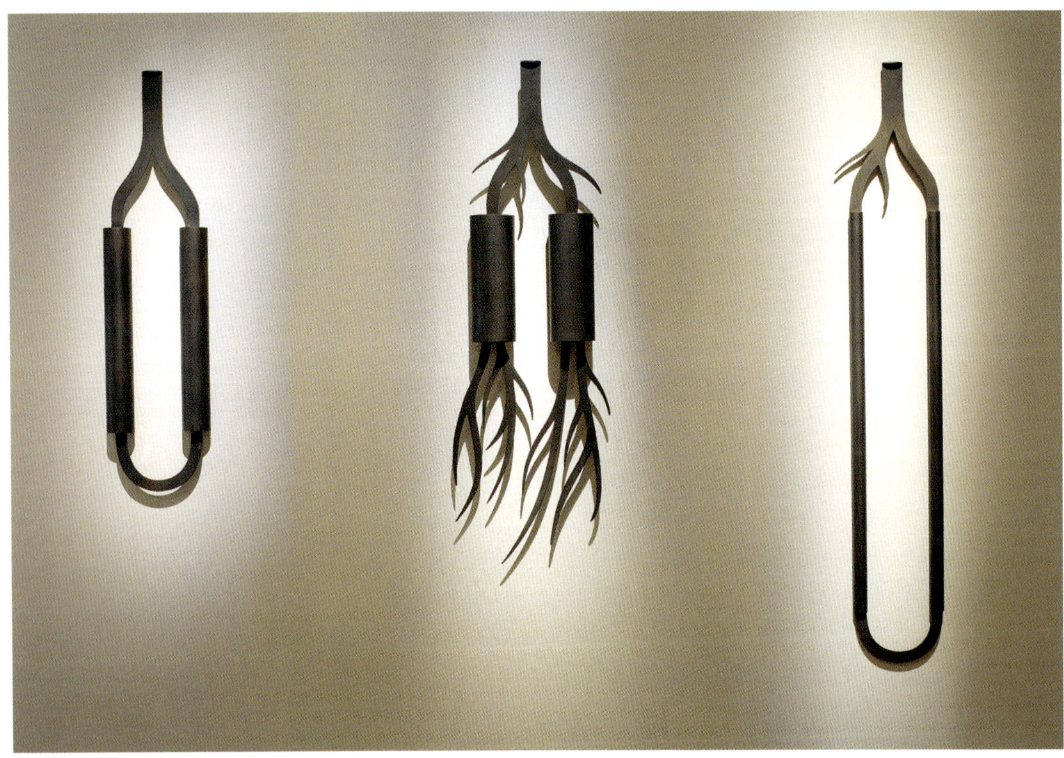

Sue **Lorraine**
left to right
Continuous model
Bronchial model
Elongated model
heat-coloured mild steel sheet and tube

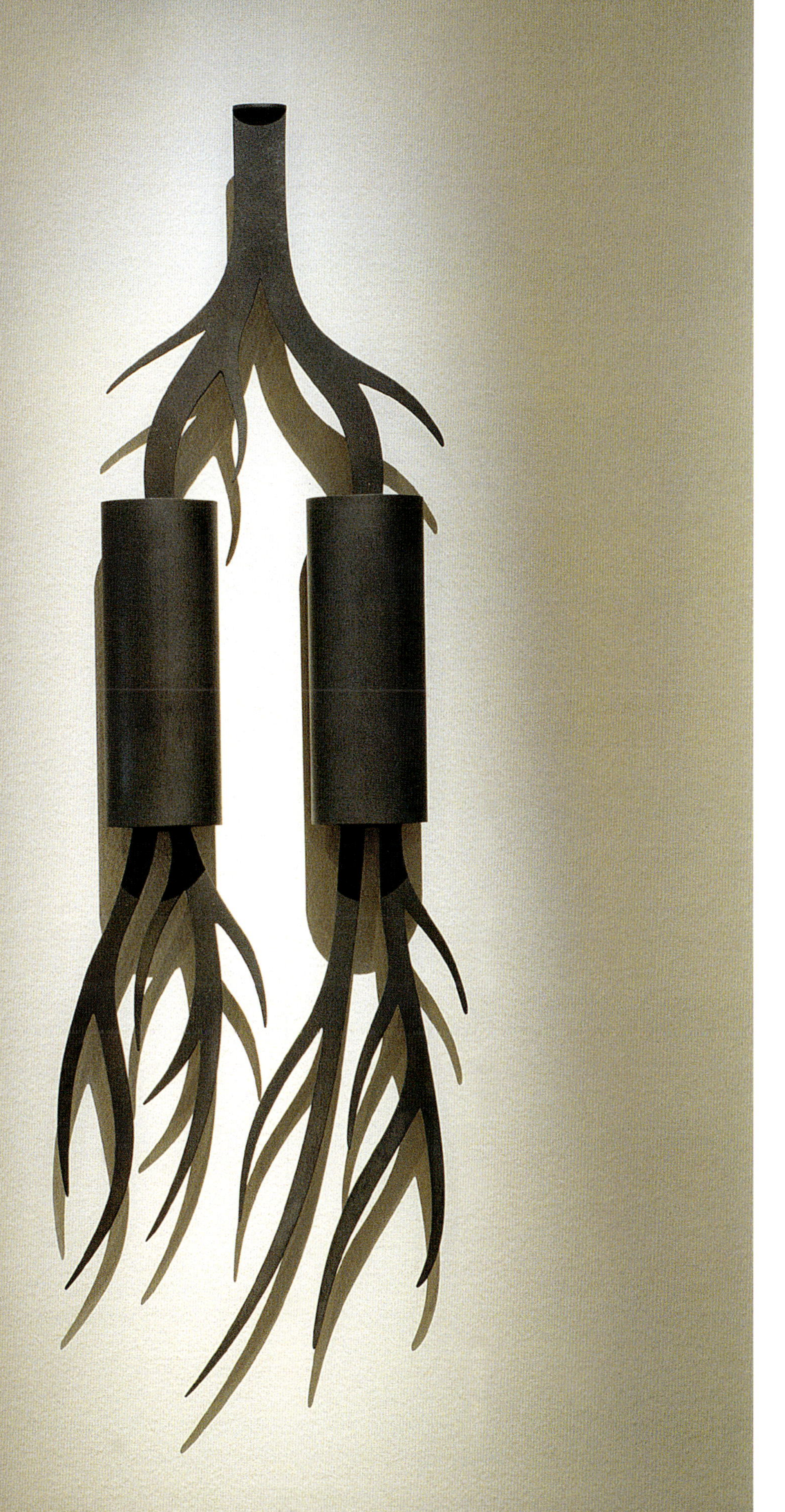

Sue **Lorraine**

As an artist working within the field of jewellery and small objects, Sue Lorraine is aware of their power to eroticise and focus attention on the parts of the body where they are worn or placed. For her, however, the more visceral, yet equally sensual aspects of the inner body are more compelling subjects for scrutiny and interpretation. She understands the way the physiology of the human body is frequently visualised through the schematised and diagrammatic representations of its functions, used to illustrate popular medical texts or didactic science museum exhibits. This work focuses on the lung, the body's organ of breath, giving form to its role of circulating air and life. Its abstracted, hard-edged construction in steel, sprung, forged and coloured with heat, is a metaphor for the strength and resilience of the lungs, as well as a reminder of its susceptibility to the effects of the industrial environment.

23

Klaus **Moje**

Tanja, New South Wales

Born Hamburg, Germany 1936,
arrived Australia 1982

Training

Journeyman's Certificate, glass cutter
and grinder in Moje family workshop,
Hamburg, Germany, 1952–55; Master's
Certificate, Rheinbach and Hadamar Glass
Schools, Germany, 1957–59.

Related professional experience

Founding Head of Glass Workshop,
Canberra School of Art, Australian
National University, Canberra, ACT,
1982–92; Australia Council Emeritus
Fellowship Award, 2001.

Selected solo exhibitions since 1991

Klaus Moje/Dale Chihuly,
The Glasmuseum, Ebeltoft, Denmark,
1991; Contemporary Art Niki, Tokyo,
Japan, 1992; *Chicago International New
Art Forms Exposition*, Navy Pier, Chicago,
IL, USA (Habatat Galleries), 1993;
Composition Gallery, San Francisco, USA,
1994; *Klaus Moje Glass: A retrospective
exhibition*, National Gallery of Victoria,
Melbourne, Vic.; Powerhouse Museum,
Sydney, NSW; Canberra School of Art
Gallery, Canberra, ACT; Museum für Kunst
und Gewerbe, Hamburg, Germany;
Charles A. Wustum Museum of Fine Arts,
Racine, WI, USA, 1995; *Seattle Art Fair*
(Ruth Summers Gallery), Seattle, USA,
1996; Craft ACT Gallery, Canberra ACT,
1997; Axia Modern Art, Melbourne, Vic.,
1998; *SOFA New York*, New York, USA
(Bullseye Connection Gallery), 2000;
The Glass World of Klaus Moje, Hsinchu
Municipal Glass Museum, Hsinchu, Taiwan,
2001.

Selected group exhibitions since 1992

A Decade of Studio Glass, Morris Museum,
New Jersey, NJ, USA, 1992; *Australian
Crafts: New works 1988–92*, Powerhouse
Museum, Sydney, NSW, 1992;
*Design Visions: Australian International
Crafts Triennial*, Art Gallery of Western
Australia, Perth, WA, 1992; *International
Kiln-formed Glass*, Bullseye Connection
Gallery, Portland OR, USA, 1992; *Art in
Glass 96*, Editions Galleries, Melbourne,
Vic., 1996; *International Contemporary
Glass*, Hsinchu Cultural Centre, Hsinchu,
Taiwan, 1996; *Venezia Aperto Vetro*,
Venice, Italy, 1996; *International Survey of
Contemporary Glass*, Concept Art Gallery,
Pittsburgh, PA, USA, 1996; *Drawing on the
Diaphanous*, Michael Nagy Fine Art,
Sydney, NSW, 1997; *From Venice to
Ebeltoft*, Glasmuseum, Ebeltoft, Denmark,
1997; *Arte en Vidrio*, Museo del Vidrio,
Monterrey, Mexico, 1997; *Via Venedig till
Varberg*, Varberg, Sweden, 1997; *The
Language of Glass*, Art Gallery of Western
Australia, Perth, WA, 1997; Gallery
Enomoto, Osaka, Japan, 1998; *Latitudes:
Bullseye glass in Australia*, Gallery
Himawari, Seto, Japan; travelling
exhibition, 1998; *Masters of Australian
Glass*, Quadrivium Gallery, Sydney, NSW,
1998; *Venezia Aperto Vetro 1998:
International New Glass*, 5 sites in Venice,
Italy, 1998; *Chongju International Craft
Biennale '99*, Chongju, South Korea, 1999;
Contemporary Australian Craft, Hokkaido
Museum of Modern Art, Sapporo, Japan;
travelling exhibition,1999; *Meister der
Moderne*, International Crafts Fair, Munich,
Germany, 1999; *National Craft Award*,
Melbourne, Vic., 1999; *At the Edge:
Australian glass art*, Brisbane City Gallery,
Brisbane, Qld; Object Galleries, Sydney,
NSW; Galerie Handwerk, Munich,
Germany; National Glass Centre,
Sunderland, UK, 2000; *Australian Crafts:
New works 1988–1992*, Powerhouse
Museum, Sydney, NSW, 2000; *Colonial to
Contemporary: A decade of collecting
Australian decorative arts and design*,

Powerhouse Museum, Sydney, NSW, 2000;
Defining Craft, American Craft Museum,
New York, USA, 2000; *Shattering
Perceptions*, Dennos Museum Centre,
Traverse City, Michigan, USA; Museo Del
Vitro, Monterrey, Mexico, 2000; *Exempla,
International Craft Fair*, Munich, Germany,
2001; *Transparent Things: Expressions in
glass*, National Gallery of Australia
Travelling Exhibition, Wagga Wagga
Regional Art Gallery, Wagga Wagga, NSW,
2001; *Facets of Australian Glass*,
Leo Kaplan Modern, New York, NY,
USA, 2002.

Public collections (Australia)

Art Gallery of South Australia, Adelaide,
SA; Art Gallery of Western Australia, Perth,
WA; National Gallery of Australia,
Canberra, ACT; National Gallery of
Victoria, Melbourne, Vic.; Parliament
House, Canberra, ACT; Powerhouse
Museum, Sydney, NSW; Queensland Art
Gallery, Brisbane, Qld; Wagga Wagga
Regional Art Gallery, Wagga Wagga, NSW.

Public collections (international)

American Craft Museum, New York, NY,
USA; Auckland Museum, Auckland, New
Zealand; Badisches Landesmuseum,
Karlsruhe, Germany; Bayerischer
Kunstgewerbe-Verein, Munich, Germany;
Carnegie Mellon Museum, Pittsburgh, PA,
USA; Cooper Hewitt Museum,
Smithsonian Institution, New York, USA;
Corning Museum of Glass, Corning, NY,
USA; Detroit Institute of Art, Detroit, MI,
USA; Fine Arts Museum of San Francisco,
CA, USA; Glasmuseum Frauenau,
Frauenau, Germany; Grassi Museum,
Leipzig, Germany; Hokkaido Museum of
Modern Art, Sapporo, Japan;
Kestnermuseum, Hannover, Germany;
Kunstgewerbemuseum, Darmstadt,
Germany; Kunstgewerbemuseum, Berlin,
Germany; Kunstmuseum Düsseldorf im
Ehrenhof, Düsseldorf, Germany;
Kunstsammlungen der Veste Coburg,
Coburg, Germany; Landesmuseum

Oldenburg, Oldenburg, Germany;
Landesmuseum Schleswig Holstein,
Schleswig, Germany; Los Angeles County
Museum of Art, Los Angeles, CA, USA;
Metropolitan Museum of Art, New York,
NY, USA; Minneapolis Museum of Art,
Minneapolis, USA; Mint Museum of
Art/Craft + Design, Charlotte, NC, USA;
Musée des Arts Décoratifs, Lausanne,
Switzerland; Museum für Angewandte
Kunst, Cologne, Germany; Museum
Bellerive, Zurich, Switzerland; Museum für
Angewandte Kunst, Frankfurt, Germany;
Museum für Kunst und Gewerbe,
Hamburg, Germany; Royal Scottish
Museum, Edinburgh, UK; Shimonoseki
City Art Museum, Shimonoseki, Japan;
The Glasmuseum, Ebeltoft, Denmark;
Toledo Museum of Art, Toledo, OH, USA;
University of Wisconsin, Madison, WI,
USA; Victoria and Albert Museum ,
London, UK; Württemburgisches
Landesmuseum, Stuttgart, Germany.

Klaus **Moje**

Fragments 1–2001
fused and ground mosaic glass

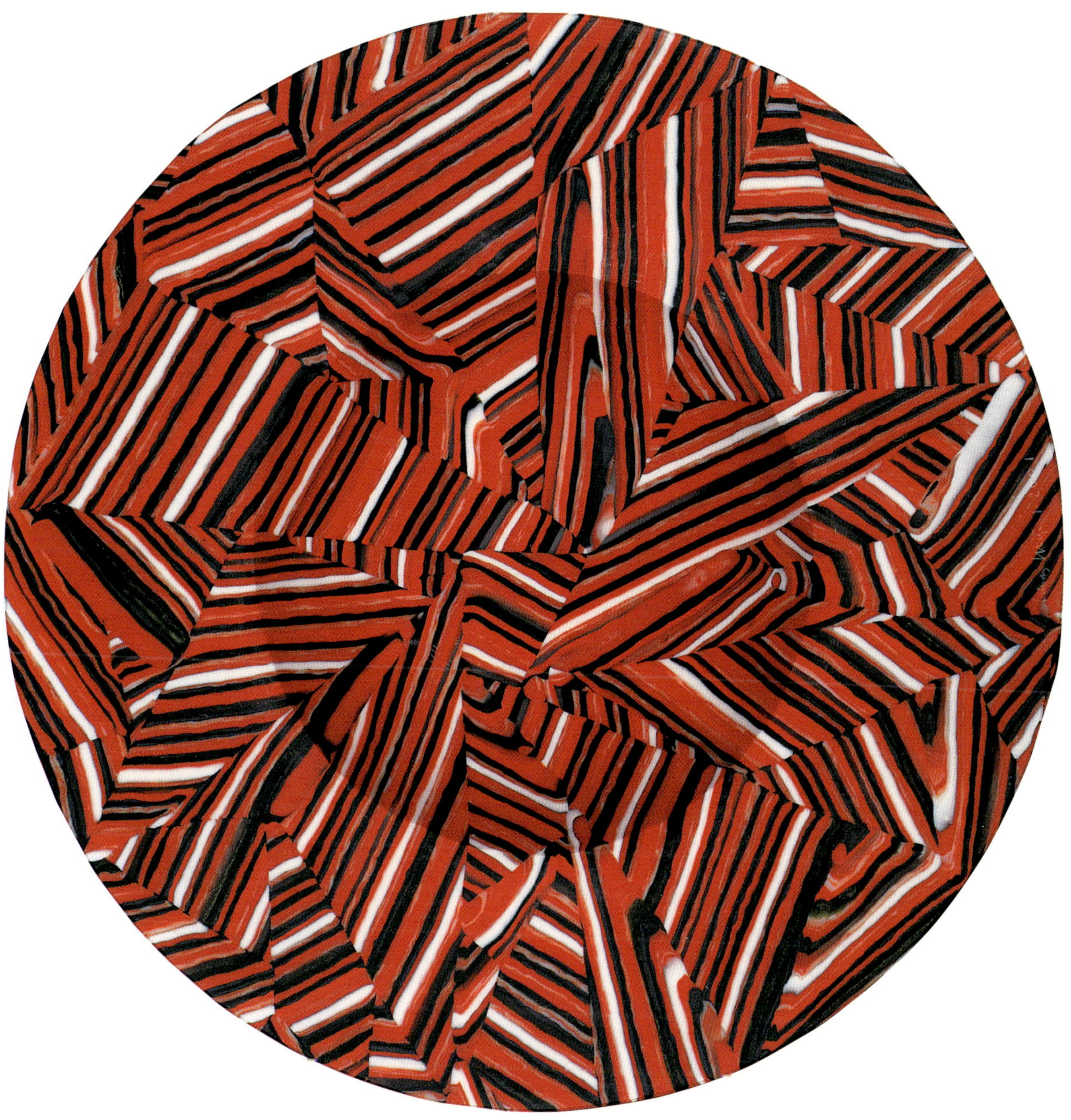

Klaus **Moje**

Working with a restricted range of forms – the shallow bowl, the flat wall panel or the cylindrical vessel – Klaus Moje draws upon the history of glassmaking to create fields of kaleidoscopic luminescence. The striated, agate-like glass produced in Germany and Austria in the 19th century and the influence of European Constructivism of the early 20th century echo through Moje's geometry. Since his arrival in Australia in 1982, he has developed this structural language to incorporate the influence of the colour and visual drama of the Australian sky and landscape.[1] His characteristic technique of cutting and composing a mosaic of coloured glass allows him to plan the structure of a work before submitting it to fusing and polishing processes that create depth and subtly alter his configurations. Close inspection of his glass reveals flashes of unexpected brilliance, graphic tensions and fluidities within the serene formality of his elemental compositions.

1 For a detailed account of Moje's career in Australia, see Geoffrey Edwards, *Klaus Moje Glass: A Retrospective Exhibition*, Melbourne: National Gallery of Victoria, 1995.

25

Catherine **Truman**
Adelaide, South Australia
Born Glenelg, South Australia 1957

Training
Diploma of Teaching (Secondary Fine Art),
1977, Bachelor of Education (Secondary
Fine Art), 1978 and Associate Diploma
(Jewellery and Metalsmithing), 1985,
South Australian College of Advanced
Education, Adelaide, SA; Japan/South
Australia Cultural Exchange Scholarship
to study netsuke carving in Japan, 1990.

Selected solo exhibitions
Blackwood Street Gallery, Melbourne, Vic.,
1984; Jam Factory Gallery, Adelaide, SA,
1984, 1992; Contemporary Jewellery
Gallery, Sydney, NSW, 1987; *Lifeboat:
Carvings by Catherine Truman*, Jam Factory
Craft and Design Centre, Adelaide, SA,
1992; Media Com, Okayama, Japan,
1993; San Francisco International Airport
Museum, San Francisco, CA, USA, 1993;
Craftwest Gallery, Perth, WA, 1995;
Craftspace, Sydney, NSW, 1995; *Catherine
Truman: Carvings*, Museum and Art
Gallery of the Northern Territory, Darwin,
NT, 1997; *Invisible Places To Be*, Fingers,
Auckland, New Zealand, 1998; *Sensuous
Interiors Under Scrutiny* (with Sue
Lorraine), Gallery Funaki, Melbourne,
Vic., 2001.

Selected group exhibitions
Schmuckszene `88, Munich, Germany;
Australian Decorative Arts 1788–1985,
Australian National Gallery, Canberra, ACT;
Australian Fashion: The contemporary art,
Powerhouse Museum, Sydney, NSW and
Victoria and Albert Museum, London, UK,
1989–1990; *First Australian Contemporary
Jewellery Biennial*, Jam Factory Gallery,
Adelaide, SA and Australian tour,
1991–92; *Family: Tradition and diversity*,
National Museum, Jakarta, Indonesia,
1994; *Turning Ten: Gray Street Workshop
10th anniversary exhibition*, Women's
Gallery, Melbourne, Vic. and Dowse Art

Museum, Wellington, New Zealand,1995;
The Somatic Object, Ivan Dougherty
Gallery, Sydney, NSW and The National
Museum of History, Taipei, Taiwan, 1997;
*Nature as Object: Craft and design from
Japan, Finland and Australia: The Third
Australian International Crafts Triennial*,
Art Gallery of Western Australia, Perth,
WA, 1998; *Seppelt Contemporary Craft
Award*, Museum of Contemporary Art,
Sydney, NSW, 1998; *Ra-expositie: New
jewellery by Australian artists*, Galerie Ra,
Amsterdam, The Netherlands, 1998;
Jewellery Moves, National Museum of
Scotland, Edinburgh, Scotland, 1998;
Contemporary Australian Craft, Hokkaido
Museum of Modern Art, Hokkaido, Japan,
1999; *Schmuck '99*, Munich, Germany,
1999; *SOFA* (Charon Kransen), New York,
USA, 1999; *Craft From Scratch: 8.
Trienniale – Form and Matters – Australia
and Germany*, Museum für Angewande
Kunst, Frankfurt, Germany, travelling
exhibition, 2000; *The Return of Beauty*,
Jam Factory Gallery, Adelaide, SA, 2000;
*Circling the Square: Gray Street Workshop
15 years*, Art Gallery of South Australia,
Adelaide, SA, 2000, and national and
international tour 2001; *Orbit*, Art
Museum, University of South Australia,
Adelaide, SA, 2001.

Public collections
Artbank; Art Gallery of South Australia,
Adelaide, SA; Art Gallery of Western
Australia, Perth, WA; Auckland Museum,
Auckland, New Zealand; Gippsland
Regional Art Gallery, Sale, Vic.; Museum
and Art Gallery of the Northern Territory,
Darwin, NT; National Gallery of Australia,
Canberra, ACT; Powerhouse Museum,
Sydney, NSW; University of Tasmania,
Hobart, Tas.; Victorian State Craft
Collection, Melbourne, Vic.

Catherine **Truman**
Interior under scrutiny no 12
carved English lime wood and paint

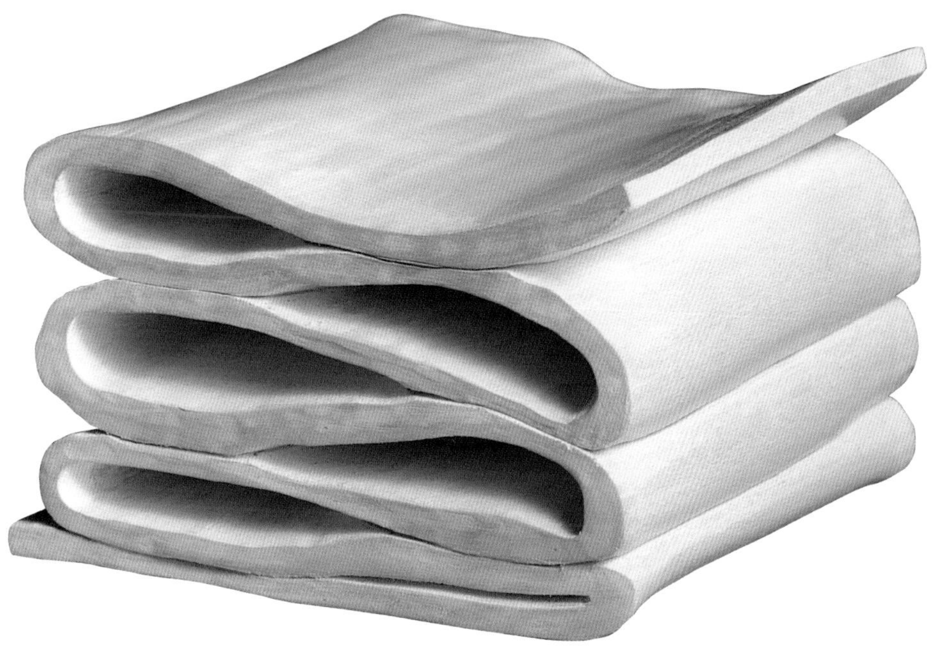

Catherine **Truman**

The structure of the human body and its systems of conduits and musculature is the point of departure for the carved wood objects of Catherine Truman. Meticulously carved and painted, they resemble antique anatomical models, yet with their elusive purpose they transcend instructive biology. A jeweller by training, Truman applies a precise logic to the production of small, hand-held objects in which the rigidity of wood is made visually subservient to the elasticity invoked by objects such as tubes, bladders and gullets. Through them, we are able to visualise the inner sensations of the body, particularly those that make us aware of our fragility, such as breathing, choking, digestion or spasm. With their talismanic and semiotic presence, an industrial ambiguity also surrounds these objects, reminding us of our increasing dependence and trust in the electromechanical systems that deliver fresh air and water to our interior environments.

27

Jenny **Turner**

Hobart, Tasmania

Born Wollongong, New South Wales 1939

Training

Bachelor of Arts, Sydney University,
Sydney, NSW, 1966; Diploma of Weaving,
Secheron Textile Centre, Hobart, Tas., 1980

Related professional experience

Established *One Off Weaving* business,
Hobart, Tas., 1980.

Solo exhibitions

Handmark Gallery, Hobart, Tas., 1982,
1983, 1984, 1990, 1993, 1994, 1997,
2000; Distelfink Gallery, Melbourne, Vic,,
1983; Beaver Galleries, Canberra, ACT,
1985, 1988; Yaizu Cultural Centre, Yaizu,
Shuko One, Tokyo, Itami Craft Centre,
Itami and Gallery Muu, Kyoto, Japan,
1992; Australia Centre, Manila,
The Philippines.

Selected group exhibitions since 1992

Celebration of a Decade, Handmark
Gallery, Hobart, TAS, 1992; *Design Visions:
Australian International Crafts Triennial*,
Art Gallery of Western Australia, Perth,
WA, 1992; *Common Threads*, Hobart,
TAS, 1992; *Wool in the Australian
Imagination*, Greenway Gallery, Hyde Park
Barracks, Sydney, NSW, 1994; *Tasmanian
Crafts*, Itami Craft Centre, Itami, Japan,
1995; Nisart Gallery, Launceston, Tas.,
1996; *The Language of Thread*, Art Gallery
of Western Australia, Perth, WA, 1996;
Tasmanian Craft Fair, Deloraine, Tas.,
1999; Tasmanian exhibition, *Create 2000*,
Sydney, NSW, 2000.

Public collections

Art Gallery of Western Australia, Perth,
WA; National Gallery of Australia,
Canberra, ACT; Queen Victoria Museum
and Art Gallery, Launceston, Tas.;
Tasmanian Museum and Art Gallery,
Hobart, Tas.; University of Tasmania,
Hobart, Tas.

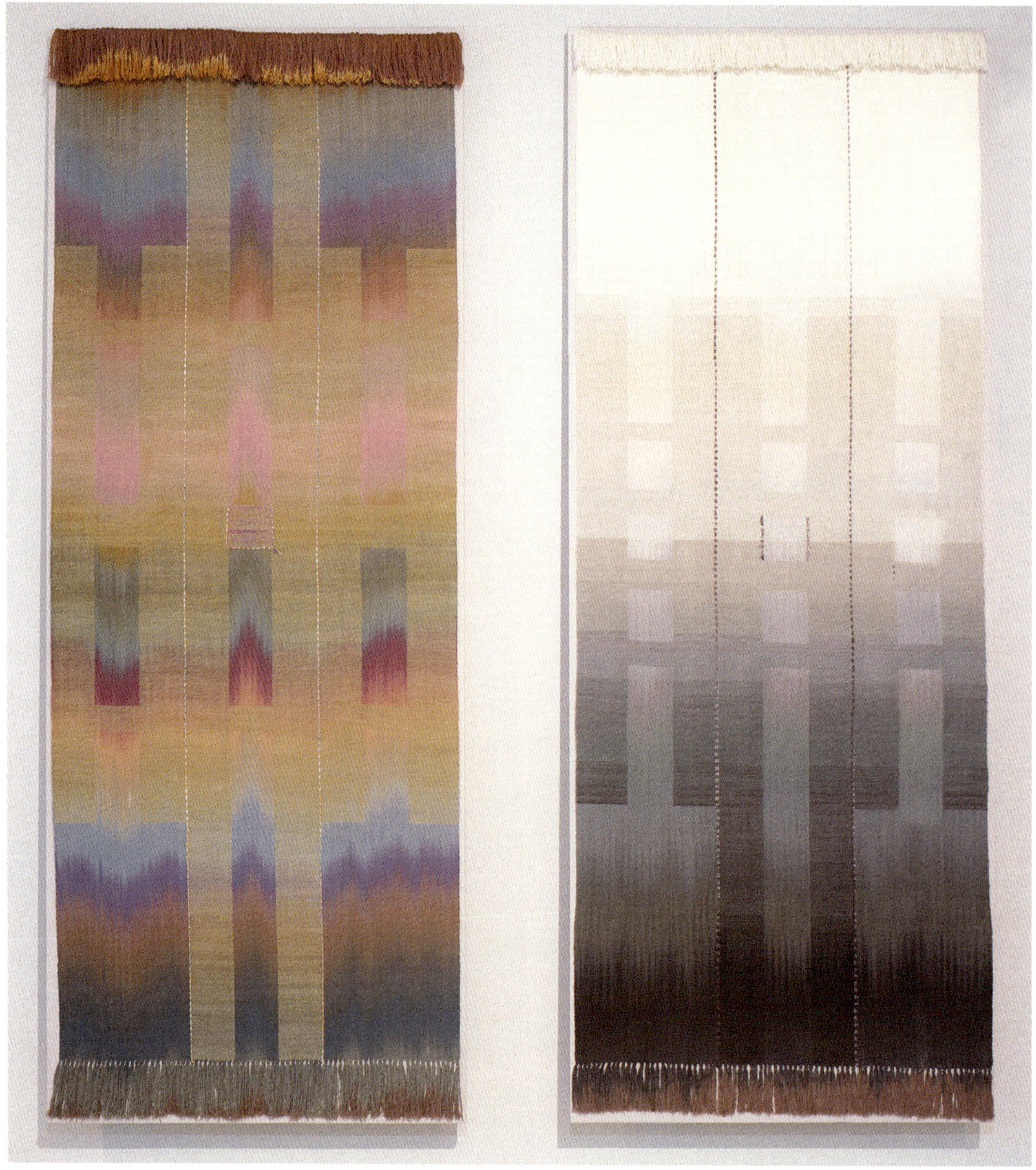

Jenny **Turner**
Shawls
woven superfine wool and silk

Jenny **Turner**

Jenny Turner is known for the refined, gradated colourings of her loom-woven wool and silk fabrics, giving them a sense of having faded with long use. This shawl shows her control of a complex dyeing process in which the fabric's warp threads reveal gradated shifts of colour, in the manner of South-East Asian *ikat* textiles. Turner's work is distinguished by its low-keyed colour and the manipulation of the thread structure to build texture into the fabric. These qualities are enhanced when the shawl is worn, allowing colour and pattern to shift direction, echoing the construction of the fabric's weave.

Richard **Whiteley**
Sydney, New South Wales
Born Great Britain 1963, arrived Australia
1963

Training
Bachelor of Arts (Visual Arts), Canberra
School of Art, Australian National
University, Canberra, ACT, 1987;
Master of Fine Art, University of Illinois,
Urbana, USA, 1993.

Related professional experience
Lecturer in Glass, Sydney College of the
Arts, University of Sydney, Sydney, NSW,
1994–2000.

Selected solo exhibitions
Gallery 105, Champaign, IL, USA, 1993;
The Glass Gallery, Bethesda, MD, USA,
1995; Wagga Wagga Regional Art Gallery,
Wagga Wagga, NSW, 1996; Craft Victoria,
Melbourne, Vic., 1998; Bullseye
Connection Gallery, Portland, OR, USA,
2000; *Symmetry x 2* (with Matthew
Curtis), Axia Modern Art, Melbourne,
Vic., 2001.

Selected group exhibitions
Glass Art from Australia, Wagga Wagga
Regional Art Gallery, Wagga Wagga, NSW;
Galerie L, Hamburg, Germany; Galerie Rob
van den Doel, The Hague, The
Netherlands; Galerie Gottschalk-Betz,
Frankfurt, Germany, 1990; *Illinois Glass*,
Marx Gallery, Chicago, IL, USA, 1992;
Critique, The Artists Museum, Sydney,
NSW, 1994; *Head Industries*, Gallery
Constantinople, Queanbeyan, NSW;
Canberra National Sculpture Forum,
Canberra, ACT, 1994; *RFC Glass Prize*,
Glass Artists' Gallery, Sydney, NSW, 1995;
Amnesty: From Strength and Hope,
The Gunnery, Sydney, NSW; Casula
Powerhouse, Casula, NSW, 1995; *Box*,
Craft Victoria, Melbourne, VIC, 1996;
University of Illinois Alumni Exhibition,
I Space, Chicago, IL, USA, 1996; *Research*,

Craft Victoria, Melbourne, Vic., 1997;
Australian Glass, Galerie Rob van den
Doel, The Hague, The Netherlands, 1977;
Light, Space and Colour (exhibition with
Steven Holl), Bellevue Art Museum,
Seattle, WA, USA, 1998; *Vitreous*,
Queensland Contemporary Craft Gallery,
Brisbane, Qld., 1999; *SOFA Chicago*,
Chicago, IL, USA (Connections Gallery),
1999; *RFC Glass Prize*, Volvo Gallery,
Sydney, NSW; travelling exhibition, 1999;
International Expo, Glass Arts Society
Conference, Tampa, FL, USA, 1999;
Fusion: Contemporary glass, Axia Modern
Art, Melbourne, Vic., 1999; *Ausglass
Members' Exhibition*, Wagga Wagga
Regional Art Gallery, Wagga Wagga, NSW,
1999; *At the Edge: Australian glass art*,
Brisbane City Gallery, Brisbane, Qld; Object
Galleries, Sydney, NSW; Galerie Handwerk,
Munich, Germany; National Glass Centre,
Sunderland, UK, 2000; *Quadrivium's
Finest*, Quadrivium Gallery, Sydney, NSW,
2000; *RFC Glass Prize*, Volvo Gallery,
Sydney, NSW; travelling exhibition, 2000;
SOFA Chicago, Chicago, IL, USA
(Connections Gallery), 2000; *Transparent
Things: Expressions in glass*, National
Galllery of Australia Travelling Exhibition,
Wagga Wagga Regional Art Gallery,
Wagga Wagga, NSW, 2001; Quadrivium,
Sydney, NSW, 2002.

Public collections
National Gallery of Australia, Canberra,
ACT; Queensland Art Gallery, Brisbane,
Qld; Victorian State Craft Collection,
Melbourne, Vic.; Wagga Wagga Regional
Art Gallery, Wagga Wagga, NSW

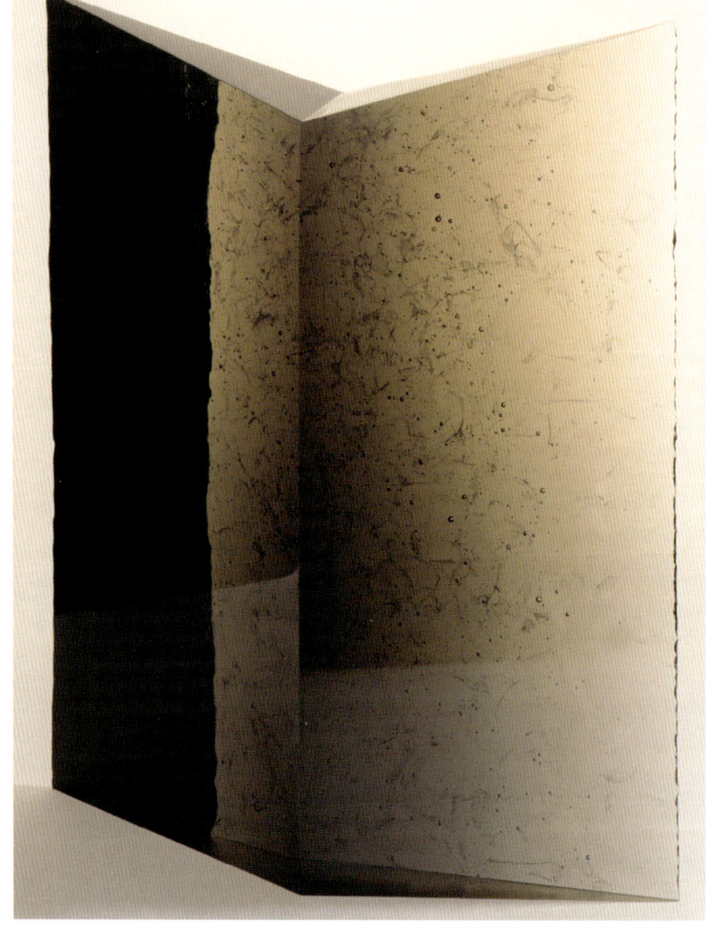

Richard **Whiteley**
Event horizon
cast and polished glass

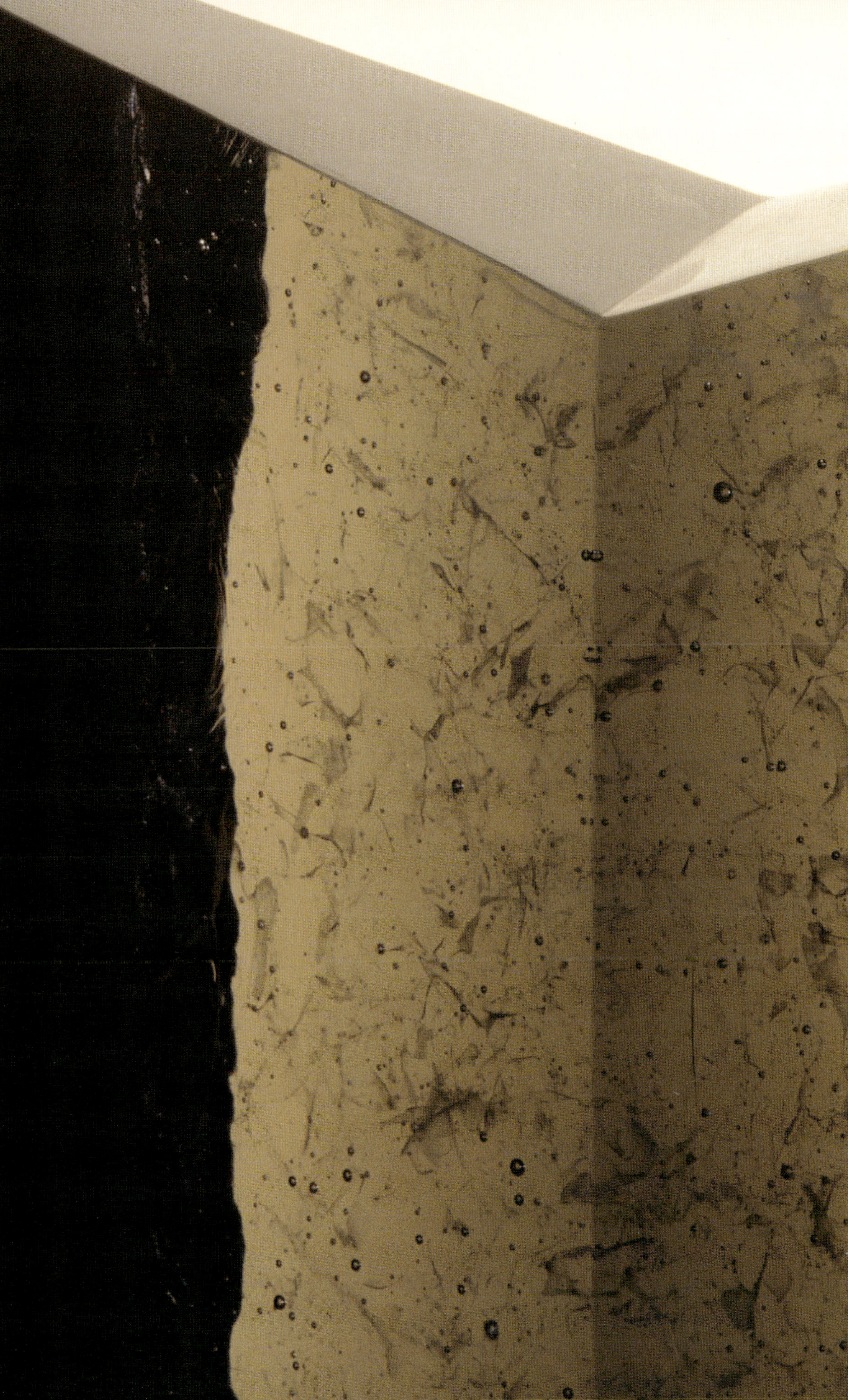

Richard **Whiteley**

In making his monumental and sentinel-like cast glass forms, Richard Whiteley draws from the technical traditions of Czech glass to articulate and reflect the Australian urban and industrial landscape.[1] His works are often blade-shaped and exploit the saturated colour only available with glass. The subtle greyness of this work evokes the crystalline quality of natural materials such as topaz and rock crystal, prized for centuries for their clarity, and cut and polished to enhance their refractiveness. Its chipped edge, however, also suggests the transformation by indigenous Australians, since European settlement, of found industrial glass fragments into precise and jewel-like spearheads. Its form and exaggerated bevelled cutting suggests a window, and acts as an agent for light, bridging and energising the space between landscape and interior.

1 While a student in 1987, Whiteley worked at the Pilchuck Glass School near Seattle with Czech glass artists, Stanislav Libenský and Jaroslava Brychtová. For an account of Whiteley's workshop experiences, see Meredith Hinchliffe, 'Richard Whiteley' in *Craft Arts International*, no 50, 2000, pp. 38–42.

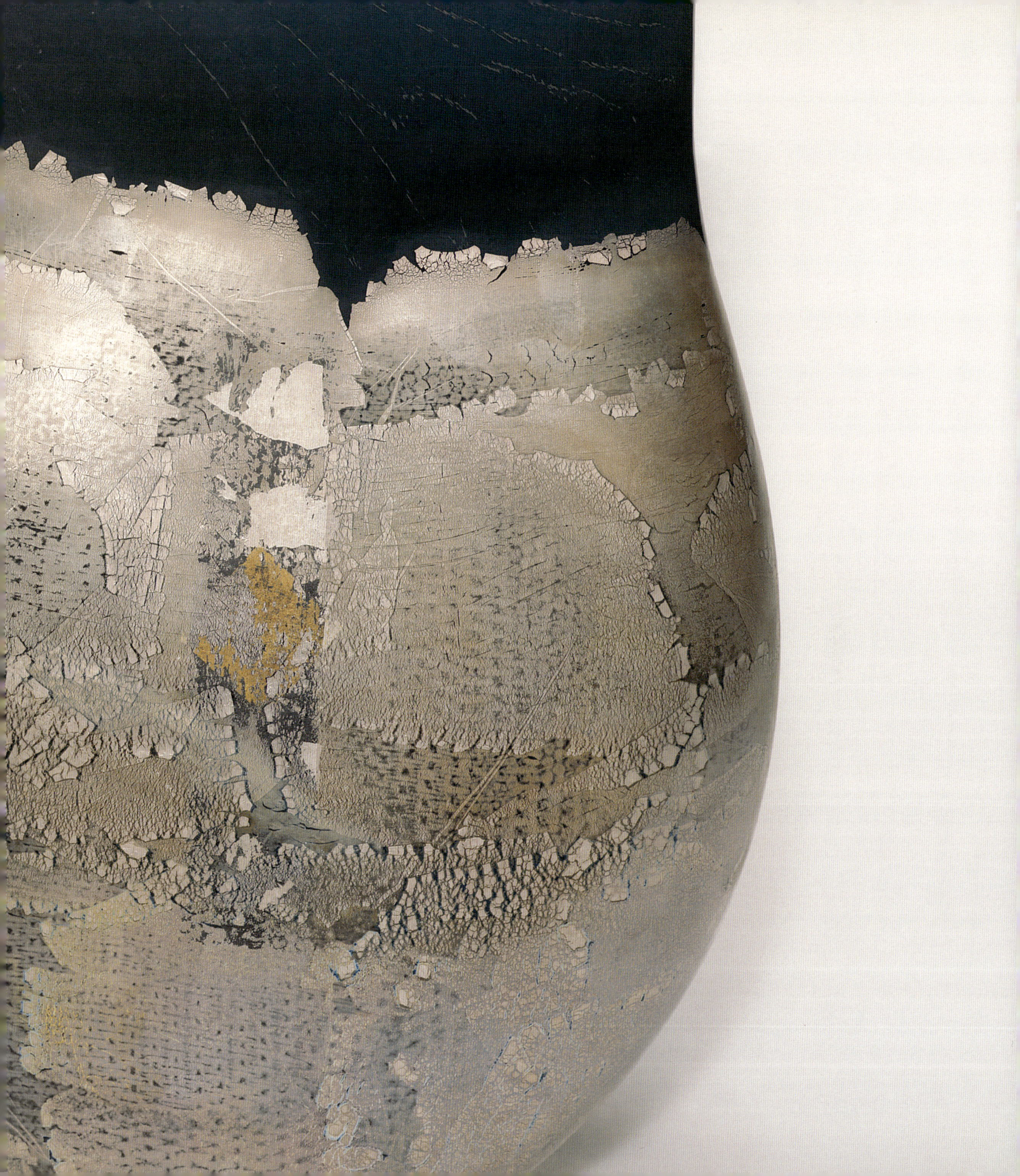

Narrative

The expression of narrative and a connection to history are part of many contemporary craft objects. Acknowledging the stylistic, technical or social histories of objects has given a number of artists a way to move through time and link the personal narratives of their work to the historical connotations and interpretations of their practice. The history of place, and the culture we have constructed within and upon it, resonates through the works illustrated in this section. The powerful physicality of Australia's natural environment pervades the narratives of light and space, growth and destruction, investigation and categorisation, and behaviour and social constructions. Through these objects, the traditions of craft and design are deconstructed and reinterpreted to refract a sense of the past into the infinitely more complex and troubled world of the present.

Uniting these works is a sense of identity resulting from the piecing together of elements and the assembly and accretion of materials and visual clues. Using traditional materials and processes and making reference to the historical language of design, the works are either built up, or pared away in layers, giving a sense of the passage of time and the inevitability of change. Through their visual and textural narrative, they provide clues by which to navigate the cultural landscape we have created and inherited, and which, in turn, will become located in a time characterised by uncertainty and renegotiation.

Janet **DeBoos** Anne **Dybka** Tony **Hanning**
Brian **Hirst** Kay **Lawrence** Jessica **Loughlin**
Helmut **Lueckenhausen** Jeff **Mincham** Milton
Moon Nick **Mount** Kevin **Perkins** Denise
Sprynskyj and Peter **Boyd**

Janet **DeBoos**

Wee Jasper, New South Wales
Born Melbourne, Victoria 1948

Training

Bachelor of Science, Sydney University,
Sydney, NSW, 1969; Ceramic Certificate,
National Art School, East Sydney Technical
College, Sydney, NSW, 1971; Fine Arts and
Italian, Sydney University, Sydney, NSW,
1974–75.

Related professional experience

Teacher, Canberra Technical College School
of Art, Canberra, ACT, 1972–75; Teacher
Ceramics, Randwick and St George
Technical Colleges, Sydney, NSW,
1976–78; Head Teacher Ceramics, East
Sydney Technical College, Sydney, NSW,
1979–80; Lecturer Ceramics (1985–97)
and Head of Ceramics Workshop,
Canberra School of Art, Australian
National University, Canberra, ACT,
1998 – present.

Selected solo exhibitions

Fusions Gallery, Brisbane, Qld., 1979;
Potters Gallery, Sydney, NSW, 1980, 1986;
Queensland Potters' Association Gallery,
Brisbane, QLD, 1985; *A Change of
Scenery*, Narek Gallery, Tharwa, ACT,
1991; *Memories of the Domestic Life*,
Ceramic Art Gallery, Sydney, NSW, 1994;
Domestic Concerns, Ceramic Art Gallery,
Sydney, NSW, 2000 (with Patsy Hely);
Memories of the Domestic Life, Weswal
Gallery, Tamworth, NSW, 1997; *Composite
of Opposites*, Drill Hall Gallery, Canberra,
ACT, 2001 (with Alan Watt); JamFactory
Galleries, Adelaide, SA, 2001.

Selected group exhibitions since 1992

National Craft Acquisition Award,
Northern Territory Museum of Arts and
Sciences, Darwin, NT, 1993, 1994;
Summer Show, European Ceramics Gallery,
Knaresborough, UK, 1993; *The Teapot
Show*, L'Unique Gallery, Adelaide, SA,
1993; *Cloudbusting*, Canberra School of
Art Gallery, Canberra, ACT, 1993; *The
Bowled and the Beautiful*, The Door
Exhibition Space, Fremantle, WA, 1994;
Newcastle Invitational Ceramic Award,
Newcastle Region Art Gallery, Newcastle,
NSW, 1995, 1997; *Bega Valley Ceramics*,
Bega Valley Regional Gallery, Bega, NSW,
1995; *Icons*, Meat Market Craft Centre,
Melbourne, Vic., 1995; *Process and
Obsession*, Performance Space, Sydney,
NSW, 1995; *Gold Coast Ceramic Award*,
Gold Coast City Gallery, Qld; *Townsville
Ceramic Acquisition Award*, Perc Tucker
Regional Gallery, Townsville, Qld, 1996;
Alice Craft Acquisition, Araluen Arts
Centre, Alice Springs, NT, 1996, 1997;
Bowled Over, The Door Exhibition Space,
Fremantle, WA, 1996; *Connected*, Craft
ACT Gallery, Canberra, ACT, 1996;
Sentinel, Manly Art Gallery, Sydney, NSW,
1996; *ANU Ceramics Staff Show*, Pastoral
Gallery, Queanbeyan, NSW, 1996; *Purple
Sands: 21 Western potters in China*, JBK
Gallery, Amsterdam, The Netherlands,
1997; *Images of Sustainability*, Watt
Space, Newcastle University, Newcastle,
NSW, 1997; *Porcelain and Stoneware*,
Contemporary Craft Space, Brisbane, Qld,
1997; *Teawares*, Distelfink Gallery,
Melbourne, Vic., 1997, 1999; *Sidney Myer
International Ceramics Award*, Shepparton
Art Gallery, Shepparton, Vic., 1998; *Salad
Days*, Ceramic Art Gallery, Sydney, NSW,
1998; *Delegates' Exhibition*, National
Ceramics Conference, WA School of Art
and Design Gallery, Perth, WA, 1999; *The
Teapot Show*, Old Bakery Gallery, Perth,
WA, 1999; *re:Searching*, Canberra School
of Art Gallery, Canberra, ACT, 1999;
White, Ceramic Art Gallery, Sydney, NSW,
1999; *Four Porcelain Artists*, Sturt Gallery,
Mittagong, NSW, 2000; *Minimal*, Fusions
Gallery, Brisbane, QLD, 2000; *Selected
Accredited Professional Members'
Exhibition*, Craft ACT Gallery, Canberra,
ACT, 2000; SOFA (Narek Gallery), Chicago,
Il, USA, 2001.

Public collections

Gold Coast City Gallery, Qld; Museum and
Art Gallery of the Northern Territory,
Darwin, NT; National Gallery of Australia,
Canberra, ACT; Shepparton Art Gallery,
Shepparton, Vic.; Toowoomba Regional
Art Gallery, Toowoomba, Qld.

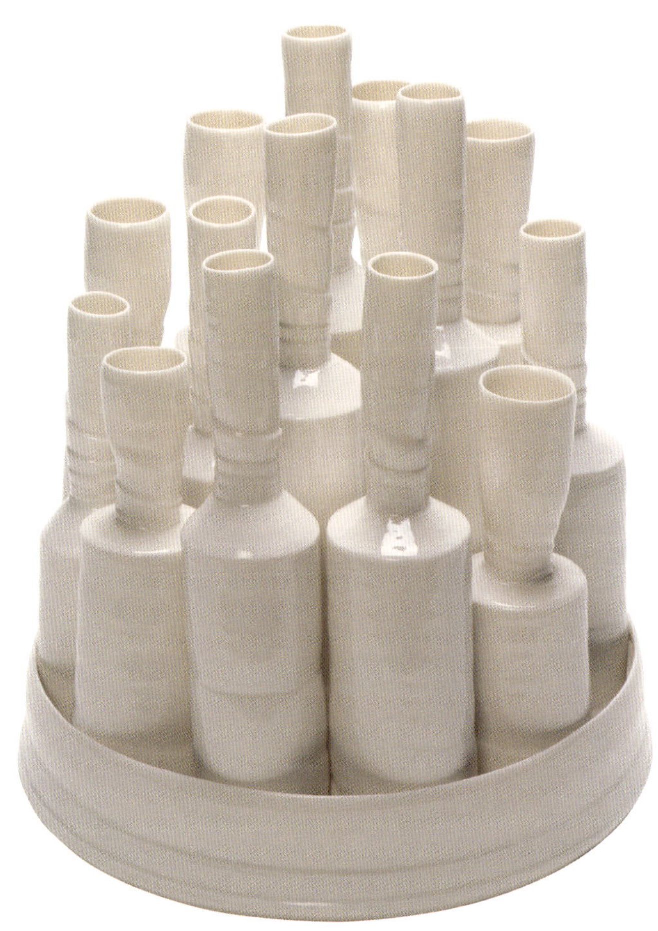

Janet **DeBoos**
Large vase
glazed porcelain

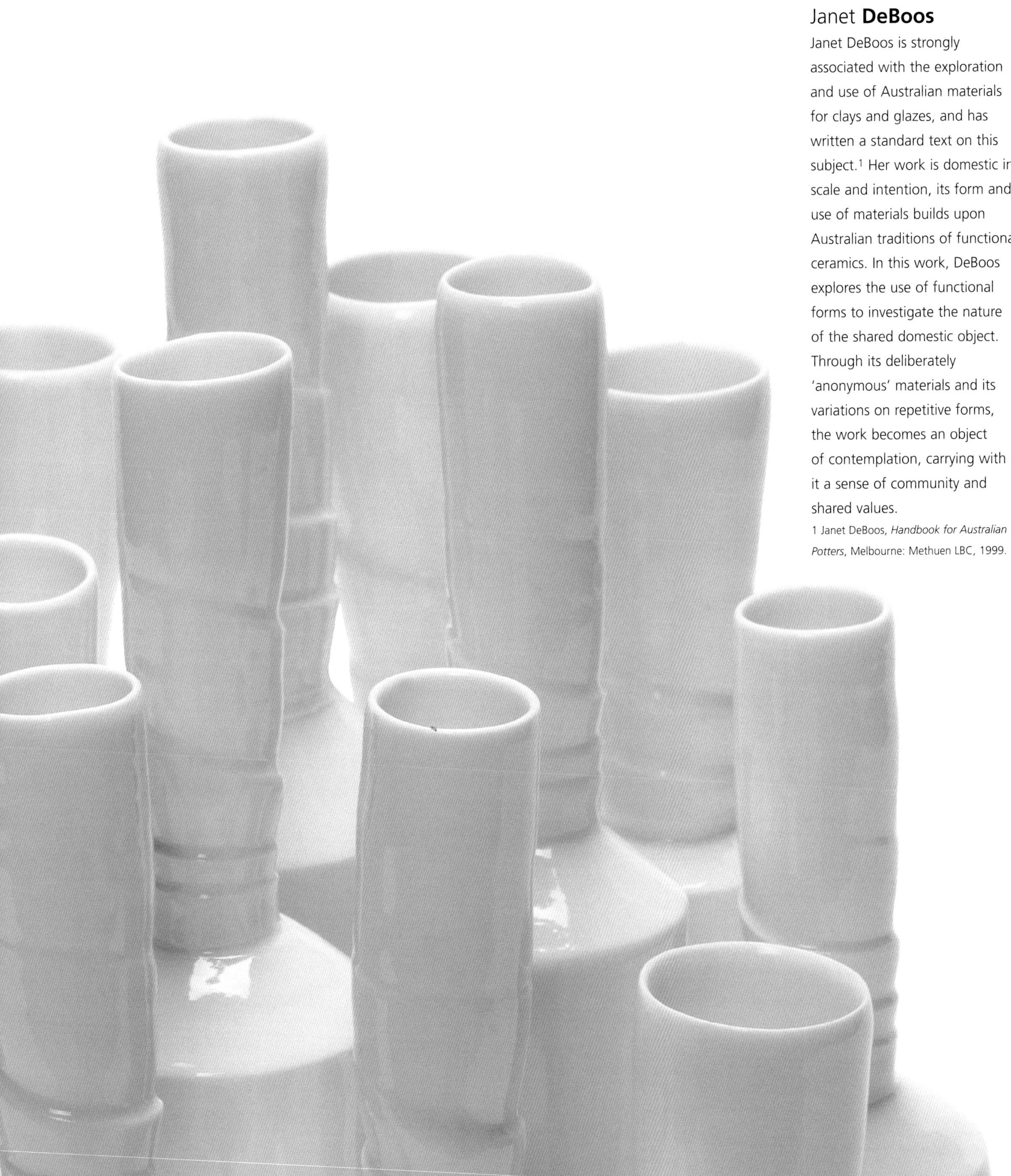

Janet **DeBoos**

Janet DeBoos is strongly associated with the exploration and use of Australian materials for clays and glazes, and has written a standard text on this subject.[1] Her work is domestic in scale and intention, its form and use of materials builds upon Australian traditions of functional ceramics. In this work, DeBoos explores the use of functional forms to investigate the nature of the shared domestic object. Through its deliberately 'anonymous' materials and its variations on repetitive forms, the work becomes an object of contemplation, carrying with it a sense of community and shared values.

1 Janet DeBoos, *Handbook for Australian Potters*, Melbourne: Methuen LBC, 1999.

Anne **Dybka**

Sydney, New South Wales

Born Portsmouth, Great Britain,
arrived Australia 1956

Training

Painting and Drawing with Martin Bloch,
London, UK, 1938–44; Graphic Arts,
London Polytecnic, London, UK, 1948–49;
Painting and Drawing, National Gallery Art
School and George Bell School,
Melbourne, Vic., late 1950s.

Related professional experience

Engraver with Crown Crystal Glass,
Sydney, NSW, 1970–76; Established own
studio in Argyle Arts Centre, Sydney, NSW,
1978; Australia Council Emeritus
Fellowship Award, 1995.

Selected solo exhibitions

Georges, Melbourne, Vic., 1970; Distelfink
Gallery, Melbourne, Vic., 1983; Beaver
Galleries, Canberra, ACT, 1992; Blaxland
Gallery, Sydney, NSW, 1993; David Jones,
Sydney, NSW, 1993; Meat Market Craft
Centre, Melbourne, Vic., 1994; Jam
Factory Craft and Design Centre Gallery,
Adelaide, SA, 1995.

Selected group exhibitions

London Guild of Glass Engravers, 1980;
Life Through Glass, Sydney Opera House,
Sydney, NSW, 1987.

Public collections (Australia)

National Gallery of Australia, Canberra,
ACT; National Gallery of Victoria,
Melbourne, Vic.; Parliament House,
Canberra, ACT; Powerhouse Museum,
Sydney, NSW; Queensland Art Gallery,
Brisbane, Qld; Wagga Wagga Regional Art
Gallery, Wagga Wagga, NSW.

Public collections (international)

The Glasmuseum, Ebeltoft, Denmark

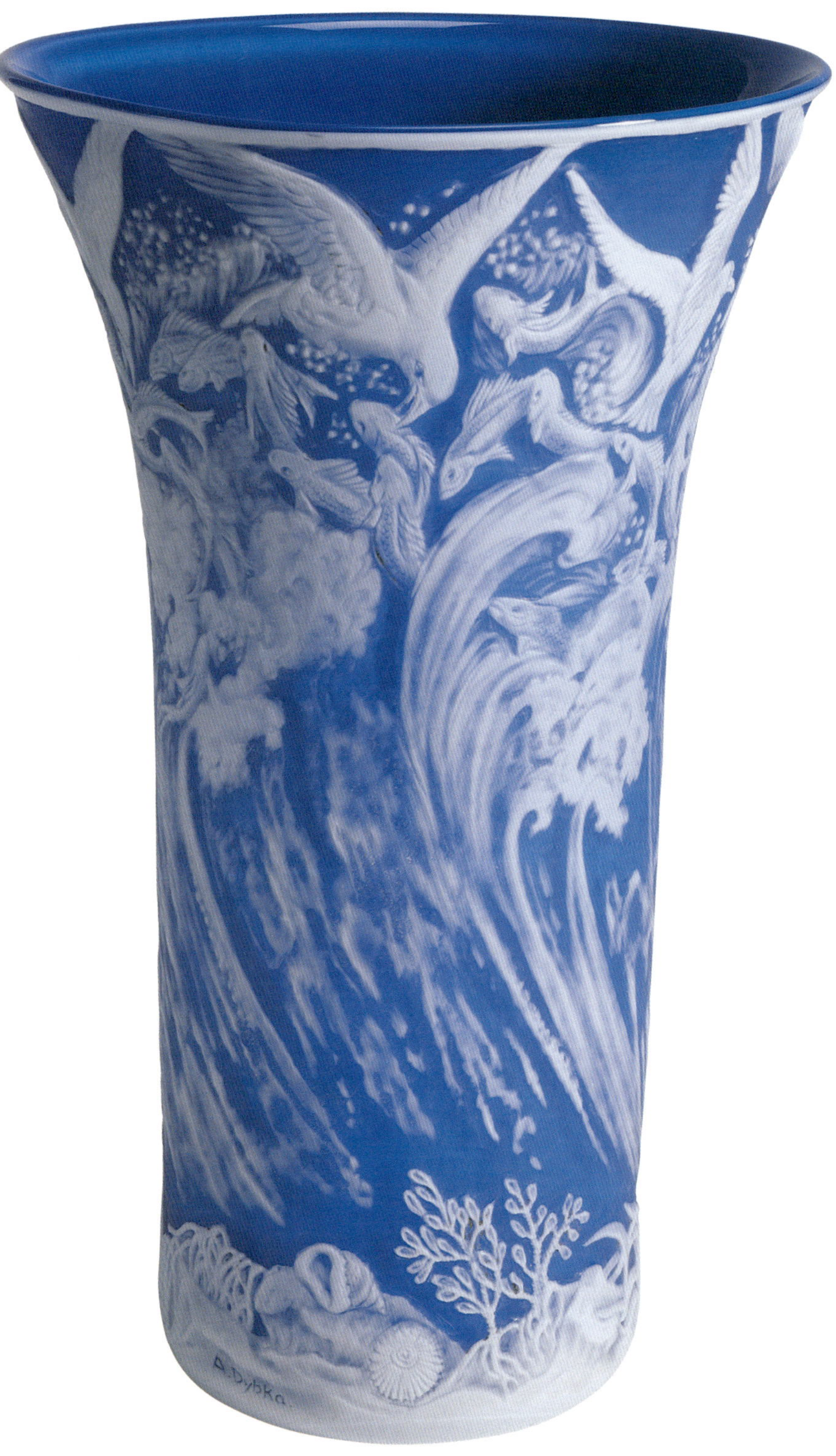

Anne **Dybka**
The shoal
engraved glass,

36

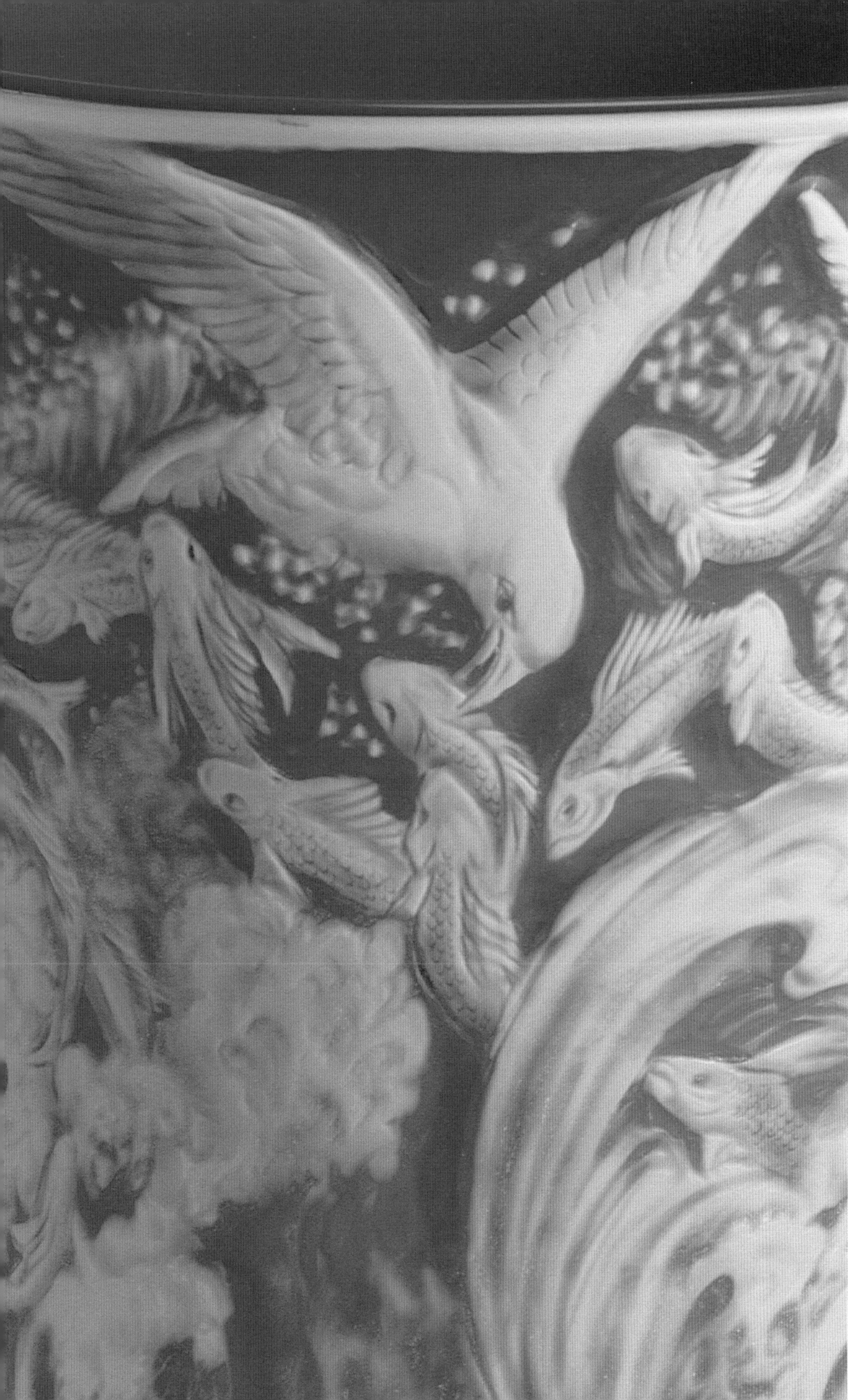

Anne **Dybka**

Anne Dybka's designs of Australian flora and fauna draw upon the technical and stylistic traditions of early modernist English and Scandinavian glass engraving. This work demonstrates Dybka's consummate skill and is engraved in a 'cameo' technique on opaque glass, blown in two layers, white over blue, by Australian glass artist, Brian Hirst. Its shape, colour and decoration evoke the swirling surf and drama of the seashore and makes stylistic references to the vivid interpretations and depictions of the natural world seen in cameo glass of the Art Nouveau movement of the late 19th century.

Tony **Hanning**

Yinnar, Victoria

Born Traralgon, Victoria 1950

Training

Master of Arts, Monash University, Melbourne, Vic., 1998; Diploma, Visual Arts, Gippsland Institute of Advanced Education, Monash University, Melbourne, Vic, 1971.

Selected solo exhibitions

Borough Galleries, Bendigo, Vic., 1985; Bairnsdale Gallery, Bairnsdale, Vic., 1985; Distelfink, Melbourne, Vic., 1986,1991, 1996; Margaret Francey Gallery, Brisbane, Qld, 1989, 1990, 1993; Powell Street Gallery, Melbourne, Vic., 1990; Flying Stone Gallery, Port Douglas, Qld, 1992; Glass Artists' Gallery, Sydney, NSW, 1994; Beaver Galleries, Canberra, ACT, 1995.

Selected group exhibitions

Four Australian Glass Artists, Australian Embassy, Washington, DC, USA, 1990; *Asia Pacific Crafts*, Kyoto, Japan, 1991; *Australian Glass Triennial*, Wagga Wagga Regional Art Gallery, Wagga Wagga, NSW, 1991; *Design Visions: Australian International Crafts Triennial*, Art Gallery of Western Australia, Perth, WA, 1992; *Australian Decorative Arts Survey: The object all sublime*, Lauraine Diggins Fine Art, Melbourne, Vic., 1994; *Four Glass Artists*, BMG Art Gallery, Adelaide, SA, 1995; *A Selection of Decorative Arts*, Lauraine Diggins Fine Art, Melbourne, VIC, 1994; Galerie L, Hamburg, Germany, 1998; SOFA New York, New York, USA, 1998; Beaver Galleries, Canberra, ACT, 1998; *Then and Now*, Metro Galleries, Melbourne, Vic., 1998; *Transparent Things: Expressions in glass*, National Gallery of Australia Travelling Exhibition, Wagga Wagga Regional Art Gallery, Wagga Wagga, NSW, 2001.

Public collections

Art Gallery of South Australia, Adelaide, SA; Art Gallery of Western Australia, Perth, WA; Devonport Gallery, Devonport, Tas.; Geelong Art Gallery, Geelong, Vic; La Trobe Regional Gallery, Morwell, Vic.; Museum and Art Gallery of Northern Territory, Darwin, NT; National Gallery of Australia, Canberra, ACT; National Gallery of Victoria, Melbourne, Vic.; Powerhouse Museum, Sydney, NSW; Queensland Art Gallery, Brisbane, Qld.; Rockhampton City Art Gallery, Rockhampton, Qld; Sale Regional Art Gallery, Sale, Vic; Tasmanian Museum and Art Gallery, Hobart, Tas.; Tweed River Regional Art Gallery, Murwillumbah, NSW; Wagga Wagga Regional Art Gallery, Wagga Wagga, NSW.

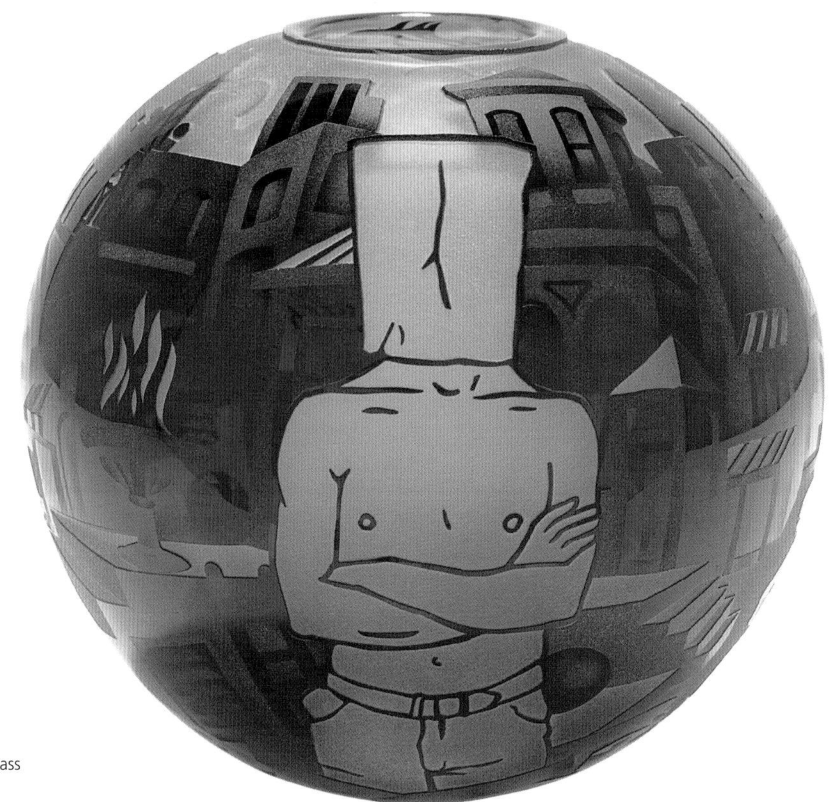

Tony **Hanning**
Mr and Mrs Anon
sandblasted and engraved glass
(two views)

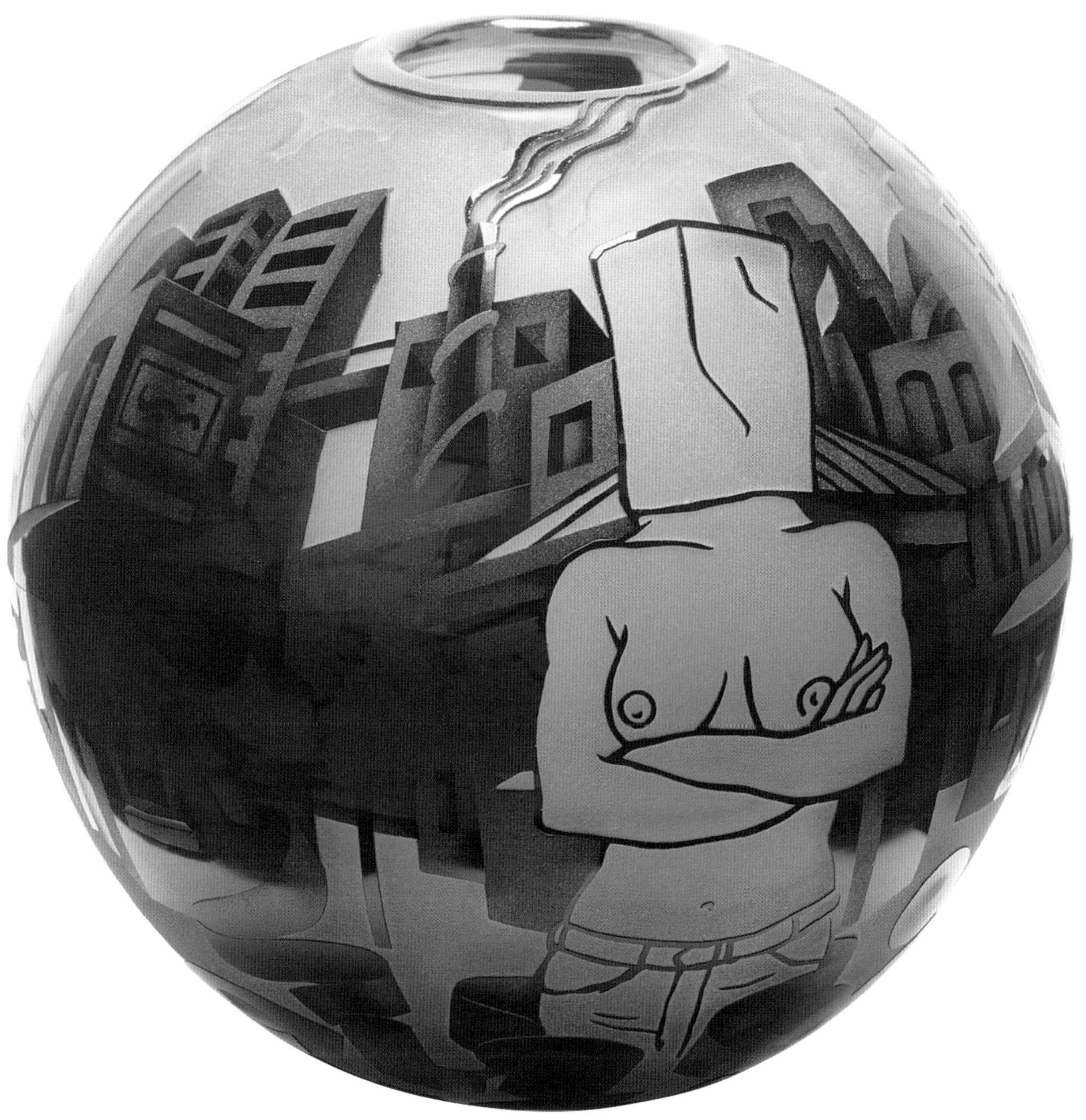

Tony **Hanning**

Tony Hanning was among the first contemporary Australian glass artists to work extensively with the techniques of cameo glass, a process where layers of glass are blown together and carved and engraved to reveal various colours beneath. This ancient technique was revived in the late 19th century by English and French glass designers, such as Thomas Webb and Emile Gallé, to express the styles of historical revival and Art Nouveau. In his early works, Hanning made reference to the work of these designers in his use of imagery of Australian flora. Later, in more complex works, he drew upon allegorical themes, employing surreal imagery of cityscapes and landscape as a background to visual puns and riddles. *Mr and Mrs Anon* shows a strong development of these ideas, drawing connections between the propaganda imagery of the Cold War period, advertising and comic book illustration of the mid-20th century.

Brian **Hirst**
Sydney, New South Wales
Born Yallourn, Victoria 1956

Training
Diploma of Arts (Visual Arts), Gippsland
Institute of Advanced Education, Churchill,
Vic., 1977–79.

Selected solo exhibitions
Object and Image Series, Blaxland Gallery,
Sydney, NSW, 1992; *A Celebration of
Glass*, Narek Galleries, Canberra, ACT,
1993; *Two Australians*, The Glass Gallery,
Bethesda, MD, USA, 1993; *Glass by Brian
Hirst*, Sale Regional Art Gallery, Sale, Vic.,
1994; *Glass Now 17*, Azabu Museum of
Arts and Crafts, Tokyo, Japan, 1995;
Makers Mark, Sydney, NSW, 1996, 2001;
Gallery Nakama, Tokyo, Japan, 1997;
Sacred Surface, University of Sydney
Gallery, Sydney, NSW, 1996; *Silent Surface*,
Quadrivium, Sydney, NSW, 1998; Beaver
Galleries, Canberra, ACT, 1999; Laurence
Miller Gallery, New York, USA, 1999;
Brian Hirst Studio Glass, Quadrivium,
Sydney NSW, 1999; *Reflection*, Lake
Russell Gallery, Coffs Harbour, NSW, 2000;
St Art, Strasbourg, France (Clara Scremini
Gallery, Paris), 2000; Clara Scremini
Gallery, Paris, France, 2001; *Surface*,
Beaver Galleries, Canberra, ACT, 2001;
Relationships in form, Quadrivium, Sydney,
NSW, 2002; *Silent Surface, Sacred Surface*,
Nancy Hoffman Gallery, New York, NY,
USA, 2002.

Selected group exhibitions since 1992
*Design Visions: Australian International
Crafts Triennial*, Art Gallery of Western
Australia, Perth, WA, 1992; *International
Invitational*, Habatat Galleries, Detroit, MI,
USA, 1993; *Two Australians* (with Robert
Knottenbelt), The Glass Gallery, Bethesda,
MD, USA, 1993; *Glass Now 16*, Tokyo,
Japan, 1994; *World Glass Now '94*,
Hokkaido Museum Of Modern Art, Japan,
1994; *Ausglass*, The Glasmuseum,
Ebeltoft, Denmark, 1995; *Venezia Aperto*

Vetro 1998: International New Glass, 5
sites in Venice, Italy, 1996; *Glass Weekend*,
Millville, NJ, USA (The Glass Gallery,
Bethesda, MD), 1997; *The Art of Gold*,
Ballarat Fine Art Gallery, Ballarat, Vic.,
1997; *Masters of Australia Glass*,
Quadrivium Gallery, Sydney, NSW, 1998;
SOFA Chicago, Chicago, IL, USA (Laurence
Miller Gallery), 1998; *Australian Glass:
10 Artists*, Gallery Enomoto, Osaka, Japan,
1998; *Contemporary Works from the Saxe
Collection*, Fine Arts Museum, San
Francisco, CA, USA, 1999; *Documenta
98*, Kanazu, Japan, 1999; *Drawn in Form*,
Brisbane City Gallery, Brisbane, Qld, 1999;
Objects of Desire, Nancy Hoffman Gallery,
New York, USA, 1999; *SOFA New York*,
New York, USA (Laurence Miller Gallery),
1999; *Canberra Glass*, Beaver Galleries,
Canberra, ACT, 2001; Clara Scremini
Gallery, Paris, France, 2001; *Glass Art in
Australia*, Quadrivium Gallery, Sydney,
NSW, 2001; *International Invitational*,
Habatat Galleries, Detroit, MI, USA, 2001;
Prime Verre, Musée-Atelier du Verre de
Sars-Poteries, Sars-Poteries, France, 2001;
At the Edge: Australian glass art, Brisbane
City Gallery, Brisbane, Qld; Object
Galleries, Sydney, NSW; Galerie Handwerk,
Munich, Germany; National Glass Centre,
Sunderland, UK, 2000; *Contemporary
Australian Craft*, Hokkaido Museum of
Modern Art, Sapporo, Japan, 1999; *Glass:
A celebration*, Nancy Hoffman Gallery,
New York, USA, 2000; Imago Galleries,
Palm Desert, CA, USA, *2000 International
Invitational*, Habatat Galleries, Detroit, MI,
USA, 2000; Museo del Vidrio, Monterrey,
Mexico, 2000; *Shattering Perceptions*,
Dennos Museum, Michigan, USA, 2001;
Transparent Things: Expressions in glass,
National Gallery of Australia Travelling
Exhibition, Wagga Wagga Regional Art
Gallery, Wagga Wagga, NSW, 2001; *19th
Annual International Glass Invitational*,
Habatat Galleries, Boca Raton, FL, USA,
2001; *Facets of Australian Glass*, Leo
Kaplan Modern, New York, NY, USA,
2002.

Public collections (Australia)
Art Gallery of Western Australia, Perth,
WA; Artbank, Sydney, NSW; Australian
National University, Canberra, ACT;
Canberra Museum and Art Gallery,
Canberra, ACT; Sale Regional Art Gallery,
Sale, Vic.; National Gallery of Australia,
Canberra, ACT; National Gallery of
Victoria, Melbourne, Vic.; Powerhouse
Museum, Sydney, NSW; Queensland Art
Gallery, Brisbane, Qld; Victorian State Craft
Collection, Melbourne, Vic.; Wagga
Wagga Regional Art Gallery, NSW

Public collections (international)
Corning Museum of Glass, NY, USA;
Evansville Museum, Indiana, USA;
Hokkaido Museum of Modern Art,
Sapporo, Japan; Koganazeki Glass
Museum, Japan; Kunstmuseum Düsseldorf
im Ehrenhof, Dusseldorf, Germany; Musée-
Atelier du Verre de Sars-Poteries, Sars-
Poteries, France; National Museum of
Modern Art, Kyoto, Japan; The Fine Arts
Museum of San Francisco, CA, USA;
The Glasmuseum, Ebeltoft, Denmark;
Yokohama Museum of Art, Yokohama,
Japan

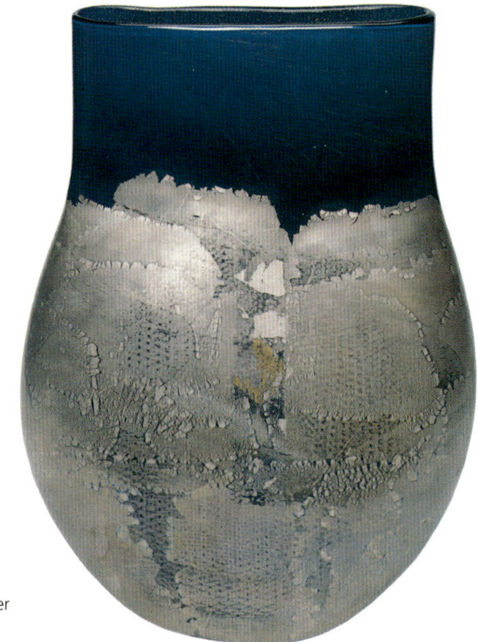

Brian **Hirst**
Flat form - Teal 2001
blown glass with gold, silver
and copper foil

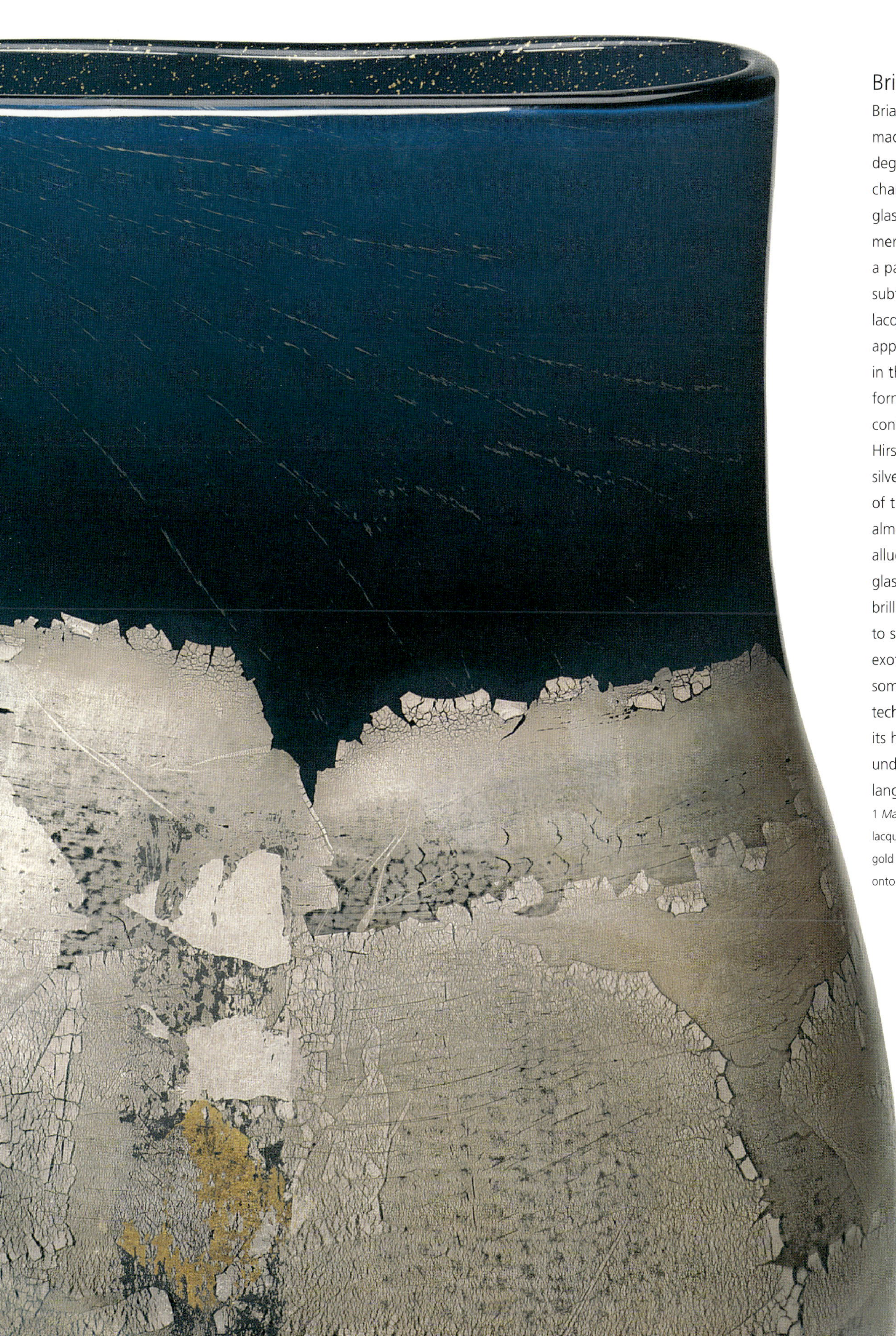

Brian **Hirst**

Brian Hirst's vessels are often made with reference to the degraded iridescent surfaces that characterise classical Roman glass. This work is a development of this theme and reflects a parallel interest in the subtleties of Japanese *makie* lacquer, through the fleeting appearance of flecked gold leaf in the vase's inner surface, a form of decoration also seen in contemporary Japanese glass. [1] Hirst's articulation of gold and silver lustre surfaces and his use of the blue-green colour teal, in almost opaque glass, also alludes to the historical use of glass in jewellery, where its brilliance and fluidity were used to suggest the arcane and the exotic. Through his mastery of some of these more demanding techniques of glass, Hirst evokes its historical richness to underscore a contemporary language of form and colour.

1 *Makie* (sprinkled picture) is a Japanese lacquer decorating technique in which gold or other metallic powders are dusted onto the surface of wet lacquer.

Kay **Lawrence**
Uraidla, South Australia
Born Canberra, ACT 1947

Training
Diploma of Art Teaching, South Australian
School of Art and Western Teachers
College, Adelaide, SA, 1965–67;
Postgraduate studies in Painting and
Printmaking, South Australian School of
Art, Adelaide, SA, 1968; Tapestry
Weaving, Edinburgh College of Art,
Edinburgh, UK, 1977–78.

Related professional experience
Lecturer Painting and Printmaking,
Salisbury C.A.E., Adelaide, SA, 1971–78;
Lecturer Textiles, Hartley C.A.E., Adelaide,
SA, 1980; Lecturer Sculpture, 1983–85,
Textiles 1988, First Year Studies, 1990,
South Australian College of Advanced
Education, Adelaide, SA, 1983–90;
Lecturer, 1992–95, Coordinator Textiles
Studio, 1995–2000, Portfolio Leader of
Research, 2001–02 and Head of School
since 2002; South Australian School
of Art, University of South Australia,
Adelaide, SA.

Selected solo exhibitions
Llewellyn Galleries, Adelaide, SA, 1971;
Yurcilla Galleries, Adelaide, SA, 1977;
Jam Factory Gallery, Adelaide, SA, 1981;
Lessness, Festival Theatre Gallery, Adelaide,
SA, 1985; Close Ties (with Marcel Marois),
University of Queensland Art Museum,
Brisbane, Qld, Object Galleries, Sydney,
NSW and University of South Australia Art
Museum, Adelaide, SA, 1999.

Selected group exhibitions since 1992
Banners of the World, McLellan Galleries,
Glasgow, UK, 1992; *Drawing 1*, University
of South Australia Art Museum, Adelaide,
SA, 1993; *Identities: Art from Australia*,
Taipei Fine Arts Museum, Taipei, Taiwan,
1993; *Texts from the Edge: Tapestry and
identity*, Jam Factory Craft and Design
Centre, Adelaide, SA, and travelling in
Australia, 1994-95; *Crossing Borders:
Contemporary Australian textile art*,
University of Wollongong, Wollongong,
NSW, for Exhibits USA, USA tour,
1995–97; *VicHealth Craft Awards*,
National Gallery of Victoria, Melbourne,
Vic., 1995; *The Language of Thread*, Art
Gallery of Western Australia, Perth, WA,
1996; *17th National Craft Acquisition
Award*, Museum and Art Gallery of the
Northern Territory, Darwin, NT, 1997;
*A Response to Lake Mungo: Works in
progress*, Long Gallery, University of
Wollongong, Wollongong, NSW, 1997;
Small Tapestries From Australia, Galleria
Forum, Lodz, Poland, 1998; *Origins and
New Perspectives: Contemporary
Australian textiles*, Queen Victoria Museum
and Art Gallery, Launceston, Tas., for tour
to Lodz, Poland, 1998–99; *Threefold: Elsje
Van Keppel, Kay Lawrence, Ernabella Arts*,
Canberra School of Art Gallery, Canberra,
ACT, 1998; *Textiles in Focus*, Parliament
House, Canberra, ACT, 1998; *Drawn in
Form*, Brisbane City Art Gallery, Brisbane,
QLD, 1999; *Frisson: 14th Tamworth Fibre
Textile Biennial*, Tamworth City Gallery,
Tamworth, NSW, 2000 and Australian tour
2000–02; *Lake Mungo Revisited*, Goulburn
Regional Art Gallery, Goulburn, NSW,
2000; *Chemistry: Art in South Australia
1990–2000*, Art Gallery of South Australia,
Adelaide, SA, 2000; *Home is Where the
Heart Is*, Burra Regional Gallery, Burra, SA,
2001.

Public collections
Ararat Gallery, Ararat, Vic.; Art Gallery of
South Australia, Adelaide, SA; Art Gallery
of Western Australia, Perth, WA; Artbank,
Sydney, NSW; National Gallery of Australia,
Canberra, ACT; Parliament House,
Canberra, ACT; Powerhouse Museum,
Sydney, NSW; Queen Victoria Museum and
Art Gallery, Launceston, Tas.; Queensland
Art Gallery, Brisbane, Qld; Riddoch Art
Gallery, Riddoch, SA; Tasmanian Museum
and Art Gallery, Hobart, Tas.; University
of Wollongong, Wollongong, NSW.

Kay **Lawrence**
Translation
woven wool, cotton and linen tapestry
Reproduced with permission of the artist

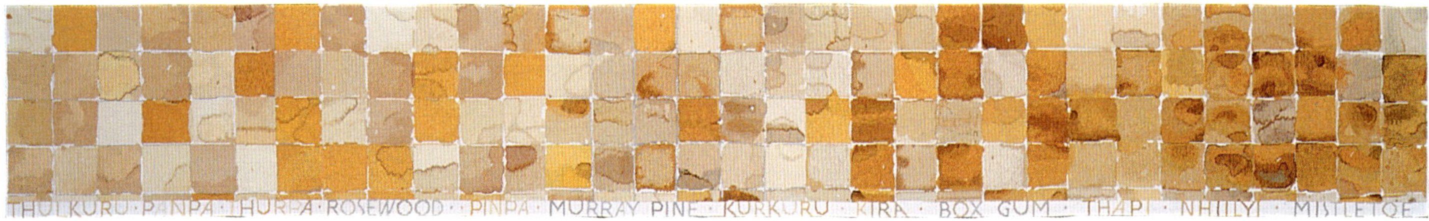

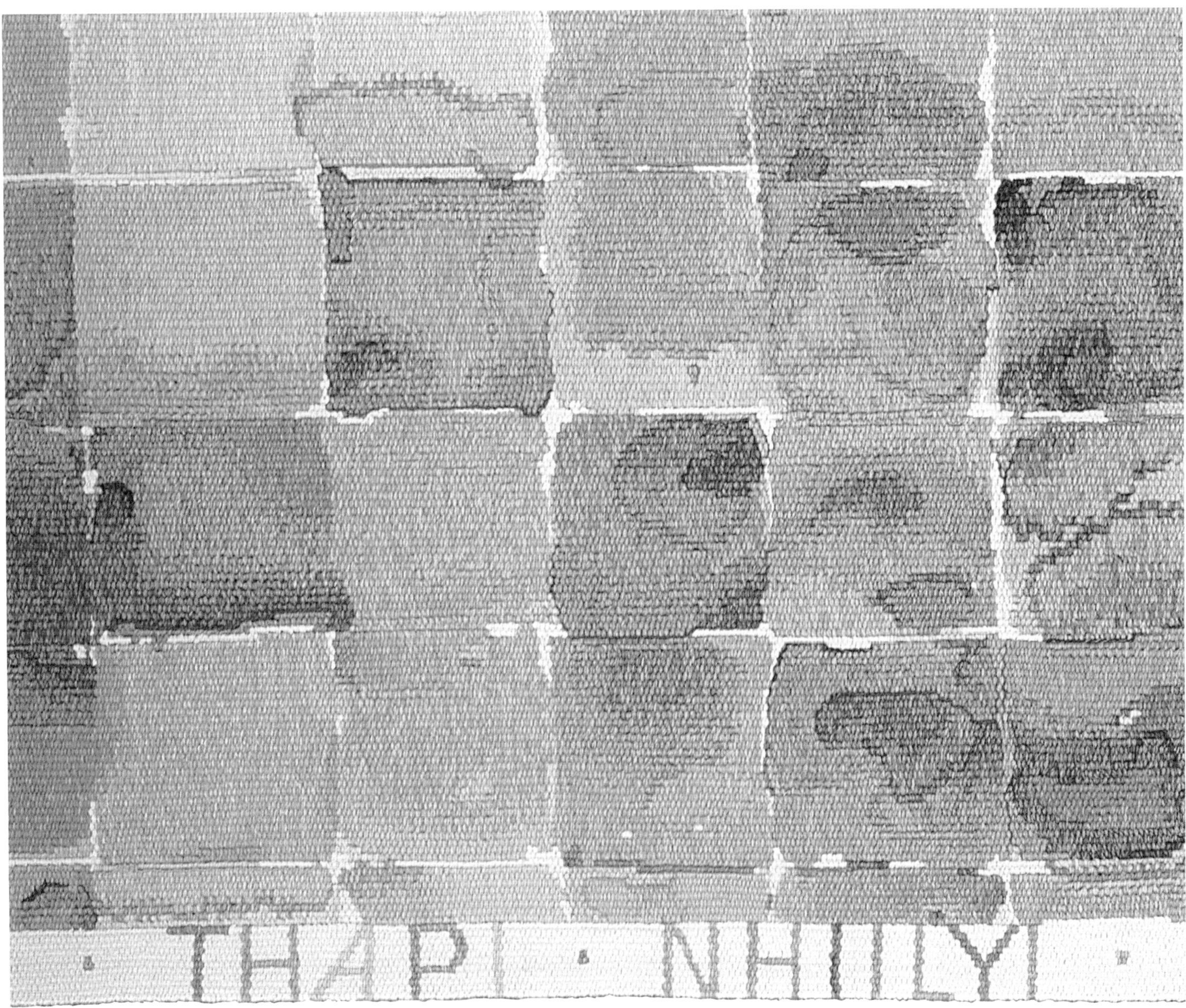

Kay **Lawrence**

Through her work on the subject of change in the landscape, Kay Lawrence is a key figure in the development of contemporary tapestry in Australia. Her tapestries on the subject of bushfires informed her design work for collaborative projects such as the monumental long horizontal embroidery for Parliament House in Canberra. Working in a similar format for this tapestry, she has used local plant dyes from Lake Mungo in south-western New South Wales, weaving a grid sequence that reflects the archaeological construct of this historic Australian cultural site. Woven along the tapestry's length are the Indigenous Paakantyi names for the dye plants, followed by English translations, suggesting the colonial mapping and appropriation of the land.[1]

1 See Jennifer Lamb, *Lake Mungo Revisited*, exhibition catalogue, Goulburn: Goulburn Regional Art Gallery and the University of Wollongong, 2000, p.12.

Jessica **Loughlin**
Adelaide, South Australia
Born Melbourne, Victoria 1975

Training
Bachelor of Arts (Visual, with Honours),
Canberra School of Art, Australian
National University, 1997.

Selected group exhibitions
RFC Glass Prize, Glass Artists' Gallery,
Sydney, 1997; *Young Glass International*,
Glasmuseum, Ebeltoft, Denmark, 1997;
*Alain & Marisa Bergou, Steve Linn, Klaus
Moje, Jessica Loughlin, Giles Bettison &
Claudia Borella*, Sanske Galerie, Zürich,
Switzerland; Venice, Italy, 1998;
International Young Artists in Glass,
Bullseye Connection Gallery, Portland OR,
USA, 1998; SOFA Chicago, Chicago, IL,
USA (Bullseye Connection Gallery), 1998;
Translucence, Quadrivium Gallery, Sydney,
NSW, 1998; *Talente '98*, Munich,
Germany, 1998; *Venezia Aperto Vetro
1998: International New Glass*, 5 sites in
Venice, Italy, 1998; Beaver Galleries,
Canberra, ACT, 1999; *Essentially Canberra*,
Object Galleries, Sydney, NSW; 1999;
*Giles Bettison, Claudia Borella and Jessica
Loughlin*, Sanske Galerie, Zürich,
Switzerland, 1999; *Glass, art & science*
(Australian studio glass exhibition), Museu
do Vidro da Marinha Grande, Marinha
Grande, Portugal, 1999; Galeria Nova
Imagem, Lisbon, Portugal, 1999; *Jessica
Loughlin & Giles Bettison,* Bullseye
Connection Gallery, Portland, OR, USA,
1999; *SOFA Chicago*, Chicago, IL, USA
(Bullseye Connection Gallery), 1999; *SOFA
New York*, New York, USA (Bullseye
Connection Gallery), 1999; *Australian
Studio Glass: Essentially Canberra*, Hsinchu
International Glass Festival, Hsinchu,
Taiwan; travelling exhibition, 2000;
Fusion: Contemporary glass, Axia Modern
Art, Melbourne, Vic., 2000; *International
Invitational*, Habatat Galleries, Pontiac, MI,
USA, 2000; New Work, Bullseye
Connection Gallery, Portland, OR, USA,
2000; *At the Edge: Australian glass art*,
Brisbane City Gallery, QLD, Galerie
Handwerk, Munich, Germany, National
Glass Centre, Sunderland, UK, 2000;
Sanske Galerie, Zürich, Switzerland, 2000;
SOFA Chicago, Chicago, IL, USA (Bullseye
Connection Gallery), 2000; *SOFA New
York*, New York, USA (Bullseye Connection
Gallery), 2000; *Vessels: International
exhibition of glass*, Koganezaki Glass
Museum, Tokyo, Japan, 2000; Christian
Braggiotti, Amsterdam, The Netherlands,
2001; *Cutting Edge*, Axia Modern Art,
Melbourne, Vic., 2001; *Glass State*,
JamFactory Galleries, Adelaide, SA, 2001;
SOFA Chicago, Chicago, IL, USA (Bullseye
Connection Gallery), 2001; *Quadrivium's
Finest*, Quadrivium Gallery, Sydney, NSW,
2001; *Transparent Things: Expressions in
glass*, National Galllery of Australia
Travelling Exhibition, Wagga Wagga
Regional Art Gallery, Wagga Wagga, NSW,
2001.

Public collections (Australia)
Australian National University, Canberra,
ACT; National Gallery of Australia,
Canberra, ACT; Wagga Wagga Regional
Art Gallery, Wagga Wagga, NSW

Public collections (international)
Museu do Vidro da Marinha Grande,
Marinha Grande, Portugal; The
Glasmuseum, Ebeltoft, Denmark

Jessica **Loughlin**
Interval between two horizons
kiln-formed, wheel-cut, enamelled and
engraved glass

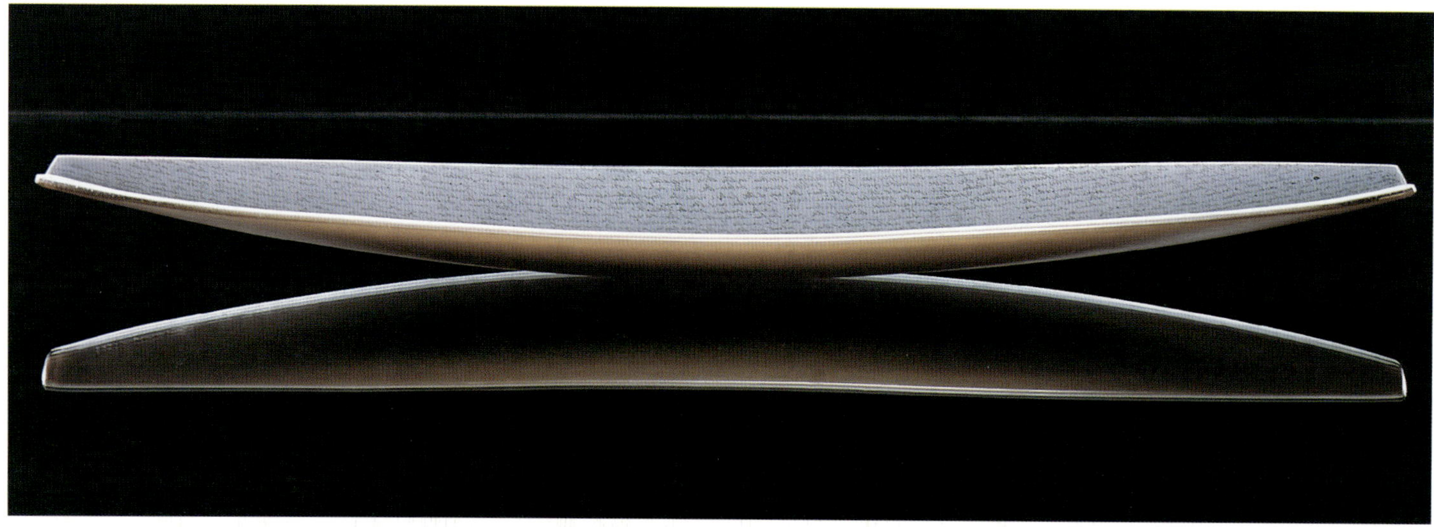

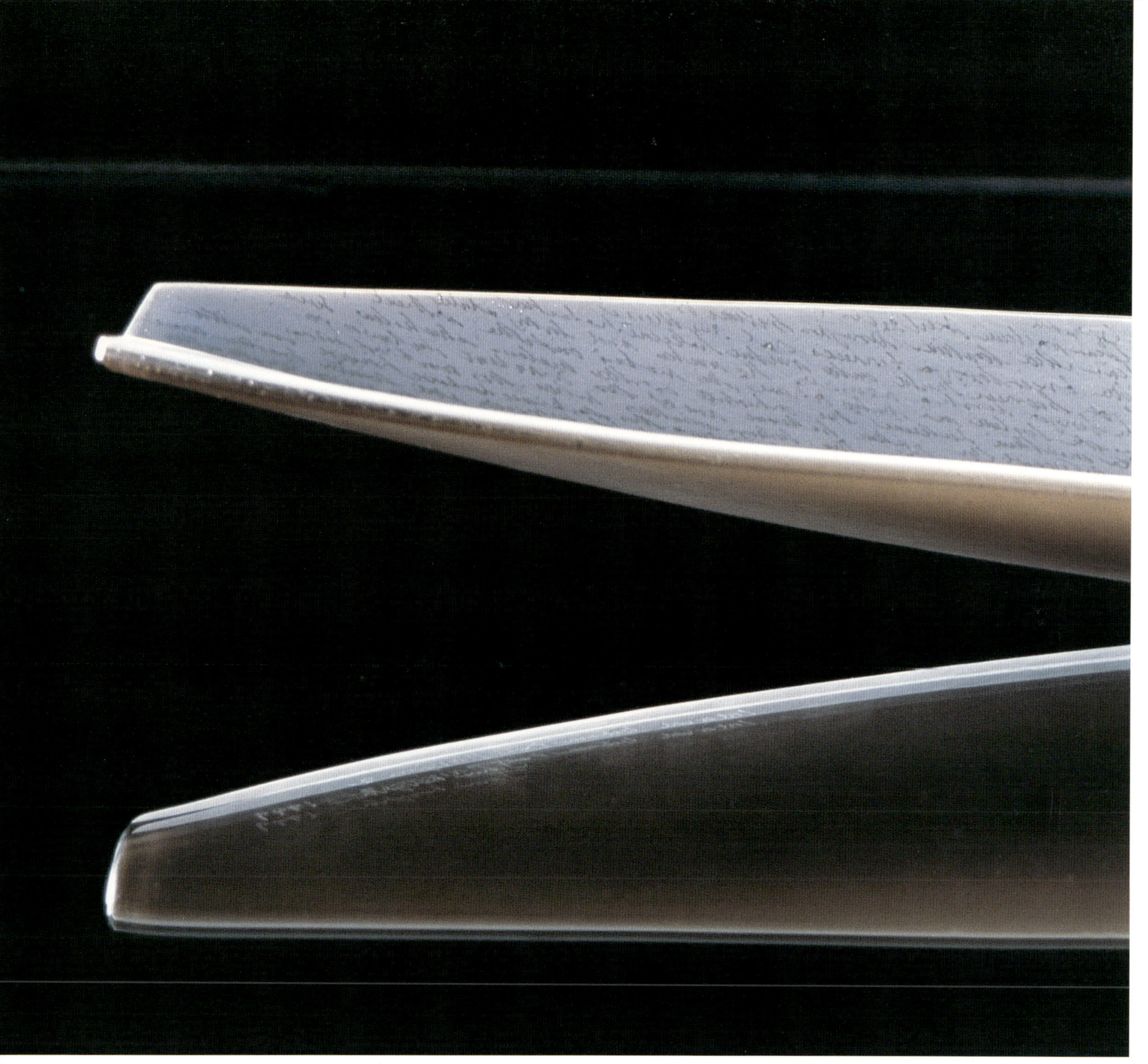

Jessica **Loughlin**

Jessica Loughlin's work explores the subject of the horizon and the flat landscapes of South Australia. In *Interval between two horizons*, she uses the form of the shallow, boat-shaped vessel, divided to delineate between actual and interpreted space. Dense handwritten text is engraved into a panel, simulating the way that colonial diarists recorded their experiences of the landscape. This faint narrative counterbalances the material physicality of the glass itself, its bleached colour evoking the shimmer of mirages and the fading of memory.

Helmut **Lueckenhausen**
Melbourne, Victoria
Born Cologne, Germany 1950, arrived
Australia 1954

Training

Diploma of Industrial Design, Royal
Melbourne Institute of Technology,
Melbourne, Vic., 1970; Diploma of
Education, State College of Victoria,
Hawthorn, Vic., 1973; Graduate Diploma
of Art (Industrial Design), Royal Melbourne
Institute of Technology, Melbourne,
Vic., 1979.

Related professional experience

Lecturer, Three Dimensional Design and
Sculpture, Box Hill College of TAFE,
Melbourne, Vic, 1974–81; Lecturer,
Furniture Design, Royal Melbourne
Institute of Technology, Melbourne, Vic.,
1982; Lecturer, Senior Lecturer, Professor
of Design, Swinburne University of
Technology, Melbourne, Vic., 1982–97;
Head of School, National School of Design,
Swinburne University of Technology,
Melbourne, Vic, since 1997.

Selected solo exhibitions

The Craft Centre, Melbourne, Vic., 1979,
1981, 1983, 1985, 1986; Blackfriars
Gallery, Sydney, NSW, 1982; Beaver
Galleries, Canberra, ACT, 1986; Queen
Victoria Museum and Art Gallery,
Launceston, Tas., travelling to Crafts
Council of Tasmania Gallery, Hobart and
Burnie Regional Art Gallery, Burnie, Tas.,
1987; BMG Fine Arts, Adelaide, SA, 1988;
Devise Gallery, Melbourne, Vic., 1988;
Devise Arts, Victorian Pavilion, *World Expo
'88, Brisbane*, Qld, 1988; BMG Fine Arts,
Sydney, NSW, 1988; Genoa Gallery,
Skaneateles, NY, USA, 1990; Erica
Underwood Gallery, Curtin University,
Perth, WA, 1991; *From the Cabinet of
Curiosity*, Lauraine Diggins Fine Art,
Melbourne, Vic., 1998.

Selected group exhibitions since 1992

Jahremesse: Gäste aus Australien, Museum
fur Kunst und Gewerbe, Hamburg,
Germany, 1992; *Design Visions: Australian
International Crafts Triennial*, Art Gallery of
Western Australia, Perth, WA, 1992;
Exhibition of Australian Design Excellence,
Department of Foreign Affairs/Australian
Academy of Design, travelling to SE Asia,
1992; *VicHealth National Craft Award*,
National Gallery of Victoria, Melbourne,
Vic., 1992; Australian Pavilion, *World Expo
'92*, Seville, Spain, 1992; *Crafts of Asia
and the Pacific*, Teheran, Iran, 1993; *The
Art of the Object*, Craft Australia travelling
exhibition, Salon Municipal de
Exposiciones, Montevideo, Uruguay and
Instituto Cultural de Las Condes, Santiago,
Chile, 1994; *Australian Decorative Arts
Survey*, Lauraine Diggins Fine Art,
Melbourne, VIC, 1994; *Contemporary
Australian Furniture*, SOFA, Chicago, IL,
USA, 1996; *Manifesto*, International Craft
Design Association, Maison & Objet, Paris,
France, 1996; *Summoning the Spirit:
Contemporary craft and folk traditions*,
Centre for Contemporary Craft, Sydney,
NSW, 1996; *Box*, Craft Victoria Gallery,
Melbourne, VIC, 1996; *Holz von nah und
vern: Artists in Wood from 5 Continents*,
Handwerkskammer Rheinhessen, Mainz,
Germany, 1997; *Von Holzstück zum
Kunststück (International Artistry in
Wood)*, Ligna, Hannover, Germany, 1997;
Objects of Ideas, Crafts Council of
Queensland, Brisbane, Qld, 1997; *Craft
Design for the Global Village*, International
Craft Design Association, Maison & Objet,
Paris France, 1998; *World Contemporary
Craft Now*, invitational exhibition of
Chongju International Craft Biennale '99,
Chongju, South Korea, 1999; *Blessed be
the Work: Australian contemporary design
in Jewish ceremony II*, The Jewish Museum
of Australia, Melbourne, Vic., 1999 and
national tour 1999-2001; *Holz in
Künstlerhand (Wood in Artists' Hands)*,
Ligna Hannover '99, Hannover, Germany,
1999; *Klein Aber Fein: International
exhibition*, Messe am Rhein, Koblenz,
Germany, 1999; *Australian Decorative
Arts Survey 2000*, Lauraine Diggins Fine
Art, Melbourne, Vic., 2000; *Against the
Grain: Australian sculptural furniture*,
Brisbane City Gallery, Qld, 2000; *From
Eltham to Memphis: An exhibition of
works from the Victorian State Craft
Collection*, Craft Victoria, Melbourne,
Vic., 2000.

Public collections

Art Gallery of Western Australia, Perth,
WA; Curtin University of Technology, Perth,
WA; Museum and Art Gallery of the
Northern Territory, Darwin, NT; National
Gallery of Australia, Canberra, ACT;
National Gallery of Victoria, Melbourne,
Vic.; Powerhouse Museum, Sydney, NSW;
Queen Victoria Museum and Art Gallery,
Launceston, Tas.; Queensland Art Gallery,
Brisbane, Qld; The Jewish Museum of
Australia, Melbourne, Vic.; Victorian State
Craft Collection, Melbourne, Vic.

Helmut **Lueckenhausen**
Wunderkabinet 2
(*from Wunderkabinet pair*)
silky oak, silky oak veneer, silver ash, silver
ash veneer, glass and sterling silver keys

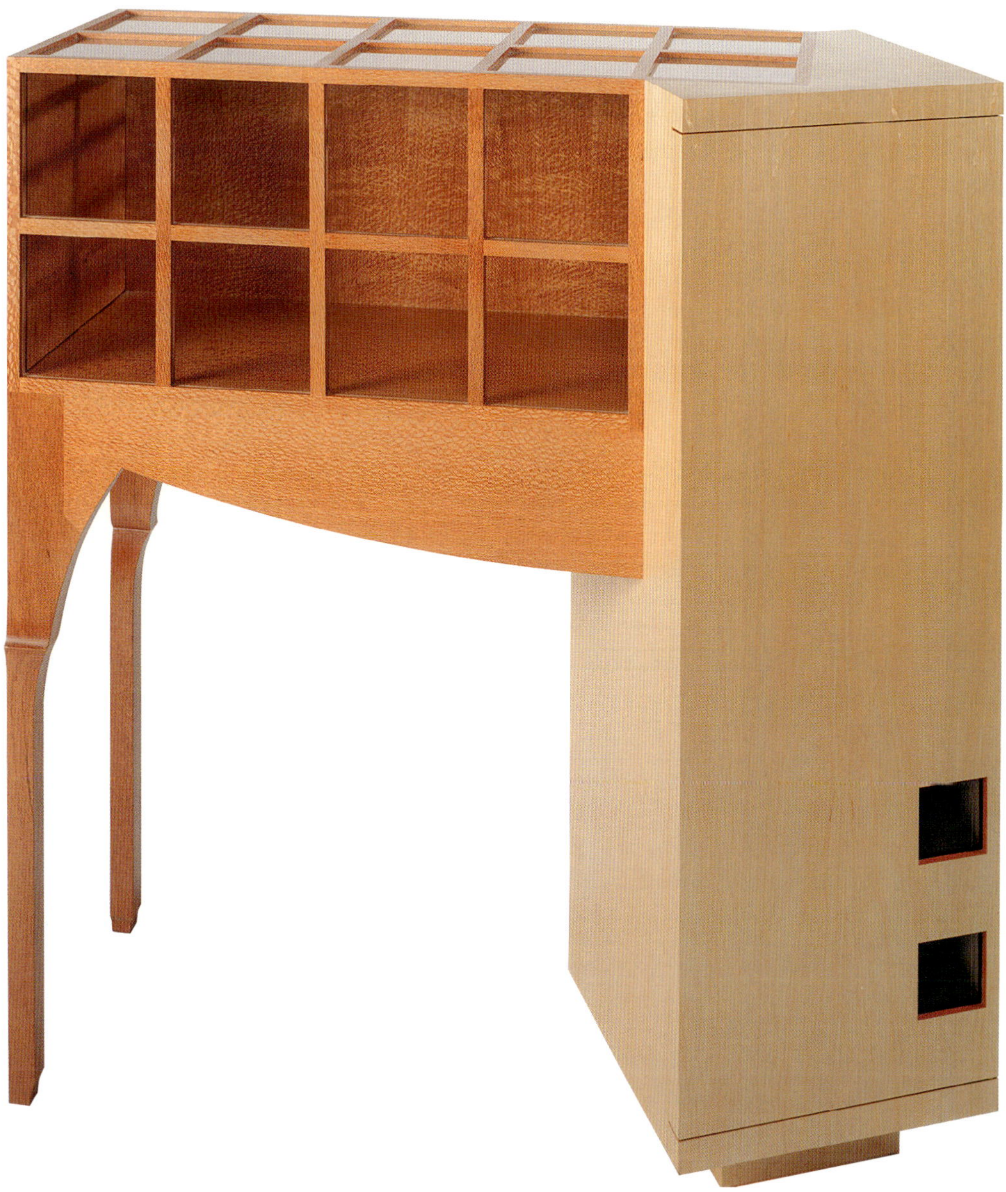

Helmut **Lueckenhausen**

The idea of the 'cabinet of curiosity' has a place in all of our histories, from collections of personal memorabilia to the taxonomic systems of our museums.[1] Helmut Lueckenhausen's *Wunderkabinets* derive from the European Wunderkammer and Kunstkabinet of the 16th and 17th centuries, in which the wonders of the natural world, such as animals, insects, birds, fish, minerals, plants and precious stones, along with crafted artefacts, were assembled together to instruct and delight. Such repositories were often objects of extraordinary craftsmanship and ingenuity, visible manifestations of the enlightened mind and the desire to find and impose order in an expanding view of the world. In this pair of cabinets, Lueckenhausen allows both enclosure and disclosure through similar structures that coexist as display cases and anonymous storage units. Each work is a gallery of refined materials and craftsmanship and, in their emptiness and potential, a theatre for the imagination.[2]

1 See Helmut Lueckenhausen, 'Wonder and despite: craft and design in museum history' in Sue Rowley (ed.), *Craft and Contemporary Theory*, Sydney: Allen and Unwin, 1997, p. 35.
2 See Jason Smith, 'Wunderkabinets' in *Object*, no 46, Sydney: Object-Australian Centre for Craft and Design, for an assessment of Lueckenhausen's *Wunderkabinet* series.

Jeff **Mincham**
Cherryville, South Australia
Born Milang, South Australia 1950

Training
Art Teacher Training, Western Teachers' College, Adelaide, SA 1972; Post Graduate Studies for Advanced Diploma of Art Teaching, South Australian School of Art, Adelaide, South Australia, 1973; Post Graduate Studies (Ceramics), Tasmanian School of Art, Hobart, Tas., 1974.

Related professional experience
Art teacher, Croydon High School, Adelaide, SA, 1975; Part-time Lecturer Ceramics, South Australian School of Art, Adelaide, SA, 1975 & 1978; Foreman and potter, Jam Factory, Adelaide, SA, 1976; Head of Ceramics, Jam Factory, Adelaide, SA, 1979; Part-time lecturer Ceramics, Murray Park College of Advanced Education, Adelaide, South Australia, 1979; Part-time Lecturer Ceramics, South Australian School of Design, Underdale, SA, 1988–1989.

Selected solo exhibitions since 1990
BMG Gallery, Sydney, NSW, 1990; Bonython-Meadmore Gallery, Sydney, NSW, 1990; Jam Factory Gallery, Adelaide, SA, 1990; Cooks Hill Gallery, Newcastle, NSW, 1990; Queensland Potters Association, Brisbane, Qld, 1990; Gasworks Gallery, Strathalbyn, SA, 1991; Realities Gallery, Melbourne, Vic., 1991; Allyn Fisher Fine Art, Bendigo, Vic., 1992; BMG Fine Art, Adelaide, SA, 1992, 1994, 1997, 1999, 2001; Holdsworth Galleries, Sydney, NSW, 1993, 1994; Lyall Burton Gallery, Melbourne, Vic., 1993, 1994, 1997, 1998; Beaver Galleries, Canberra, ACT, 1997, 2000; Mira Fine Art Gallery, Melbourne, Vic., 2001.

Selected group exhibitions since 1990
Austceram, Perth, WA, 1990; *Fletcher Challenge Ceramic Award*, Auckland Museum, Auckland, New Zealand, 1991; *International Triennial of Ceramics*, Warsaw, Poland, 1991; National Gallery of Victoria, Melbourne, Vic., 1992; *Design Visions: Australian International Crafts Triennial*, Art Gallery of Western Australia, Perth, WA, 1992; *Alice Springs Craft Award*, Araluen Arts Centre, Alice Springs, NT, 1992; *11th Gold Coast Ceramic Award*, Gold Coast City Art Gallery, Gold Coast, Qld, 1992; *3rd Mino International Ceramic Award*, Nagoya, Japan, 1992; *Clay, Fibre, Glass, Metal, Wood*, Lyall Burton Gallery, Melbourne, Vic., 1995; *Ceramics Survey 1965 to 1995*, Bathurst Regional Art Gallery, Bathurst, NSW, 1995; Lyall Burton Gallery, Melbourne, Vic., 1997; *The Language of Clay*, Art Gallery of Western Australia, Perth, WA, 1999; *Chemistry: Art in South Australia 1990–2000*, Art Gallery of South Australia, Adelaide, SA, 2000; *Place and Identity: Contemporary South Australian ceramists*, University of South Australia Art Museum, Adelaide, SA, 2000; *Landscape, Memory and the Imagination*, Brisbane City Gallery, Brisbane, Qld, 2001.

Public collections (Australia)
Art Gallery of South Australia, Adelaide, SA: Art Gallery of Western Australia, Perth, WA; Bathurst Regional Art Gallery, Bathurst, NSW; Castlemaine Art Gallery, Castlemaine, Vic.; Geelong Art Gallery, Geelong, Vic.; Gold Coast City Art Gallery, Gold Coast, Qld.; Manly Art Gallery, Sydney, NSW; Museum and Art Gallery of the Northern Territory, Darwin, NT; National Gallery of Australia, Canberra, ACT; National Gallery of Victoria, Melbourne, Vic.; Newcastle Region Art Gallery, Newcastle, NSW; Parliament House, Canberra, ACT; Powerhouse Museum, Sydney, NSW; Queen Victoria Museum and Art Gallery, Launceston, Tas.; Queensland Art Gallery, Brisbane, Qld; Rockhampton City Art Gallery, Rockhampton, Qld; Shepparton Art Gallery, Shepparton, Vic.; Stanthorpe Art Gallery, Stanthorpe, Qld.

Public collections (international)
National Gallery of Malaysia, Kuala Lumpur, Malaysia; National Gallery of Taiwan, Taipei, Taiwan.

Jeff **Mincham**
Highland journey
glazed earthenware

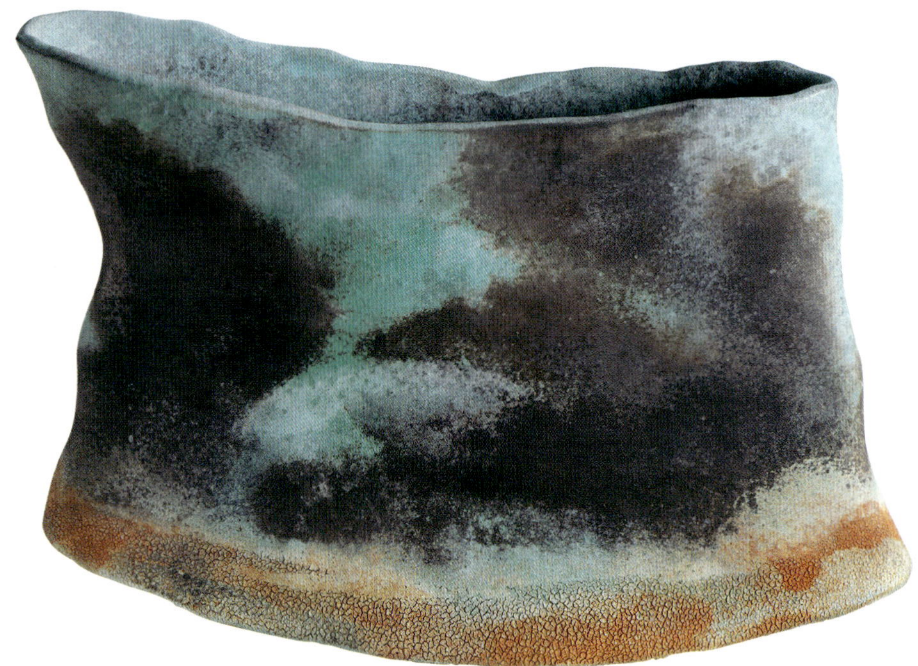

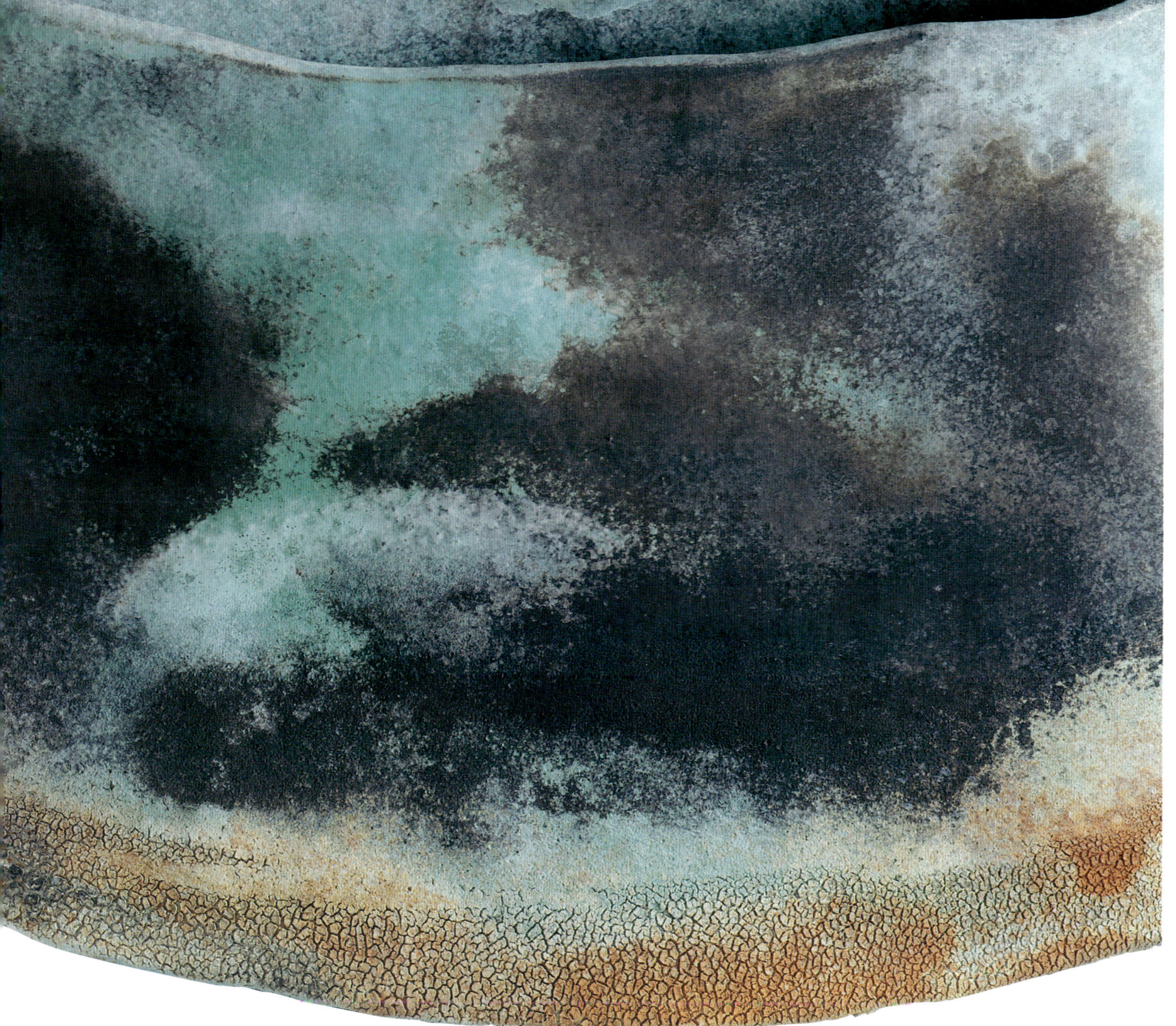

Jeff **Mincham**

Throughout his career as a ceramicist, Jeff Mincham has pursued the subject of the South Australian landscape through the firing and glazing of his characteristic large, sculptural vessel forms in the raku technique, a process through which the ceramic surface is defined by the marks of combustible, natural materials. *Highland journey* shows Mincham's vigorous handling of patinated alkaline glazes to evoke the scarred and scorched earth resulting from bushfires near his home in the Adelaide Hills. The charred surface of its undulating form is overlaid with verdant colour, an abstraction of the renewal of the bush after burning.

Milton **Moon**
Adelaide, South Australia
Born Melbourne, Victoria 1926

Training
Private ceramic tuition with Mervyn
Feeney, Brisbane, Qld, 1950; Painting and
Drawing, Central Technical College,
Brisbane, Qld, 1951; Private tuition with
Margaret Cilento, Brisbane, Qld, 1951.

Related professional experience
Senior Pottery Instructor, Department of
Technical Education, Central Technical
College, Brisbane, Qld, 1962–69; Art Tutor,
Department of Architecture, University of
Queensland, Brisbane, Qld, 1967–68;
Senior Lecturer, Head of Ceramics, South
Australian School of Art, Adelaide, SA,
1969–75; Myer Foundation Geijutsu
Fellow, Japan, 1974.

Selected solo exhibitions
Johnstone Gallery, Brisbane, Qld, 1959,
1962, 1964, 1965, 1967, 1969, 1970,
1971; Rudy Komon Gallery, Sydney, NSW,
1962; Von Bertouch Gallery, Newcastle,
NSW, 1963, 1969; Hungry Horse Gallery,
Sydney, NSW, 1965; Macquarie Galleries,
Sydney, NSW, 1968, 1969, 1979;
Bonython Galleries, Adelaide, SA, 1969,
1971, 1973, 1975, 1977, 1979; Skinner
Galleries, Perth, WA, 1972; Australian
Galleries, Melbourne, VIC, 1972;
Collectors Gallery, Perth, WA, 1976; De
Gruchy Gallery, Brisbane, Qld, 1976, 1982,
1989; Greenhill Galleries, Adelaide, SA,
1976, 1982, 1988; Solander Gallery,
Canberra, ACT, 1976, 1988;
The Craft Centre, Melbourne, VIC, 1977,
1979; Jam Factory Gallery, Adelaide, SA,
1979; Market Row Gallery, Sydney, NSW,
1982; Distelfink Gallery, Melbourne, Vic.,
1982, 1983, 1985; Bonython Meadmore
Galleries, Adelaide, SA, 1984; Potters
Gallery, Sydney, 1985; Cooks Hill Gallery,
Newcastle, NSW, 1985; Christine
Abrahams Gallery, Melbourne, Vic., 1990,
1996, 1999; Stafford Studios, Perth, WA,
1990, 1993, 1999; Philip Bacon Galleries,
Brisbane, Qld., 1991, 1995; *Milton Moon
Retrospective*, Art Gallery of South
Australia, Adelaide,1991; Gallery,
Okayama, Japan, 1993; Aptos Cruz
Galleries, Stirling, SA, 1993, 1998; Ray
Hughes Gallery, Sydney, NSW, 1995.

Selected group exhibitions since 1992
Form and Essence, Aptos Cruz Galleries,
Stirling, SA, 1993; Solander Gallery,
Canberra, ACT, 1994; *Ceramics Survey
1969 to 1995*, Bathurst Regional Art
Gallery, Bathurst, NSW, 1995; *The Japan
Inspiration: Influence in crafts and design*,
Art Gallery of Western Australia, Perth,
WA, 1997; *The Language of Clay*, Art
Gallery of Western Australia, Perth, WA,
1999; University of South Australia,
Adelaide, SA, 2000.

Public collections
Art Gallery of New South Wales, Sydney,
NSW; Art Gallery of South Australia,
Adelaide, SA; Art Gallery of Western
Australia, Perth, WA; Artbank, Sydney,
NSW; Brisbane City Art Gallery, Brisbane,
Qld; Carrick Hill, Adelaide, SA; Museum
and Art Gallery of the Northern Territory,
Darwin, NT; National Gallery of Australia,
Canberra, ACT; National Gallery of
Victoria, Melbourne, Vic.; Newcastle
Region Art Gallery, Newcastle, NSW;
Parliament House, Canberra, ACT;
Powerhouse Museum, Sydney, NSW;
Queensland Art Gallery, Brisbane, Qld;
Queensland University of Technology,
Brisbane, Qld; Reserve Bank of Australia;
Shepparton Art Gallery, Shepparton, Vic;
Tasmanian Museum and Art Gallery,
Hobart, Tas.; The High Court of Australia,
Canberra, ACT; Victorian Ministry of the
Arts, Melbourne, Vic.

Milton **Moon**
Yandicoogina
glazed stoneware

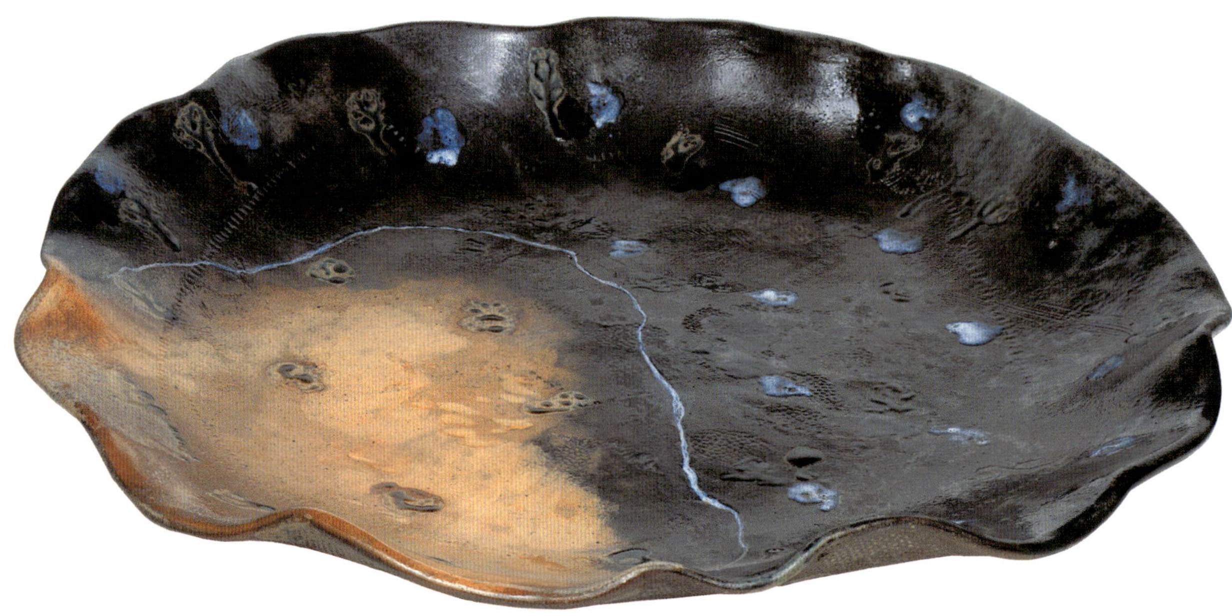

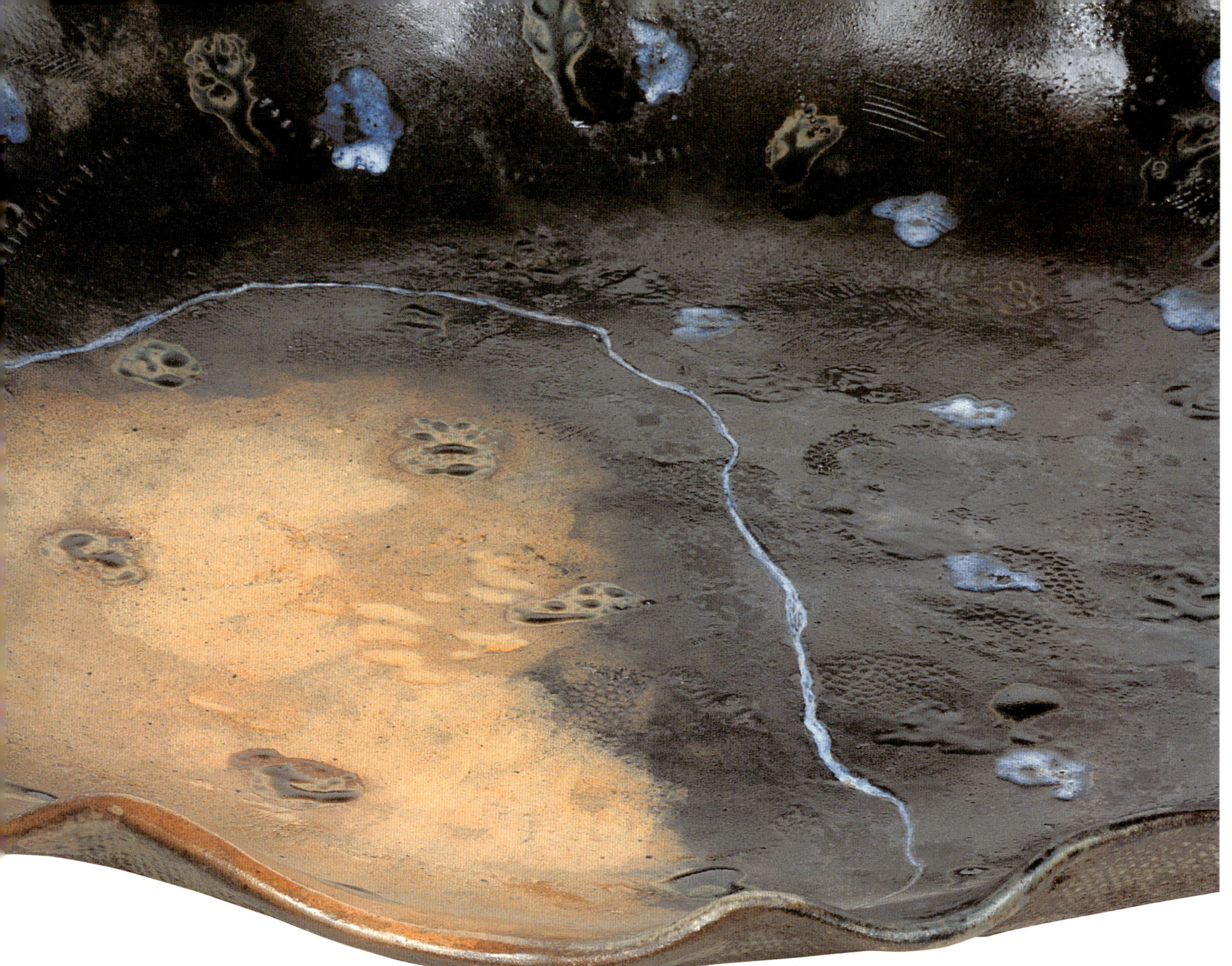

Milton **Moon**

Milton Moon purchased his first Japanese pots while travelling to Japan on military duty at the end of the Second World War. In 1950 he began making pottery in Brisbane. Subsequent trips to Japan intensified his interest in all aspects of its ceramic traditions and practices and their relationship to the philosophies of Zen Buddhism. Through this understanding of Japanese painting and ceramic techniques, Moon has developed a language of form, texture and colour that has allowed him to build strong references to the Australian landscape and flora in his work.[1] This platter is the result of time spent in the Pilbara and Kimberley areas of northern Western Australia, where Moon experienced the way the harsh physicality of the region is humanised and made intimate through the ancient rock engravings of its Indigenous inhabitants. In this work, Moon alludes to this sense of spiritual permanency by interpreting the night sky, with its endlessly repeating patterns, as a metaphor for the cyclical nature of life on earth.

1 See Christopher Menz, *Milton Moon Retrospective*, Adelaide: Art Gallery of South Australia, 1991, for a complete account of Moon's ceramic work.

51

Nick **Mount**
Adelaide, South Australia
Born Adelaide, South Australia 1952

Training
South Australian School of Art, Adelaide,
SA, 1970–71; Visual Arts, Gippsland
Institute of Advanced Education, Churchill,
VIC, 1972–74; Australia Council VACB
Grants for glass study in Europe, 1975
and USA, 1980.

Related professional experience
Tutor, established Hot Glass Studio,
Caulfield Institute of Technology,
Melbourne, Vic., 1977; Head of Glass
Workshop, Jam factory Craft and Design
Centre, Adelaide, SA, 1994–97; Teaching
Assistant, Pilchuck Glass School,
Washington, USA, 1985, 1987, 1992,
1993, 1995, 1999, 2001.

Selected solo exhibitions
The Crafts Centre, Melbourne, Vic., 1977;
La Trobe Regional Art Gallery, Morwell,
Vic., 1978; Solander Gallery, Canberra,
ACT, 1980; Jam Factory Craft and Design
Centre Gallery, Adelaide, SA, 1980, 1982;
Robin Gibson Gallery, Sydney, NSW, 1981;
Distelfink Gallery, Melbourne, Vic., 1981;
Scotchmer Gallery, Melbourne, Vic., 1986;
Bonython Meadmore Gallery, Adelaide,
SA, 1986; Macquarie Galleries, Sydney,
NSW, 1986; BMG Gallery, Adelaide, SA,
1992, 1993; Beaver Galleries, Canberra,
ACT, 1992; Artworks Gallery, Nungurner,
Vic., 1992; *Pagliaccio, Plates and Popolo*,
Distelfink Gallery, Melbourne, Vic., 1993;
Recent Works, Lyall Burton Gallery,
Melbourne, Vic., 1996; *Les Grands
Fabliers*, BMG Art, Adelaide, SA, 1997;
The Artist Formerly Known as Lucky,
Beaver Galleries, Canberra, ACT, 1997;
Nick Mount, Galerie L, Hamburg,
Germany, 1998; *New Glass*, Makers Mark,
Melbourne, Vic., 1998; *Nick Mount Glass*,
Brisbane City Gallery, Brisbane, Qld, 1999;
Fabricated Vessels, BMG Art, Adelaide, SA,
1999; *Nick Mount*, BIJ Van Zielst Goed

Wonen, Middelharnis Zuid-Holland, The
Netherlands, 2000; *Compilation*,
Quadrivium, Sydney, NSW, 2001.

Selected group exhibitions since 1992
Small Works, Glass Artists Gallery, Sydney,
NSW, 1993; *Origins and Originality*,
Canberra School of Art Gallery, Canberra,
Act, 1993; *Studio Glass*, Bendigo Art
Gallery, Bendigo, Vic., 1993; *The Cutting
Edge: 1994 Wagga Glass Triennial*, Wagga
Wagga Regional Art Gallery, Wagga
Wagga, NSW, 1994; *The Australian Glass
Show*, Contemporary Art NIKI, Tokyo,
Japan, 1994; *The Art of the Object*, Craft
Australia travelling exhibition, Salon
Municipal de Exposiciones, Montevideo,
Uruguay and Instituto Cultural de Las
Condes, Santiago, Chile, 1994; *Glass in
Australia*, Meat Market Craft Centre,
Melbourne, Vic., 1995; *Ausglass*, The
Glasmuseum, Ebeltoft, Denmark and
Galerie L, Hamburg, Germany, 1995;
Celebrate! Twenty One Years, Jam Factory
Craft and Design Centre, Adelaide, SA,
1995; *National Glass Art Collection*,
Wagga Wagga Regional art Gallery,
Wagga Wagga, NSW, travelling exhibition
in Australia, 1996; *City of Hobart Art Prize*,
Carnegie Gallery, Hobart, Tas., 1996;
Portrait der Meister, Internationale
Handwerksmesse München, Munich,
Germany, 1997; *Glass*, Arica Gallery, Perth,
WA, 1997; *Australian Glass*, Galerie Rob
van den Doel, The Hague, The
Netherlands, 1997; *Contemporary Glass*,
Quadrivium, Sydney, NSW, 1997;
Translucence, Quadrivium, Sydney, NSW,
1998; *Venezia Aperto Vetro 1998:
International New Glass*: 5 sites in Venice,
Italy, 1998; *Creative Australia*, Osaka,
Japan, 1999; *Presiding Officers' Acquisitive
Craft Prize*, Parliament House, Canberra,
ACT, 1999; *Alla Maniera Veneziana*, Jam
Factory Craft and Design Centre Gallery,
Adelaide, SA, 1999; *Glass, Art & Science*
(Australian studio glass exhibition), Museu
do Vidro da Marinha Grande, Marinha
Grande, Portugal, 1999; *GAS International*

Expo 2, Tampa, FL, USA, 1999; *Desire*,
Quadrivium, Sydney, NSW, 2000; *SOFA*,
Navy Pier, Chicago, IL, USA, 2000, 2001;
SOFA, New York, NY, USA, 2000, 2001;
Contemporary Art Glass, Despard Gallery,
Hobart, Tas., 2000; *Vessels*, Koganezaki
Glass Museum, Koganezaki, Japan, 2000;
At the Edge: Australian glass art, Brisbane
City Gallery, Brisbane, Qld; Object
Galleries, Sydney, NSW; Galerie Handwerk,
Munich, Germany; National Glass Centre,
Sunderland, UK, 2000; *Glass Art in
Australia*, Quadrivium, Sydney, NSW, 2001;
Ranamok Glass Prize, Volvo Gallery,
Sydney, NSW and travelling in Australia,
2001–02; *Glass State*, JamFactory
Galleries, Adelaide, SA, 2001; *Facets of
Australian Glass*, Leo Kaplan Modern,
New York, NY, USA, 2002.

Public collections (Australia)
Ararat Gallery, Ararat, Vic; Art Gallery of
South Australia, Adelaide, SA; Art Gallery
of Western Australia, Perth, WA; Artbank,
Sydney, NSW; La Trobe Regional Art
Gallery, Morwell Vic.; National Gallery of
Australia, Canberra, ACT; National Gallery
of Victoria, Melbourne, Vic.; Parliament
House, Canberra, ACT; Powerhouse
Museum, Sydney, NSW; Queensland Art
Gallery, Brisbane, Qld; Sale Regional Art
Gallery, Sale, Vic.; Victorian State Craft
Collection, Melbourne, Vic.; Wagga
Wagga Regional Art Gallery, Wagga
Wagga, NSW;

Public collections (international)
The Glasmuseum, Ebeltoft, Denmark

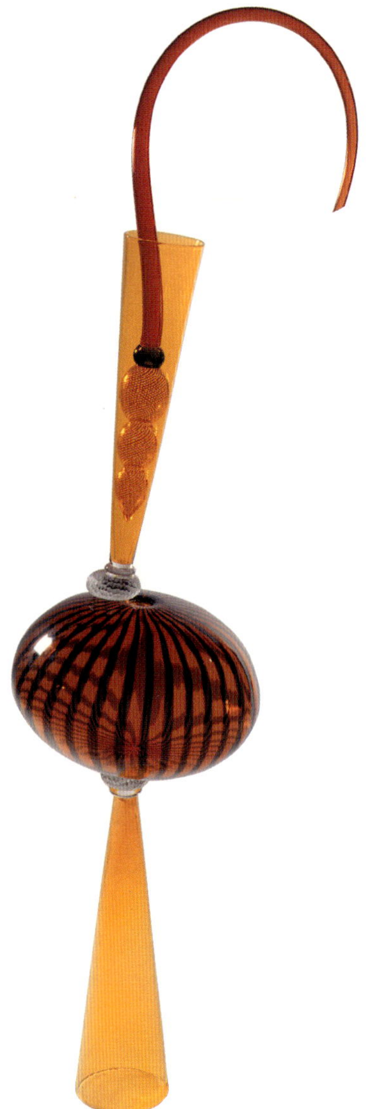

Nick **Mount**
Scent Bottle
blown double-overlay glass, fabricated,
ground and polished

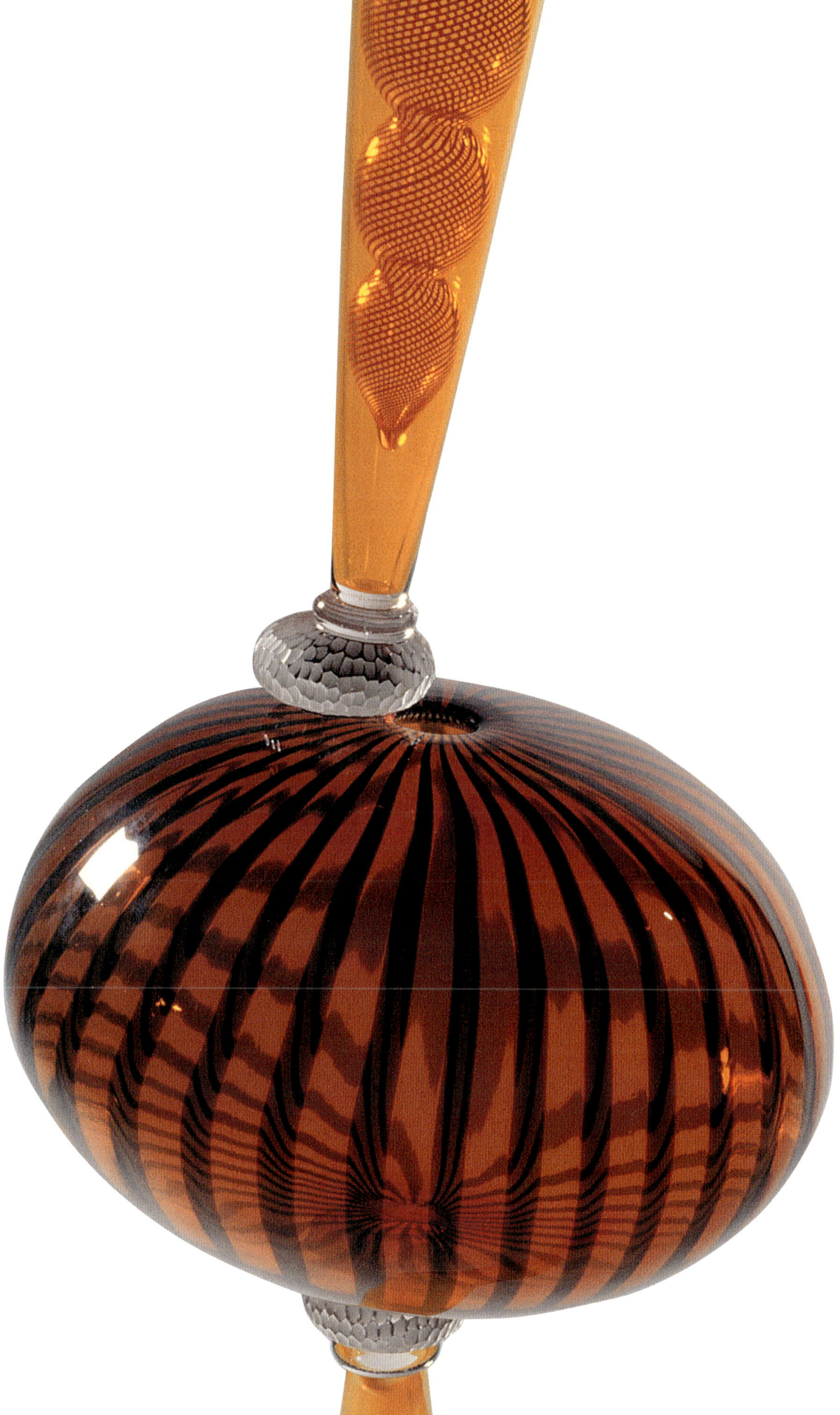

Nick **Mount**

Nick Mount was among the group of glass artists who developed the craft in Australia during the late 1970s.[1] This work, a blown glass form with references to the tradition, design and function of the scent bottle, shows his strong sense of design and colour and his development of the Venetian glass traditions that engaged his interest early in his career. The continuity of these traditions also alludes to the power of scent to trigger memory. His enjoyment of his technical virtuosity is evident in the audaciously balanced form of this object. Its dramatic and witty presence suggests the over-scaled flasks of coloured liquids used in traditional pharmacies and the merchandising displays in perfume shops and department stores, with their exaggerated emphasis on 'designer' brands and signatures.

1 See Noris Ioannou, *Australian Studio Glass – The movement, its makers and their art*, Sydney: Craftsman House, 1995, pp. 30–33.

Kevin **Perkins**

Franklin, Tasmania

Born Launceston, Tasmania 1945

Training

Training in carpentry and joinery, industrial
arts and sculpture.

Related professional experience

Lecturer Furniture Design, University of
Tasmania.

Solo exhibitions

Design Centre of Tasmania, Launceston,
Tas., 1978, 1984; Watters Gallery (with
Peter Taylor), Sydney, NSW, 1979; *Tables*,
Salamanca Art Centre, Hobart, Tas., 1988;
Handmark Gallery, Hobart, Tas., 1996.

Selected group exhibitions since 1992

Tasmanian Wood Design Exhibition,
Hobart, Tas., 1993, 1995, 1999; *Designer
Furniture*, Plimsoll Gallery, University of
Tasmania, Hobart, Tas., 1994; *Home
Made*, Plimsoll Gallery, University of
Tasmania, Hobart, Tas., 1995; *Places of
Importance*, Crafts Council of the ACT
Gallery, Canberra, ACT, 1995; *Points of
Diversity*, Tasmanian Museum and Art
Gallery, Launceston, Tas., 1996; Handmark
Gallery, Hobart, Tas., 1996; Wood Trust,
Sydney, NSW, 1996; *International
Contemporary Furniture Fair*, CSS, New
York, NY, USA, 1996; *Designex*, Sydney,
NSW, 1996; *Design For Production*,
Hobart, Tas., 1998; *Tasmanian Tiger*,
Tasmanian Museum and Art Gallery,
Hobart, Tas., 1999; *Against the Grain:
Australian sculptural furniture*, Brisbane
City Gallery, Brisbane, Qld, 2000; *Rings of
History*, Craft ACT Gallery, Canberra, ACT,
2001; *One Tree*, Tasmanian Museum and
Art Gallery, Hobart, Tas., 2001; *Response
to the Island*, Long Gallery, Salamanca Arts
Centre, Hobart, Tas., 2001.

Public collections

Art Gallery of Western Australia, Perth,
WA; National Gallery of Australia,
Canberra, ACT; Powerhouse Museum,
Sydney, NSW; Tasmanian Museum and Art
Gallery, Hobart, Tas.; Tasmanian Wood
Design Collection, Launceston, Tas.

Kevin **Perkins**

Cape Barren Goose cabinet
Huon pine, purpleheart, ebony,
sycamore and glass,
224 x 140 x 90 cm

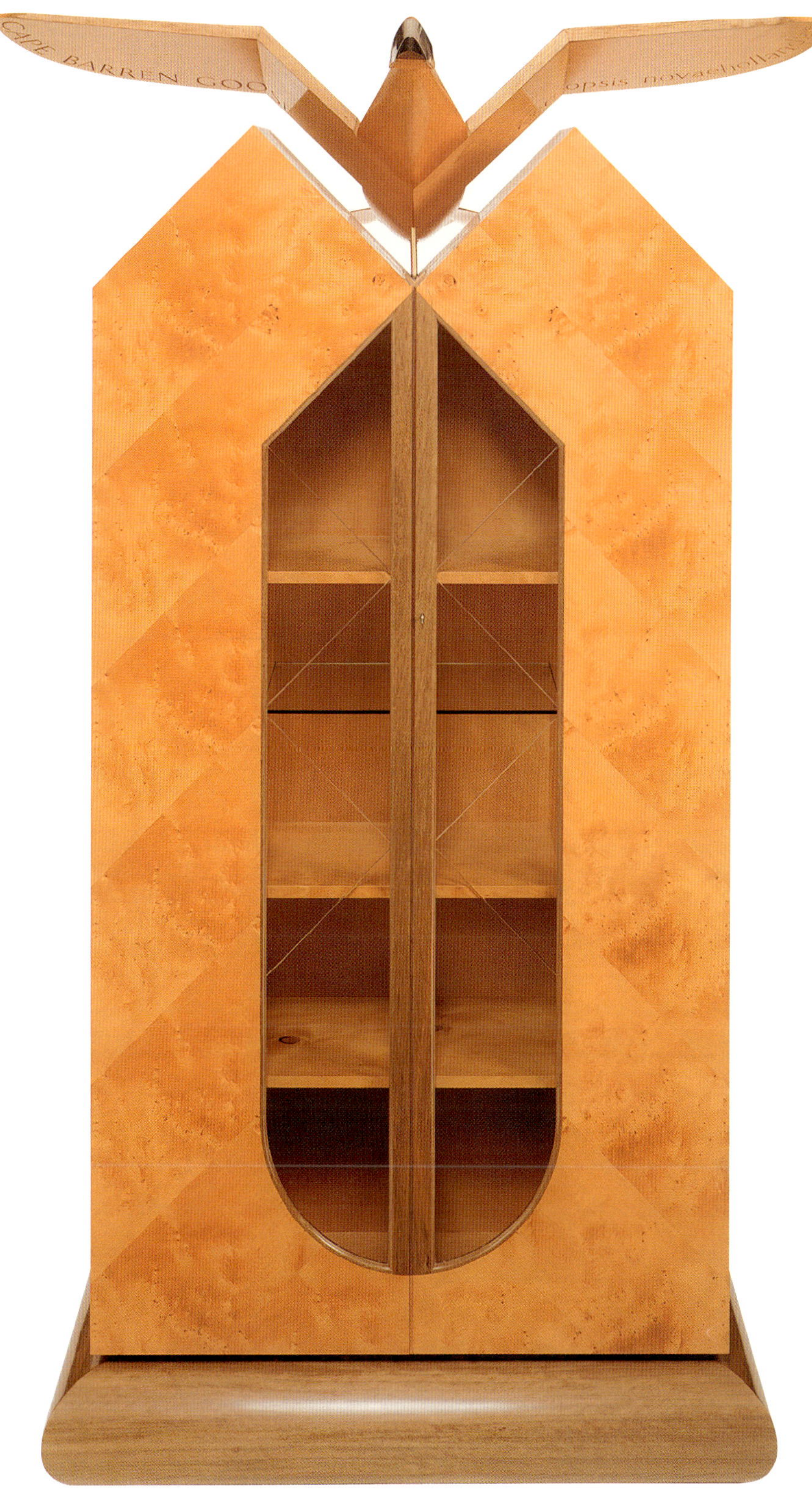

Kevin **Perkins**

This cabinet is surmounted with a carved, stylised Huon pine figure of a flying Cape Barren Goose, its beak made from ebony and silver with its scientific and common name incised under each wing. The doors open to reveal three shelves incorporating three drawers on each side, each group incorporating a further, secret drawer. Kevin Perkins has used 'crossfire' and 'birdseye' Huon pine veneers in geometric patterns on the door fronts and case back, along with sycamore for the base plinth and ebony and purpleheart woods as accents. This cabinet is part of a series of furniture with design themes based on the endanger-ment of the Cape Barren Goose and of Tasmania's native Huon pine forests.[1] Additionally, Perkins' design makes reference to the neoclassical furniture of Tasmania's colonial period (particularly the Chippendale-style 'swan neck' cabinets of the late 18th century) and to the use of local animal imagery in the Tasmanian Arts and Crafts Movement of the late 19th century.[2]

1 See Tom Darby, *Making Fine Furniture – Designer-makers and their projects*, pp.37–44.

2 See Caroline Miley, *Beautiful and Useful: The Arts and Crafts Movement in Tasmania*, Hobart: Queen Victoria Museum and Art Gallery, 1987.

Denise **Sprynskyj**
Melbourne, Victoria
Born Melbourne, Victoria 1960

Training
Bachelor of Arts (Fashion and Textiles),
Royal Melbourne Institute of Technology,
1992; Master of Arts, RMIT University,
Melbourne, Vic., 1999.

Related professional experience
Established S!X design label and studio
with Peter Boyd, Melbourne, Vic., 1994.

Peter **Boyd**
Melbourne, Victoria
Born Melbourne, Victoria 1971

Training
Bachelor of Arts (Fashion and Textiles),
Royal Melbourne Institute of Technology,
1992.

Related professional experience
Established S!X design label and studio
with Denise Sprynskyj, Melbourne, Vic.,
1994.

**Selected group exhibitions (Denise
Sprynskyj and Peter Boyd partnership,
S!X)**
Austrade exhibition, Mitsokoshi
Department Store, Taipei, Taiwan, 1994;
Couture to Chaos, National Gallery of
Victoria, Melbourne, Vic., 1996; *Autopsy*,
Melbourne Fringe Festival, Melbourne,
Vic., 1997; *Undress*, Melbourne Fashion
Festival, Melbourne, Vic., 1998; *Emerging
Craft*, Craft Victoria Gallery, Melbourne,
Vic., 1998; *Past Tense, Future Perfect*,
Craftwest, Perth and The Moores Building,
Fremantle, WA and travelling in Australia,
1999; *50 Years of Japanese Lifestyle:
Postwar fashion & design*, Utsonomiya
Museum of Art, Utsonomiya, Japan, 1998;
Male Order: Addressing menswear, Ian
Potter Museum of Art, Melbourne, Vic.,
1999; *Tokyo Vogue*, Brisbane City Gallery,
Brisbane, Qld., 1999; *Dis-Placement*, Span

Gallery, Melbourne, Vic., 2000; *Cycle of
Decomposition*, Creation Baumann, Paris,
France, 2000, *City of Hobart Art Prize
2000*, Tasmanian Museum and Art Gallery,
Hobart, Launceston, Tas., 2000; *Cycle of
Decomposition II*, Melbourne Fashion
Festival, Melbourne, Vic., 2001.

**Public collections (Denise Sprynskyj
and Peter Boyd partnership, S!X)**
National Gallery of Australia, Canberra,
ACT; National Gallery of Victoria,
Melbourne, Vic.

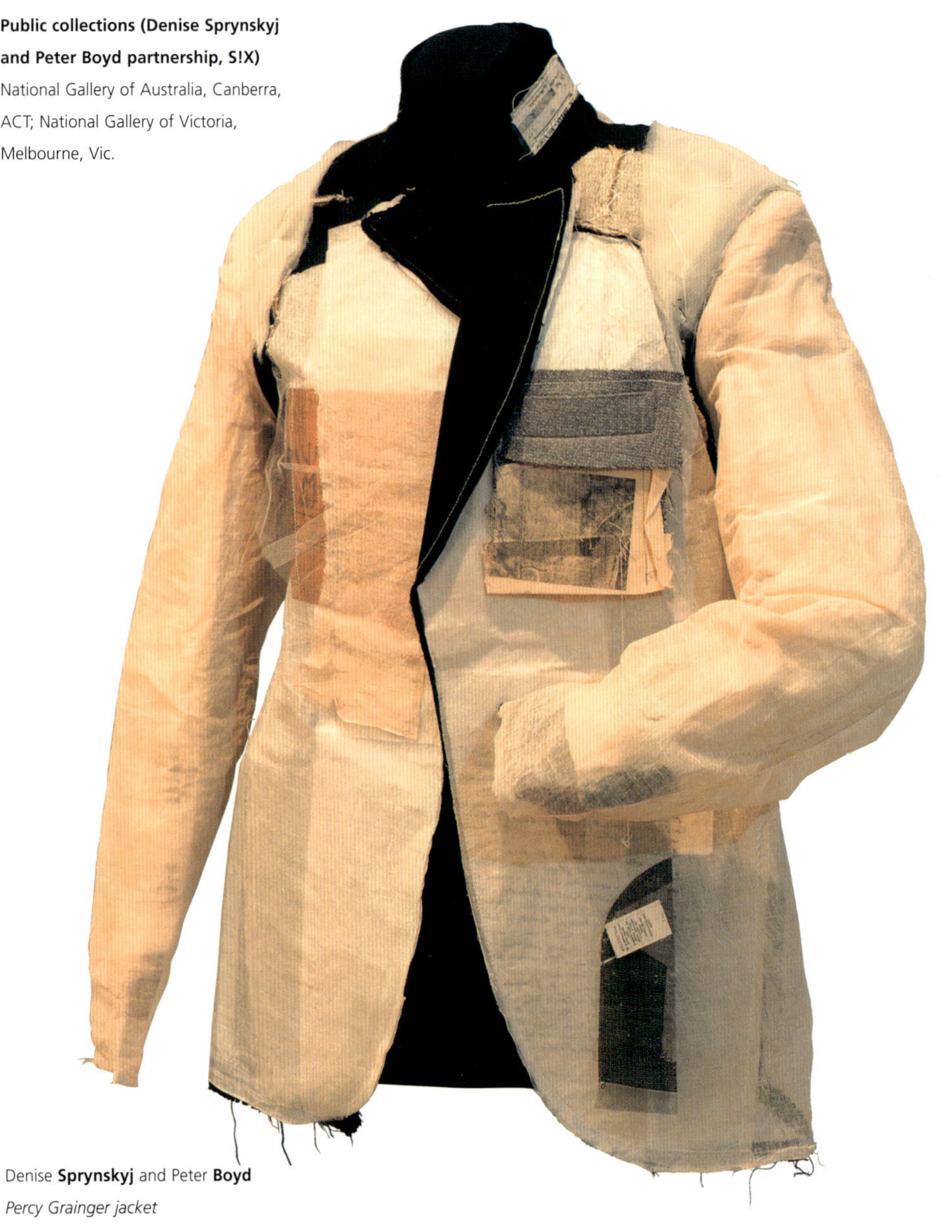

Denise **Sprynskyj** and Peter **Boyd**
Percy Grainger jacket
'Remixed Movement No 6'
wool, silk, cotton, paper, Mylar
and heat-transfer print,

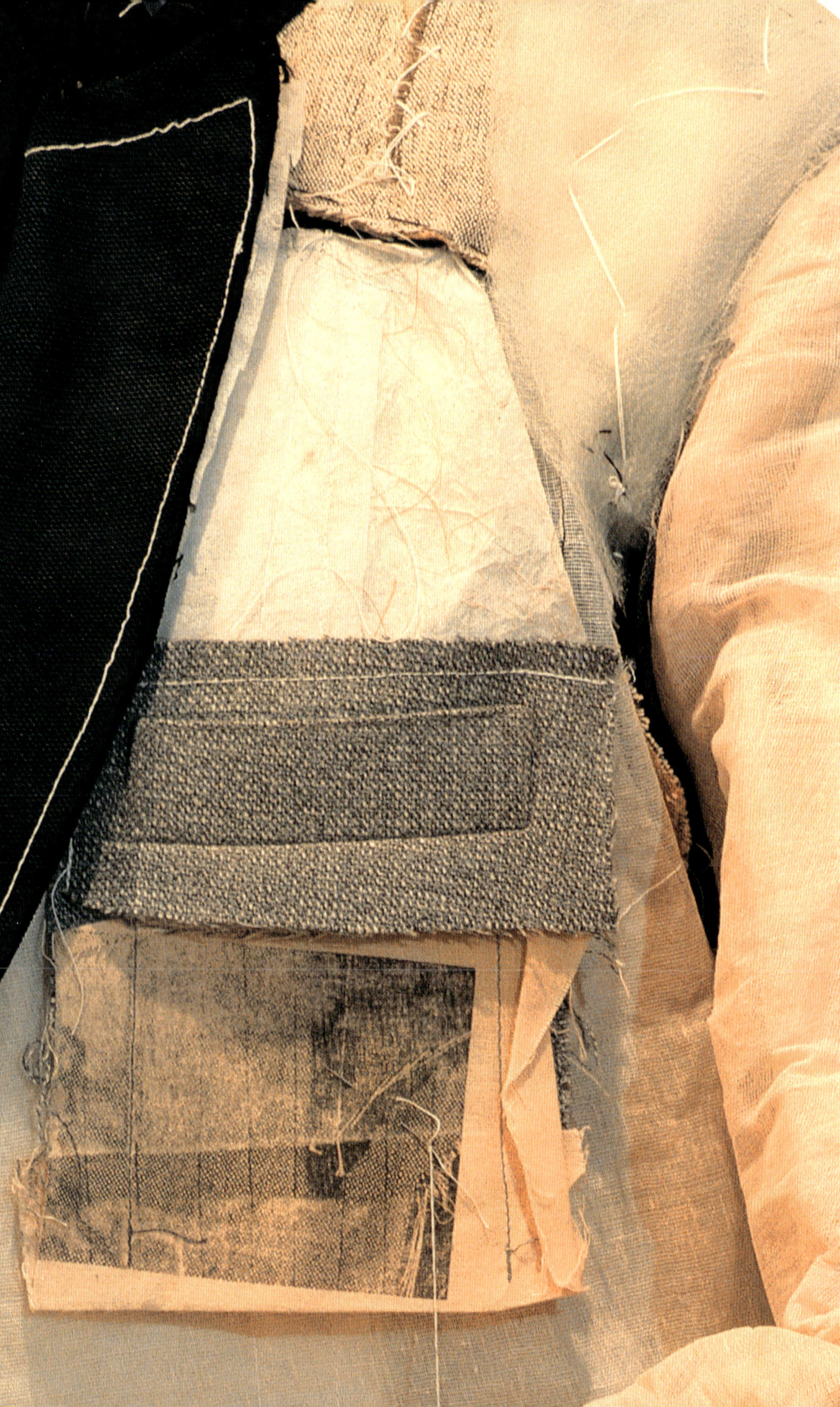

Denise **Sprynskyj** and Peter **Boyd**

The life, work and clothes of
the early 20th–century
Australian composer and
experimental musician,
Percy Grainger, inspired this
garment. Like Grainger, who
also created his own experimental clothing, Denise
Sprynskyj and Peter Boyd,
working together for their
fashion label, S!X, have a
fascination with found objects
and the dissonance created
when making new works from
old. With wit and ingenuity,
their deconstruction of garments
makes light of the practice of
tailors and dressmakers by
allowing raw, cut edges to
remain as evidence of the
process of construction and
modification. Upending the
lexicon of male tailoring, a man's
traditional tailored jacket has
been turned inside out and
taken apart, and large sections
removed, with only key details
such as the collar and breast
pocket remaining. Its silhouette
is reconfigured in transparent
silk, cotton, handmade paper
and tulle, with copies of Percy
Grainger's music and handwritten notes (transferred to
Mylar) dispersed throughout the
body of the jacket.

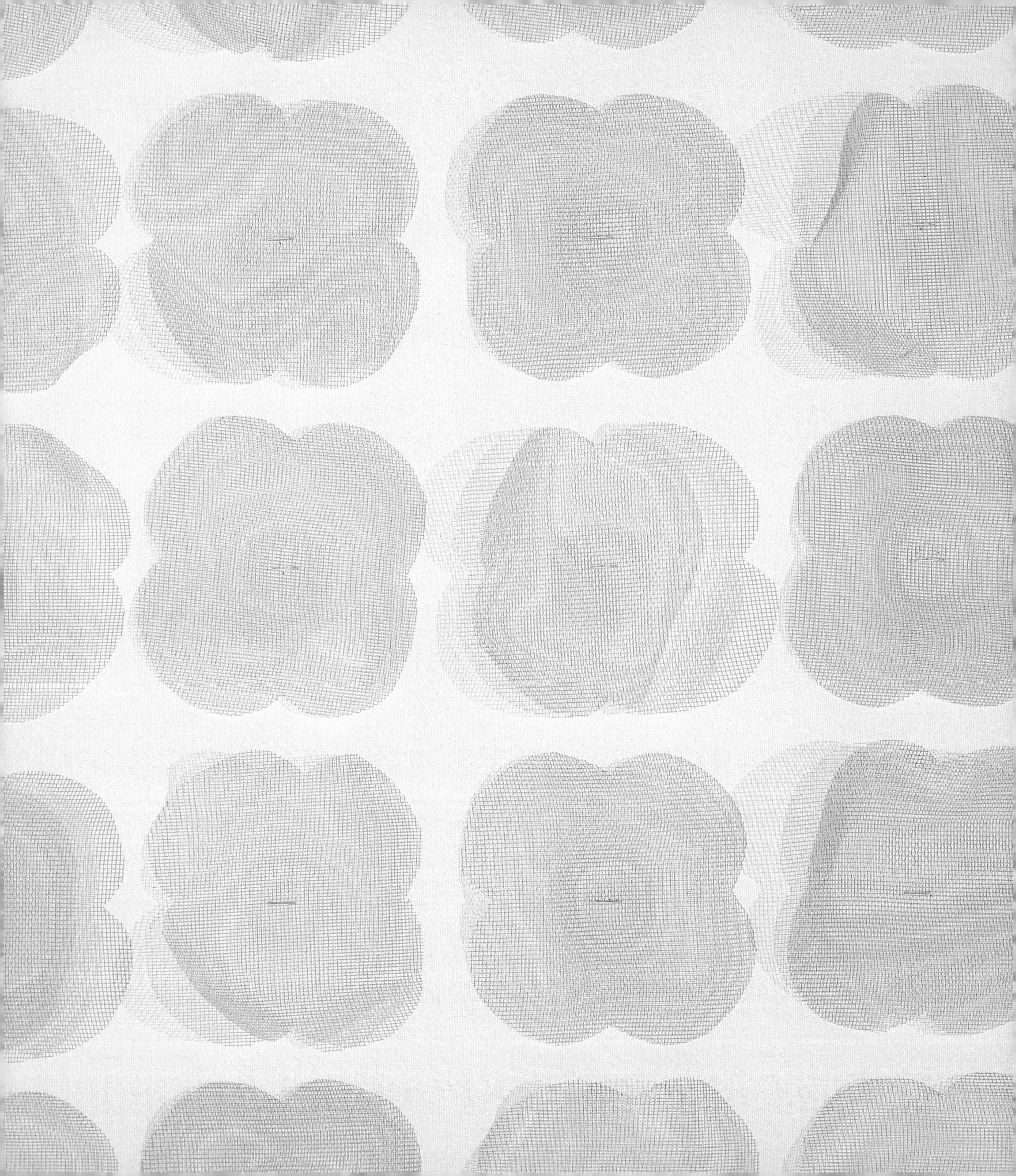

Transformation

The transformation of raw materials through the traditional techniques of the crafts has been a measure of achievement and material culture for millennia. The resulting objects have provided us with physical manifestations of artists' imagination and ingenuity and a pride in skill and the effective use of natural resources. Contemporary makers preside over not only the technical transformation of materials, such as silica to glass, clay to porcelain or digital signals to fabric, but also the transformation of their meaning and value. The manipulation of graphic imagery and surface design, the juxtaposition of materials, the recycling of objects and the subversion of techniques and traditions bring a new understanding to familiar forms and imbue everyday materials with a poetic presence.

Objects play a part in our perception of space by involving us visually and physically, and even the most arcane still engage us with visual and tactile clues to their origin. Although we can sense the temperature of glass, the weight of ceramic or the texture of fabric through our prior experience of materials, we are in turn transformed by objects that challenge our expectations and hint at other, unknown experiences. Even though the group of objects illustrated in this section may never be exhibited together again, in this context their relationship to each other transforms their meaning and intensifies their presence.

Les **Blakebrough** Pippin **Drysdale**
Marian **Hosking** Helge **Larsen** and Darani
Lewers Mitsuo **Shoji** Alan **Watt** Margaret
West Maureen **Williams** Liz **Williamson**

Les **Blakebrough**

Hobart, Tasmania

Born Kingston, Surrey, Great Britain 1930,
arrived Australia 1948

Training

Painting and Ceramics, East Sydney
Technical College, Sydney, NSW, 1957;
Apprenticed to Ivan McMeekin, Sturt
Pottery, Mittagong, NSW, 1957–59;
Studied under Takeichi Kawai, Kyoto,
Japan, 1963–64.

Related professional experience

Manager, Sturt Pottery, Mittagong, NSW,
1960–72; Director, Sturt Craft Centre,
Mittagong, NSW, 1964–72; Senior
Lecturer, Ceramics, School of Art, Hobart,
Tas., 1973–81; Associate Professor, Head
of Ceramics, Tasmanian School of Art,
University of Tasmania, Hobart, Tas.,
1989–94; Principal Research Fellow,
Ceramic Research Unit, University of
Tasmania, Hobart, Tas., 1996 – present.

Selected solo exhibitions since 1980

Bowerbank Mill Gallery, Deloraine, Tas.,
1981; Distelfink Gallery, Melbourne, Vic.,
1981, 1986, 1989, 1993, 1996; Cooks Hill
Gallery, Newcastle, NSW, 1985, 1990,
1996; Bonython-Meadmore Gallery,
Adelaide, SA, 1986; Saddlers Crescent,
Richmond, Tas., 1987; Handmark Gallery,
Hobart, Tas., 1987; Macquarie Galleries,
Sydney, NSW, 1987, 1988, 1989; *Les
Blakebrough: Retrospective*, University of
Tasmania, Hobart, Tas., 1988, and touring
to five Australian venues, 1989; Ceramic
Art Gallery, Sydney, NSW, 1995, 1997;
Beaver Galleries, Canberra, ACT, 1996,
2001; Savode Gallery, Brisbane, Qld, 1997;
BMG Fine Art, Adelaide, SA, 1998, 2000;
Sturt Gallery, Mittagong, NSW, 2000.

Selected group exhibitions since 1992

Gold Coast Ceramic Award, Gold Coast
City Art Gallery, Gold Coast, Qld, 1993;
Home Made, Plimsoll Gallery, University of
Tasmania, Hobart, Tas., 1995; *Ceramics
Survey 1969-1995*, Bathurst Regional Art
Gallery, Bathurst, NSW, 1995;
*Delinquent Angel: Australian historical,
Aboriginal and contemporary ceramics*,
Museo Internazionale delle Ceramiche,
Faenza, Italy and travelling in Asia and
Australia, 1995–97; *Newcastle Purchase
Award Exhibition*, Newcastle Region Art
Gallery, Newcastle, NSW, 1996; *Triaxial
Blend*, Rochester Institute of Technology,
Rochester, NY, USA, 1996; *Four Visions of
Antarctica*, Newcastle Region Art Gallery,
Newcastle, NSW, 1997; *Sidney Myer Fund
International Ceramics Award*, Shepparton
Art Gallery, Shepparton, Vic., 1997; *The
Japan Inspiration: Influence in crafts and
design*, Art Gallery of Western Australia,
Perth, WA, 1997; *Southern Light:
Contemporary Australian porcelain*, SOFA
98, Chicago, USA, 1998; *Contemporary
Australian Craft*, Hokkaido Museum of
Modern Art, Sapporo, Japan, 1999; *The
Language of Clay*, Art Gallery of Western
Australia, Perth, WA, 1999: *Response to
the Island*, Long Gallery, Salamanca Arts
Centre, Hobart, Tas., 2001.

Public collections (Australia)

Art Gallery of New South Wales, Sydney,
NSW; Art Gallery of South Australia,
Adelaide, SA; Art Gallery of Western
Australia, Perth, WA; Australian National
University, Canberra, ACT; Flinders
University, Adelaide, SA; National Gallery
of Australia, Canberra, ACT; National
Gallery of Victoria, Melbourne, Vic.;
Newcastle Regional Art Gallery, Newcastle,
NSW; Parliament House, Canberra, ACT;
Queen Victoria Museum and Art Gallery,
Launceston, Tas.; Queensland Art Gallery,
Brisbane, Qld; Shepparton Art Gallery,
Shepparton, Vic.; Tasmanian Museum and
Art Gallery, Hobart, Tas.; University of
Queensland, Brisbane, Qld; University of
Tasmania, Hobart, Tas.; University of
Western Australia, Perth, WA; Victorian
State Craft Collection, Melbourne, Vic..

Public collections (international)

Kunstindustrimuseet i Oslo, Oslo, Norway;
Museo Internazionale delle Ceramiche,
Faenza, Italy.

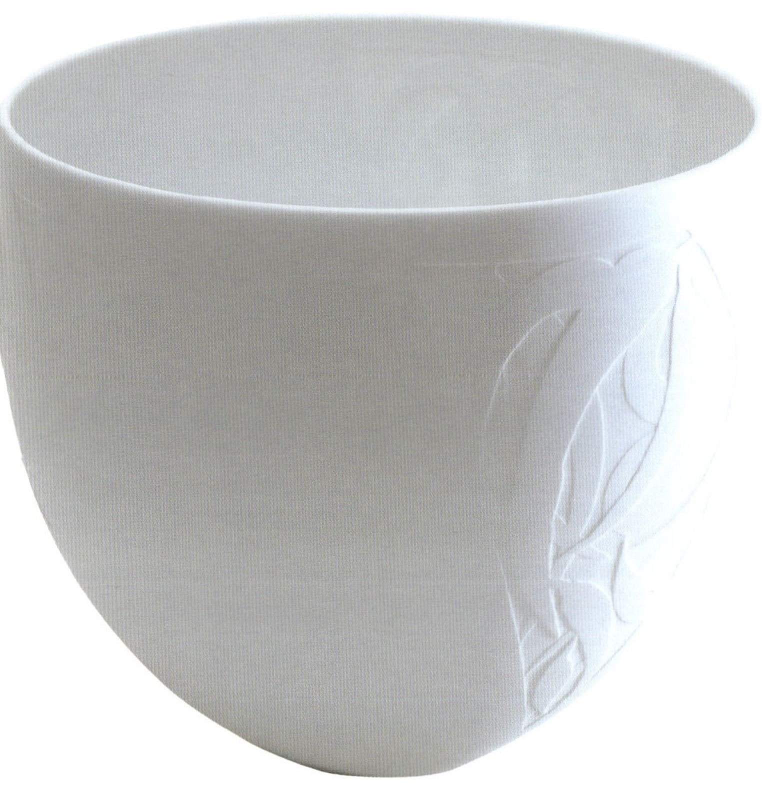

Les **Blakebrough**
Forest Floor
carved Southern Ice porcelain

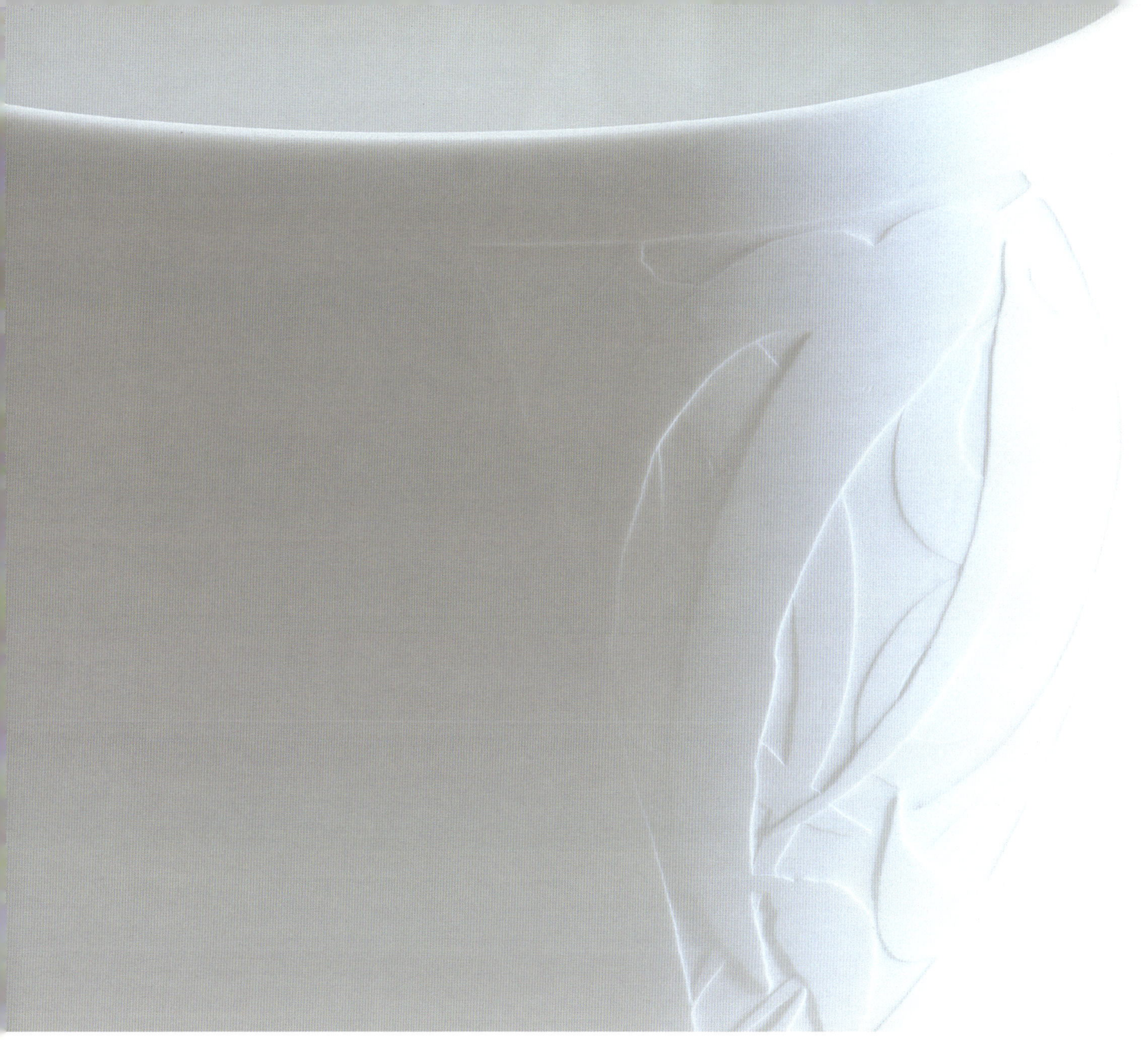

Les **Blakebrough**

Les Blakebrough is one of Australia's most experienced ceramic artists and brings to this work a distillation of a number of themes that have characterised his work over the past 50 years. Developing and using his own porcelain clay has encouraged him to explore its particular qualities of translucency and crystalline whiteness.[1] This bowl's raised relief decoration has been achieved by masking areas of the unfired clay surface with shellac before sponging away the background to a thinness that, when fired, will allow the passage of light. The resulting effect has the subtlety of a watermark and a sense of transience and luminosity that one might expect from a coating of frost or ice on foliage or rocks. While visually reductive, Blakebrough's forms are strong and grounded in a precise and generous functionality, reflecting his finely-honed design sensibility and a celebration of the science of craft.

1 With five Australian Research Council grants since 1991, Blakebrough has undertaken research into Tasmanian porcelain, flexible kiln design, porcelain clay development, and industrial processes for craft-based industry.

Pippin Drysdale
Fremantle, Western Australia
Born 1943, Melbourne, Victoria

Training
Diploma of Advanced Ceramics, Perth
Technical College, Perth, WA, 1981;
Bachelor of Arts (Fine Art), Curtin
University, Perth, WA, 1985.

Solo exhibitions
Editions Gallery, Fremantle, WA, 1986;
Greenhill Galleries, Perth, WA, 1987;
Handmark Gallery, Hobart, Tas., 1988;
Fremantle Art Centre, Fremantle, WA,
1988; Potter's Gallery, Brisbane, Qld, 1989;
Narek Gallery, Canberra, ACT, 1989, 1992;
Distelfink Gallery, Melbourne, Vic., 1990,
1995, 1997; Perth Galleries, Perth, WA,
1990, 1993, 1999; Tomsk State Gallery
and Museum, Russia, 1991; Novosirbirsk
State Gallery and Museum, Russia, 1991;
Gallery 2, Launceston, TAS, 1993; The
Door Gallery, Fremantle, WA, 1995;
Contemporary Art Gallery, Sydney, NSW,
1996; Beaver Galleries, Canberra, ACT,
1997; Pots on Ponsonby, Auckland, New
Zealand, 1997; Quadrivium, Sydney, NSW,
2000; BMG ART, Adelaide, SA, 2001.

Selected group exhibitions since 1992
*Design Visions: Australian International
Crafts Triennial*, Art Gallery of Western
Australia, Perth, WA, 1992; *The Bowl*,
Narek Gallery, Canberra, ACT, 1993;
Gallery 2, Launceston, Tas., 1993; *Pride of
Place: New acquisitions 1990–1994*, Art
Gallery of Western Australia, Perth, WA,
1994; *Delinquent Angel: Australian
historical, Aboriginal and contemporary
ceramics*, Museo Internazionale delle
Ceramiche, Faenza, Italy and travelling in
Asia and Australia, 1995–97; *Juggling the
Elements*, Manly Art Gallery, Sydney, NSW,
1995; *Fletcher Challenge Ceramics Award*,
Auckland Museum, Auckland, New
Zealand, 1996; *Sidney Myer Fund
Invitational Ceramics Award*, Shepparton
Art Gallery, Shepparton, Vic., 1996;
City of Perth Craft Award, Craftwest
Gallery, Perth, WA, 1996; Cooks Hill
Gallery, Newcastle, NSW, 1996; Beaver
Galleries, Canberra, ACT, 1996; *Art in
Gold*, Ballarat Fine Art Gallery, Ballarat,
Vic., 1997; *Decorated Clay*, Queensland
Art Gallery, Brisbane, Qld, 1998;
Contemporary Australian Craft, Hokkaido
Museum of Modern Art, Sapporo, Japan,
1999; *A Generous Vessel*, Centre for
Contemporary Craft, Sydney, NSW, 1999;
The Language of Clay, Art Gallery of
Western Australia, Perth, WA, 1999;
Vitalità Perenne del Lustro, Palazzo dei
Consoli, Gubbio, Italy, 1999; *Quadrivium's
Finest*, Quadrivium, Sydney, NSW, 2000.

Public collections (Australia)
Art Gallery of Western Australia, Perth,
WA; Campbelltown City Art Gallery,
Campbelltown, NSW; Manly Art Gallery,
Sydney, NSW; Museum and Art Gallery of
the Northern Territory, Darwin, NT,
National Gallery of Australia, Canberra,
ACT; Newcastle Region Art Gallery,
Newcastle, NSW; Powerhouse Museum,
Sydney, NSW; Queensland Art Gallery,
Brisbane, Qld; Shepparton Art Gallery,
Shepparton, Vic.; Tasmanian Museum and
Art Gallery, Hobart, Tas.

Public collections (international)
Auckland Art Gallery, Auckland, New
Zealand; Novosirbirsk State Gallery, Siberia,
Russia; Tomsk State Gallery and Museum,
Siberia, Russia.

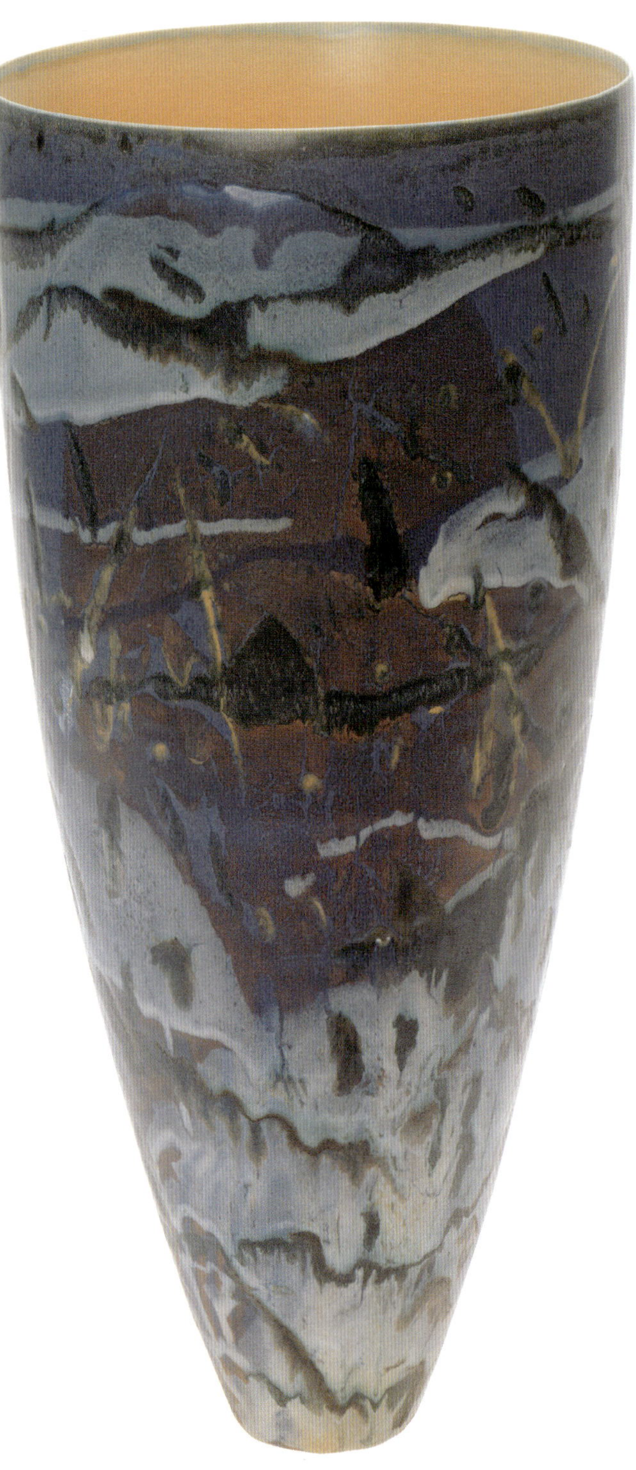

Pippin **Drysdale**
Koh-E-Nida
glazed porcelain
© Pippin Drysdale, 2000.
Licensed by VISCOPY Ltd, Sydney 2002.

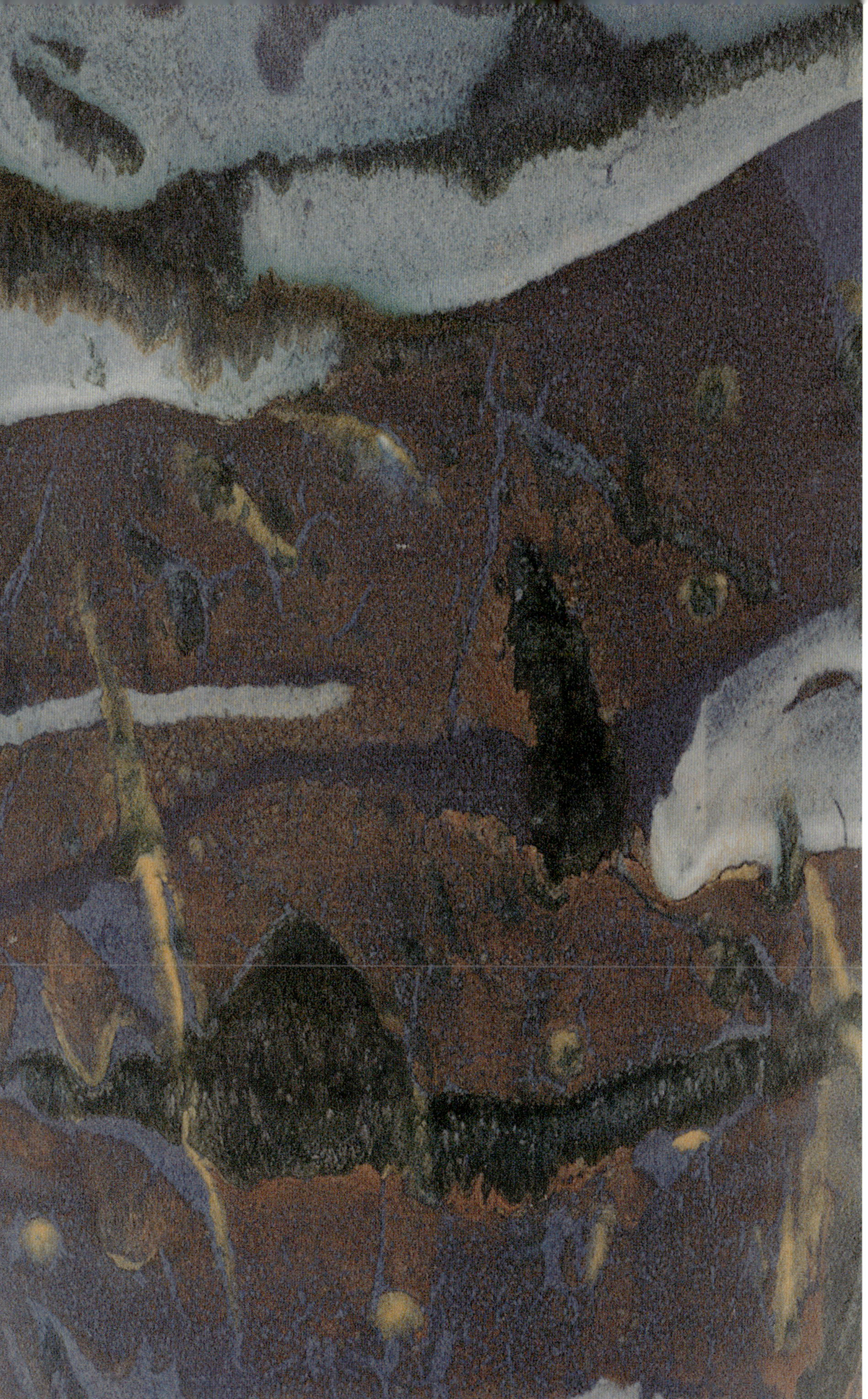

Pippin **Drysdale**

Pippin Drysdale produces series of ceramics based on her experiences abroad and extensive travel and research in outback Australia. This work is from a series she developed after a period of research in Pakistan. Its surface decoration of multicoloured and multiple-fired glazes derives from her earlier ceramics depicting the colour and landforms of Australia's north-west. Drysdale's innovative glazes are realised with particular brilliance in this work, giving it a richness and intensity of surface that suggests the shifting colour of Pakistan's mountain landscapes and the vivid, layered and wrapped silk garments typical of this region.

Marian **Hosking**

Melbourne, Victoria

Born Melbourne, Victoria 1948

Training

Diploma of Art (Gold and Silversmithing), 1969 and Master of Arts, 1995, Royal Melbourne Institute of Technology, Melbourne, Vic., 1969; Fachhochschule für Gestaltung, Pforzheim, Germany, 1971–72.

Related professional experience

Lecturer, Gold and Silversmithing, Charles Sturt University, Wagga Wagga, NSW, 1973–75; Lecturer, Gold and Silversmithing, Royal Melbourne Institute of Technology, Melbourne, Vic., 1987–97; Lecturer and Studio Coordinator, Metals/Jewellery, Faculty of Art and Design, Monash University, Melbourne, Vic., 1997-present.

Selected solo exhibitions

Recent Work, Makers Mark, Melbourne, Vic., 1979; Standfield Gallery, Melbourne, Vic., 1989; Contemporary Jewellery Gallery, Sydney, NSW, 1989; Gray Street Gallery, Adelaide, SA, 1990; Gallery Funaki, Melbourne, Vic., 1996; *Pattern, Perception*, Crawford Gallery, Sydney, NSW, 1996; *People, Patterns, Place*, Gippsland Regional Art Gallery, Sale, Vic., 1997; *Intimate Variations*, Gallery Funaki, Melbourne, Vic., 1998; *Haku-Box, Sara-Plate*, Matsuya Ginza, Tokyo, Japan, 1999; *Scattered Similarities*, Gallery Funaki, Melbourne, Vic. and Object Galleries, Sydney, NSW, 2001.

Selected group exhibitions since 1992

Australian Contemporary Design in Jewish Ceremony, Jewish Museum of Australia, Melbourne, Vic., 1991–92; *Australian Contemporary Hollow Ware*, Australian Exhibitions Touring Agency, travelling in Australia, Indonesia, Korea, The Philippines and USA, 1991–93; *Market, Kitsch and Cultural Production*, Craft Victoria, Melbourne, Vic., 1993; *Metalgefasse, Form and Function, Wechselspeil*, Germany, 1993; *Australia Gold: Contemporary Australian jewellery and metalwork*, Asialink/Royal Melbourne Institute of Technology, travelling in Australia, Indonesia, Japan, Korea, Malaysia, The Philippines and Singapore, 1993; *Production/Reproduction*, Gallery 101, Melbourne, Vic., 1995; *Five Contemporary Jewellers*, Studio COM, Kyoto, Japan, 1997; *Contemporary Vessels and Jewels: Australian fine metalwork*, Queensland Art Gallery, Brisbane, Qld, 1997; *Cecily and Colin Rigg Craft Award*, National Gallery of Victoria, Melbourne, Vic., 1997; *Seven Contemporary Jewellers From Four Countries*, Craft A, Ishikawa, Japan, 1998; *Circles About the Body*, Plimsoll Gallery, University of Tasmania, Hobart, Tas., 1998; *12th Silver Triennial*, Deutsches Goldschmiedehaus, Hanau, Germany, 1998; *6th Ernest Levigny Exhibition*, Buda, Castlemaine, Vic., 1999; *Drawn in Form*, Object Galleries, Sydney, NSW, 1999; *Metal Element III: Japan, Korea, Australia*, International Design Center, Nagoya, Japan, 1999 and Australian Embassy, Tokyo, Japan, 2000; *Skill*, Craft Victoria, Melbourne, Vic., 1999; *Ways of Working: Contemporary objects and jewellery from Japan, Korea and Australia*, Faculty Gallery, Monash University, Melbourne, Vic., 2000; *Australian Silversmithing*, Victoria and Albert Museum, London, UK, 2000; *Australia 2000*, Lesley Craze Gallery, London, UK, 2000; *National Jewellery Award*, Griffith Regional Art Gallery, Griffith, NSW, 2000; *Metal Element of Five Countries*, International Design Center, Nagoya, Japan, 2001; *Micromegas*, Galerie für Angewandte Kunst, Bayerischer Kunstgewerbe-Verein, Munich, Germany, 2001; *Chongju International Craft Biennale, Chongju*, South Korea, 2001.

Public collections (Australia)

City of Banyule Art Collection, Banyule, Vic.; Griffith Regional Gallery, Griffith, NSW; Hamilton Art Gallery, Hamilton, Vic.; National Gallery of Australia, Canberra, ACT; National Gallery of Victoria, Melbourne, Vic.; Powerhouse Museum, Sydney, NSW; Queen Victoria Museum and Art Gallery, Launceston, Tas.; Queensland Art Gallery, Brisbane, Qld.; Sale Regional Art Gallery, Sale, Vic.; Victorian State Craft Collection, Melbourne, Vic..

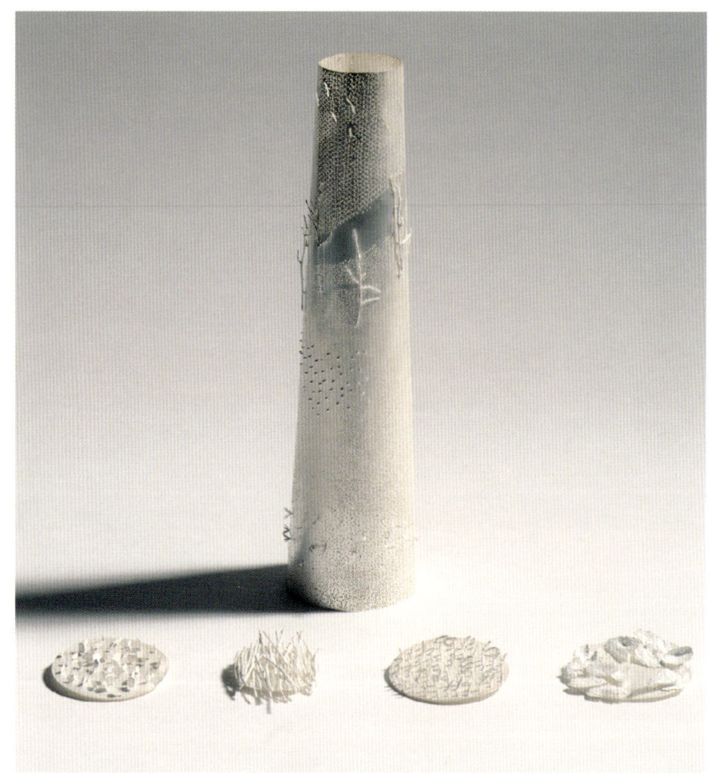

Marian **Hosking**

Vessel with four brooches: Leptospermum, Casaurina, Banksia, Angophora

sterling silver and stainless steel

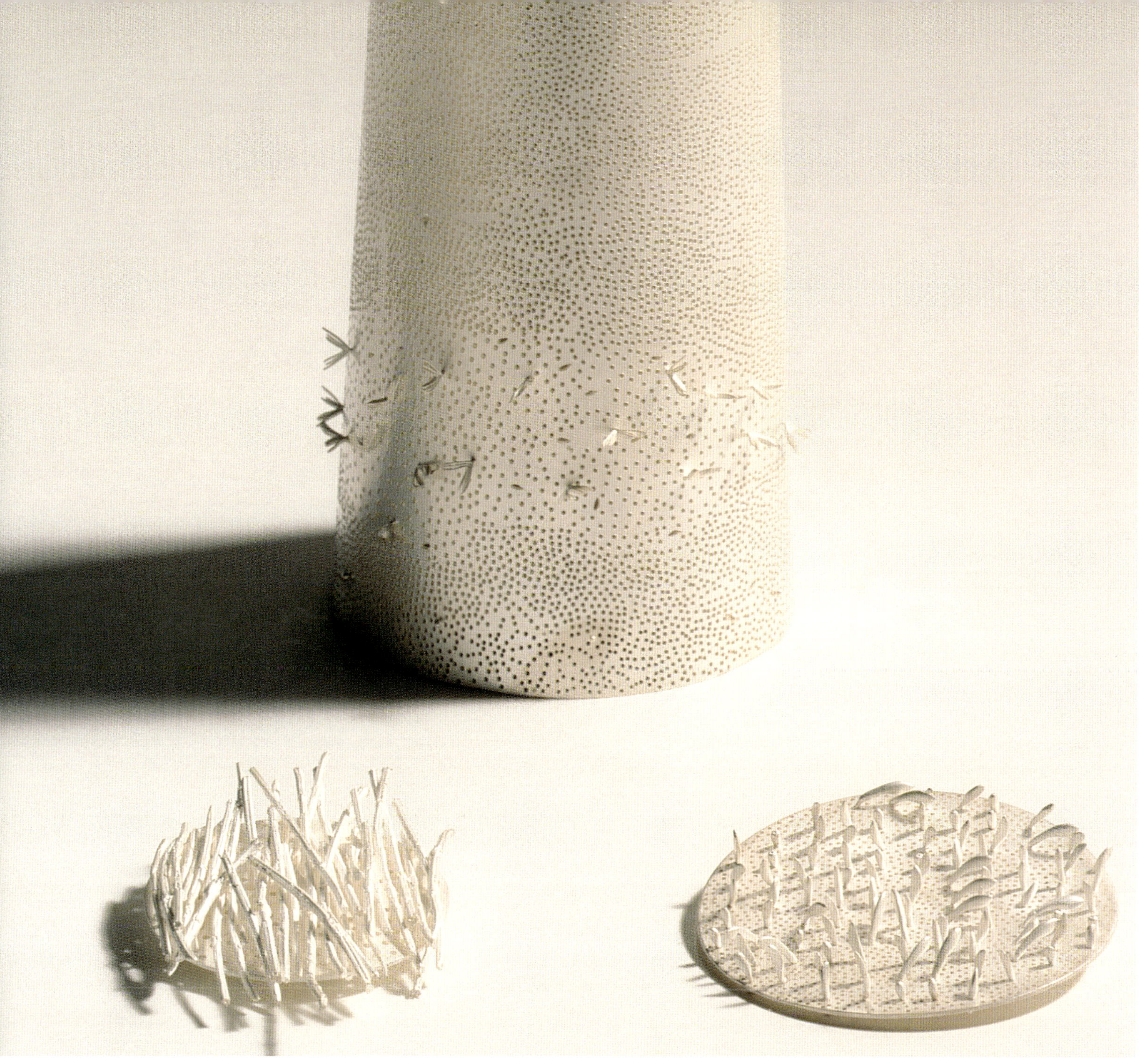

Marian **Hosking**

A close observation of the Australian bush environment informs the jewellery and objects of Marian Hosking. In this work, she celebrates the qualities of four familiar plants, abstracting their physical characteristics through intricate metalwork. Her familiar technique of piercing shapes into the metal, and loosely affixing to it myriad elements that move with the slightest touch, is seen in these brooches and their accompanying branch-like vessel. While conjuring the fragile texture and constant transformation of the micro-environment of the forest floor, such objects are not frozen as specimens, rather they gain a new life through being worn and used.

Helge **Larsen**

Sydney, New South Wales

Born Copenhagen, Denmark 1929, arrived Australia 1961.

Training

National Diploma, Guldsmedehojskolen (College of Craft and Design), Copenhagen, Denmark, 1953

Related professional experience

Established workshop in Copenhagen, Denmark, 1955; Senior Instructor, Department of Industrial Arts, University of New South Wales, Sydney, NSW, 1962–74; Head of Jewellery,1977–90, and Associate Professor, 1990–97, Sydney College of the Arts, University of New South Wales, Sydney, NSW; Head of School, School of Visual Arts, Sydney College of the Arts, 1991–94.

Darani **Lewers**

Sydney, New South Wales

Born Sydney, New South Wales 1936

Training

Trainee with Nina Ratsep, Sydney, NSW, 1957; Trainee with Helge Larsen, Copenhagen, Denmark, 1958–59.

Related professional experience

Formed partnership with Helge Larsen, Sydney, NSW, 1961.

Selected solo exhibitions (Helge Larsen and Darani Lewers partnership)

Macquarie Gallery, Sydney, NSW, 1961, 1963, 1967, 1971; Skinner Gallery, Perth, WA, 1961; Bonython Gallery, Adelaide, SA, 1962; Johnstone Gallery, Brisbane, Qld, 1962, 1963,1964; Gallery A, Melbourne, Vic., 1962, 1966; Von Bertouch Gallery, Newcastle, NSW, 1963, 1966; Gallery A, Sydney, NSW, 1967, 1970; Macquarie Galleries, Canberra, ACT, 1971; Realities Gallery, Melbourne, Vic., 1972, 1976; Det Danske

Kunstindustimuseum, Copenhagen, Denmark, 1973, 2000; Galerie Galtung, Oslo, Norway, 1973; Bonython Gallery, Sydney, NSW, 1974, 1975; Galerie Traklhaus, Salzburg, Austria, 1975; Crafts Council of Queensland, Brisbane, Qld, 1976; Galerie am Graben, Vienna, Austria, 1976,1988; Berrima Gallery, Berrima, NSW, 1978; *Helge Larsen and Darani Lewers: A Retrospective: Jewellery, hollow ware and sculpture*, National Gallery of Victoria, Melbourne, Vic, 1986 and Australian tour, 1986–88, Schmuckmuseum, Pforzheim, Germany, 1988; Irving Sculpture Gallery, Sydney, NSW, 1989; Solander Gallery, Canberra, ACT, 1990; Christine Abrahams Gallery, Melbourne, Vic., 1992; Sherman Galleries, Sydney, NSW, 1995,1998, 2001; Galerie Tactus, Copenhagen, Denmark, 1996; Australian Embassy, Paris, France, 1997; The Applied Art Museum of Estonia, Tallinn, Estonia, 1998; Beaver Galleries, Canberra, ACT, 1999; Brisbane City Gallery, Brisbane, Qld, 2000; Museet på Koldinghus, Kolding, Denmark, 2000; Australian Embassy, Washington, DC, USA, 2002.

Selected group exhibitions since 1992 (Helge Larsen and Darani Lewers partnership)

Australian Contemporary Hollow Ware, Australian Exhibitions Touring Agency, travelling in Australia, Indonesia, Korea, The Philippines and USA, 1991–93; *20th Century Silverware*, Victoria and Albert Museum, London, UK, 1993; *Art of Adornment*, Queen Victoria Museum and Art Gallery, Launceston, Tas., travelling exhibition in Japan and SE Asia, 1993–94; *Contemporary Wearables '93*, Toowoomba Art Gallery, Toowoomba, Qld, 1993; Second Australian Contemporary Jewellery Biennial, Jam Factory Craft and Design Centre, Adelaide, SA, 1993; *Armed*, The Door, Fremantle, WA, 1994; *Der Becher und Loffel*, Gisela Seibert-Philuppen Gallery, Berlin, Germany, 1995; *Makers*

Mark 20 Years Retrospective, Makers Mark, Melbourne, Vic., 1997; *Fire in the Heart: Australian Enamel*; Craft Space, Sydney, NSW, 1997; *Creative Capital*, Centre for Contemporary Craft, Sydney, NSW, 1998; *Contemporary Australian Craft*, Hokkaido Museum of Modern Art, Sapporo, Japan, 1999; *Australia 2000*, Lesley Craze Gallery, London, UK, 2000; *Fifty Years of Design in Australia*, Rose Seidler House, Historic Houses Trust of New South Wales, Sydney, NSW, 2000; *Herman's Art Award*, Sherman Galleries, Sydney, NSW, 2001.

Public collections (Australia) (Helge Larsen and Darani Lewers partnership)

Art Gallery of South Australia, Adelaide, SA; Art Gallery of Western Australia, Perth, WA; Hamilton Art Gallery, Hamilton, Vic.; National Gallery of Australia, Canberra, ACT; National Gallery of Victoria, Melbourne, Vic.; Powerhouse Museum, Sydney, NSW; Queen Victoria Museum and Art Gallery, Launceston, Tas.; Queensland Art Gallery, Brisbane, Qld; Parliament House, Canberra, ACT; Toowoomba Art Gallery, Toowoomba, Qld; University of New South Wales, Sydney, NSW.

Public collections (international) (Helge Larsen and Darani Lewers partnership)

Australian Embassy, Tokyo, Japan; The Applied Art Museum of Estonia, Tallinn, Estonia; Det Danske Kunstindustrimuseum, Copenhagen, Denmark; Museet på Koldinghus, Kolding, Denmark; Museum fur Angewandte Kunst, Vienna, Austria; Schmuckmuseum, Pforzheim, Germany; Umeleckoprumyslové Muzeum v Praze, Prague, Czech Republic; Wuppertaler Uhren Museum, Wuppertal, Germany.

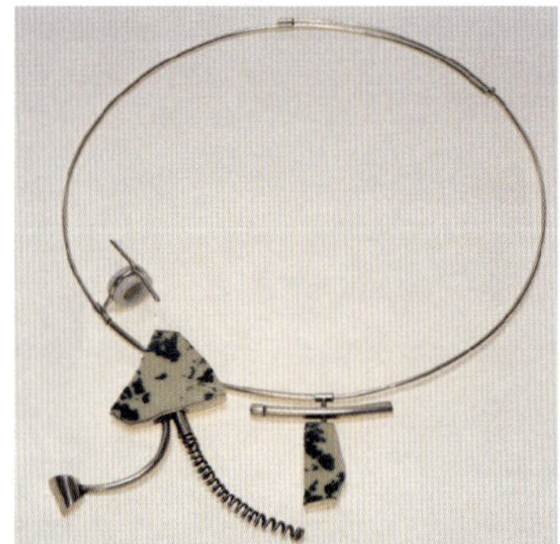

Helge **Larsen** and Darani **Lewers**
Traces neck ring
sterling silver, stone, iron and glazed ceramic shard

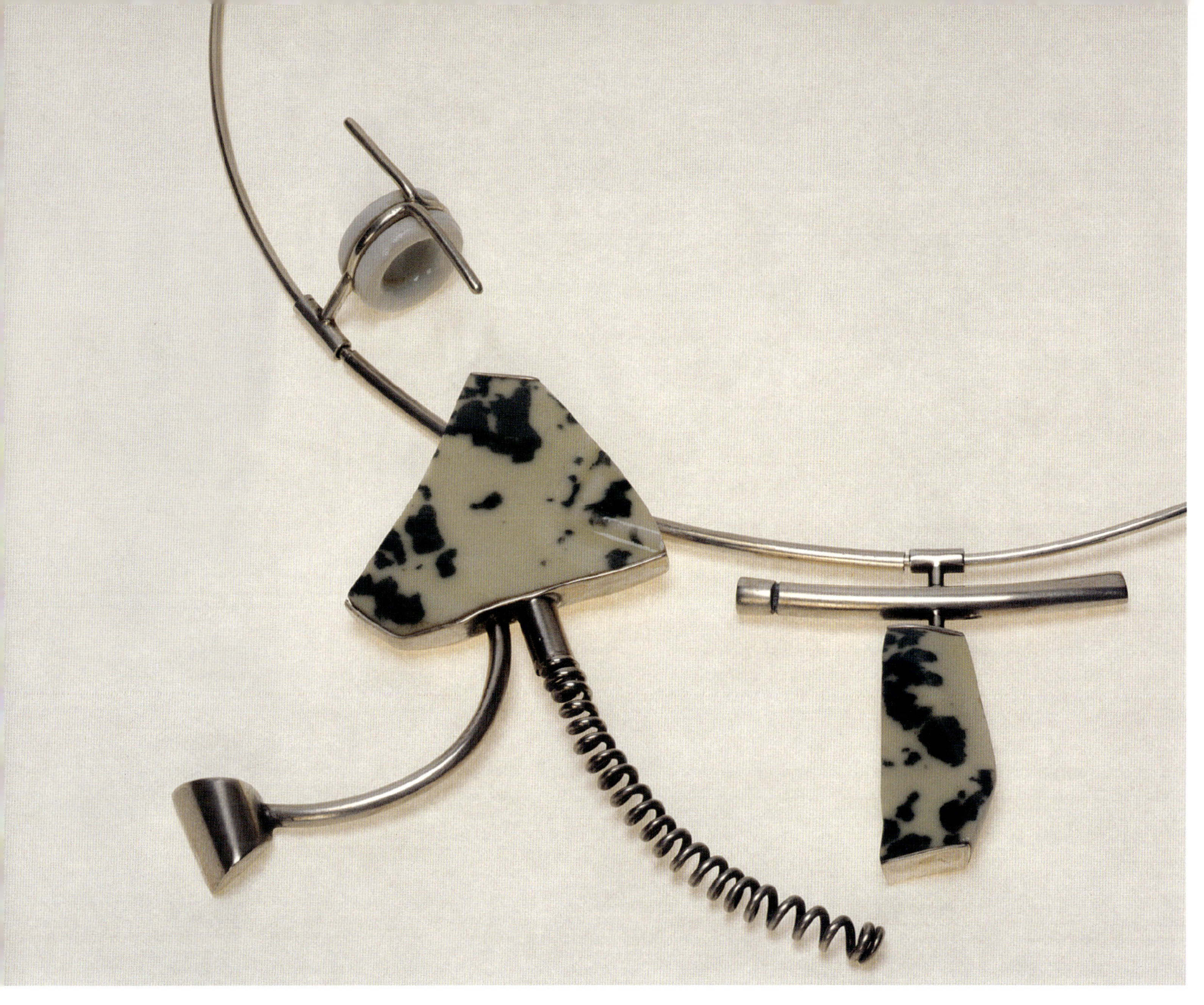

Helge **Larsen** and Darani **Lewers**

In this work, we see the influence of the organic design and functionalism that characterised Scandinavian jewellery and metalwork from the 1950s. Helge Larsen, in partnership with Darani Lewers, was instrumental in the establishment of these principles in Australia and they have developed work that expresses a highly individual interpretation of the Australian environment.[1] The genesis of these objects can be seen in their work from the early 1980s, in which fragmentary images of the Australian environment are combined in flexible jewellery objects. This work is from the artists' most recent production, following a period of travel and research in Central Australia, North Africa and Europe. It reflects their long interest in the structures and systems that underpin the natural and the built environment, and in combining precious metals and stones with found natural and industrial materials, in this case, a fragment of the ubiquitous, organically-shaped ceramic electric kettles found in Australian homes from the 1930s.

1 See Judith O'Callaghan, *Helge Larsen & Darani Lewers – A retrospective*, Melbourne: National Gallery of Victoria, 1986, for an account of the development of Larsen and Lewers' partnership and work to 1986.

Mitsuo **Shoji**
Sydney, New South Wales
Born Osaka, Japan 1946,
arrived Australia 1973

Training
Studied art and design, Art Institute of
Osaka City Museum and Nakanoshima
School of Arts, Osaka, Japan, 1967;
Bachelor of Arts and Teaching Certificate,
1971, and Master of Fine Arts, Kyoto City
University of Arts, Kyoto, Japan, 1973.

Related professional experience
Lecturer Ceramics, 1978–92,
Senior Lecturer Ceramics, since 1992,
Sydney College of the Arts, University of
New South Wales, Sydney, NSW.

Selected solo exhibitions
Mitsuo Shoji Ceramics, Meat Market Craft
Centre, Melbourne, Vic., 1974; *Ceramic
Objects*, Nakamiya Gallery, Osaka, Japan,
1977; *Wet Clay Installation*, Iteza Gallery,
Kyoto, Japan, 1977; *Pottery Works*, David
Jones Art Gallery, Sydney, NSW, 1979;
Pottery Works, Victor Mace Art Gallery,
Brisbane, Qld, 1980; *Clay Work*, John
Clark Gallery, Sydney, NSW, 1980; *Black
Fire and Clay Painting*, Blackfriars Gallery,
Sydney, NSW, 1981; *Mitsuo Shoji
Ceramics*, Gryphon Gallery, Melbourne,
Vic., 1982; *Mitsuo Shoji Ceramics*, Queen
Victoria Museum and Art Gallery,
Launceston, touring to three Tasmanian
venues, Tas., 1984; *Objects – Painting –
Installation*, Shepparton Art Gallery,
Shepparton, Vic. and Canberra School of
Art Gallery, Canberra, ACT, 1984; *Recent
Pottery* by Mitsuo Shoji, Aladdin Gallery,
Sydney, NSW, 1985; *Colour Inlay Ceramics*
by Mitsuo Shoji, Cuppacumbalong Craft
Centre Gallery, Canberra, ACT, and
Australian Craftworks Gallery, Sydney,
NSW, 1986; *Recent Ceramics by Mitsuo
Shoji*, Victor Mace Gallery, Brisbane, Qld,
1986; *Black Fire and Clay Painting*, Devise
Gallery, Melbourne, Vic., 1986; *Pottery –
Recent Works by Mitsuo Shoji*, Cooks Hill
Gallery, Newcastle, NSW, 1986;
*Mitsuo Shoji – Glass installation and
ceramic paintings*, Roz MacAllan Gallery,
Brisbane, Qld, 1987; *Colour Inlay Ceramics
and Painting*, Bonython Meadmore Gallery,
Sydney, NSW, 1987; *Mitsuo Shoji Ceramics
and Glass Objects*, Waikato Museum of
Art and History, Hamilton, New Zealand,
1989; *Mitsuo Shoji Ceramic Sculptures and
Paintings*, Irving Sculpture Gallery, Sydney,
NSW, 1989; *Travail en Cours*, Art Gallery
Ecole d'Art, Aix-en-Provence, France,
1990; *Recent Mitsuo Shoji Pottery with
Traditional Manners*, Cooks Hill Gallery,
Newcastle, NSW, 1991; *Mitsuo Shoji
Ceramics*, A.B.C. Art Gallery, Osaka, Japan,
1992; *Mitsuo Shoji: Recent works*, Cooks
Hill Gallery, Newcastle, NSW, 1995;
Ceramic Paintings by Mitsuo Shoji, Japan
Foundation Gallery, Sydney, NSW, 1997;
*Mitsuo Shoji: Is our life a square, circle or
triangle?*, Quadrivium, Sydney, NSW, 2000.

Selected group exhibitions since 1992
3rd International Ceramic Competition,
Sopot, Poland, 1992; *Fresh Clay: Australia*,
Meat Market Craft Centre, Melbourne,
Vic., 1993; *International Academy of
Ceramics Members' Exhibition*, Museum of
Decorative Arts, Prague, Czech Republic,
1994; *The Bechyne International Ceramics
Symposium Exhibition*, Louny, Czech
Republic, 1994; *Fletcher Challenge
Ceramics Award*, Auckland Museum,
Auckland, New Zealand, 1994; *Australian
Contemporary Ceramics*, Concorso
Internazionale della Ceramica d'Arte,
Faenza, Italy, touring to Japan and
Singapore, 1995; *Panavezys International
Ceramics Symposium Exhibition*, Art
Gallery of Panavezys, Panavezys, Lithuania,
1995; *Delinquent Angel: Australian
historical, Aboriginal and contemporary
ceramics*, Museo Internazionale delle
Ceramiche, Faenza, Italy and travelling in
Asia and Australia, 1995–97; *The Japan
Inspiration: Influence in crafts and design*,
Art Gallery of Western Australia, Perth,
WA, 1997; *In-Context*, Manly Art Gallery,
Sydney, NSW, 1997; *Salad Days*, Ceramic
Art Gallery, Sydney, NSW, 1998; *The
Language of Clay*, Art Gallery of Western
Australia, Perth, WA, 1999; *The Masters
Series*, Gallery Qdos, Lorne, Vic., 1999;
Icarus as Metaphor, Goulburn Regional Art
Gallery, Goulburn, NSW, touring to
regional Australian galleries, 1999.

Public collections (Australia)
Ararat Art Gallery, Ararat, Vic.; Art Gallery
of Western Australia, Perth, WA; Brisbane
City Gallery, Brisbane, Qld; National Gallery
of Australia, Canberra, ACT; National
Gallery of Victoria, Melbourne, Vic.;
Newcastle Region Art Gallery, Newcastle,
NSW; Powerhouse Museum, Sydney, NSW;
Queensland Art Gallery, Brisbane, Qld;
Shepparton Art Gallery, Shepparton, Vic.;
Tasmanian Art Gallery and Museum,
Hobart, Tas.; Victorian State Craft
Collection, Melbourne, Vic.

Public collections (international)
International Ceramics Museum, Shigaraki,
Japan; Museo Internazionale delle
Ceramiche, Faenza, Italy; Museum of Art
and Design, Helsinki, Finland;
Umeleckoprumyslové Muzeumv Praze,
Prague, Czech Republic.

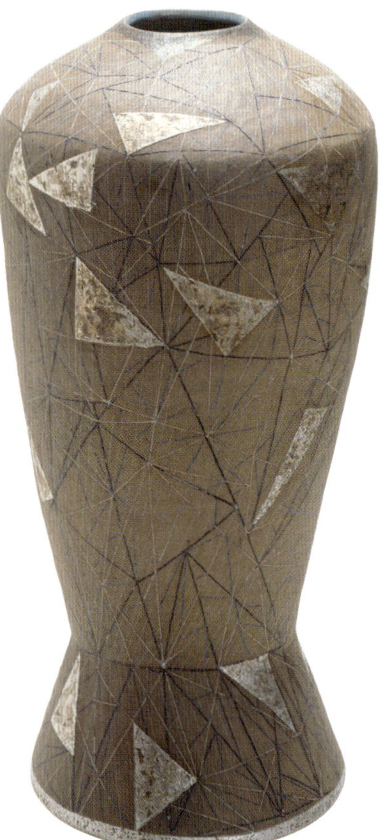

Mitsuo **Shoji**
Gaman I – Tattoo
stoneware with gold and silver leaf foil
and coloured inlays

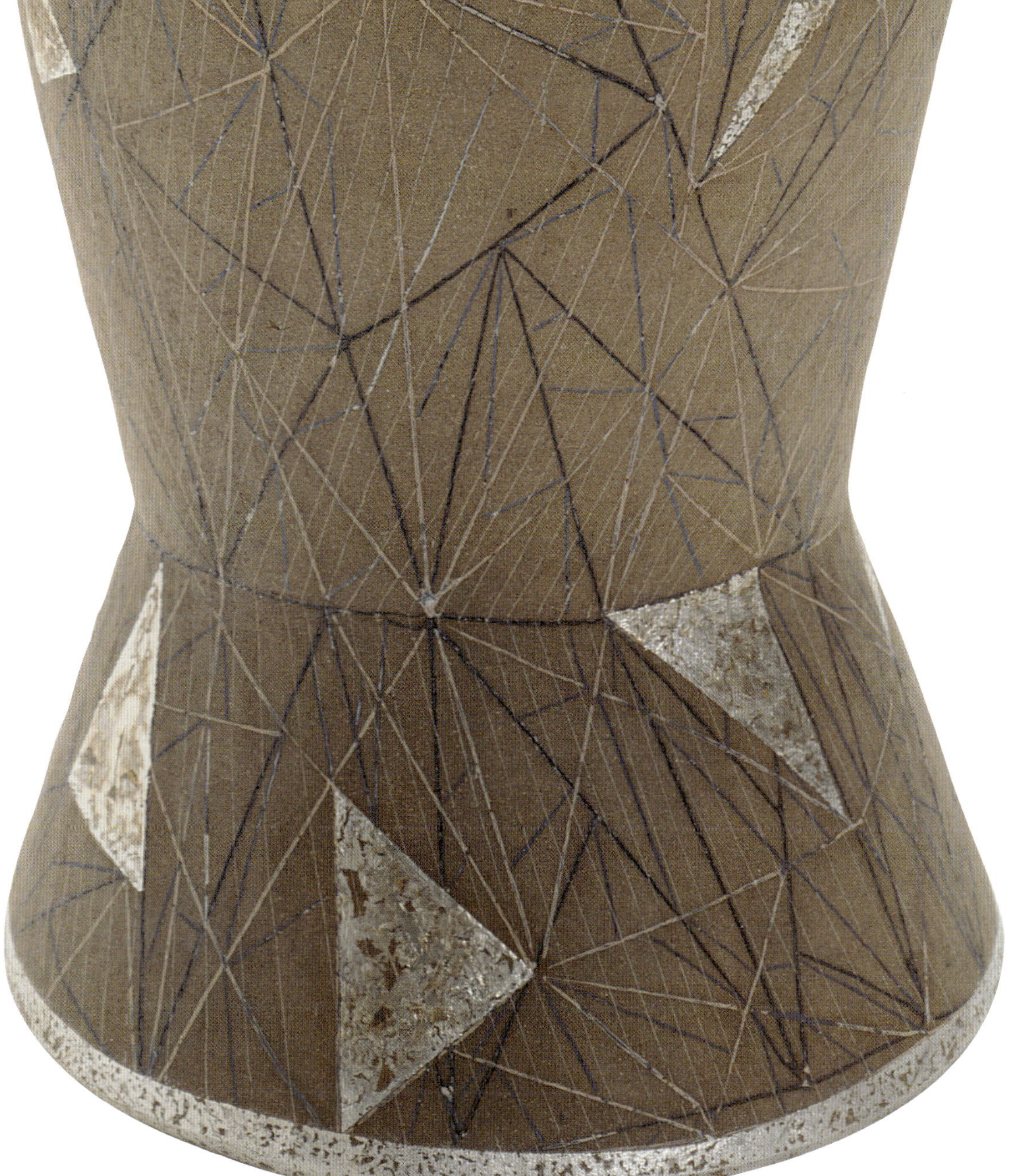

Mitsuo **Shoji**

Mitsuo Shoji's work, like that of a number of Japanese ceramicists, encompasses both functional and sculptural objects, united in an approach to surface decoration.[1] His repertoire of design ranges from gestural brushwork in the traditional Japanese *mingei* tradition, to black-fired works with torch-fired decoration of gold leaf and, more recently, works with formal geometric decoration of coloured clay inlays. Using the square, the circle and the triangle, the design of this large vessel is a synthesis of Shoji's investigations into the relationship between volume and surface. It reveals his interest in the marks of human intervention in the landscape, scarification and the tradition of the Japanese tattoo. Like these tattoos, which envelop the body and cannot be fully revealed at any one time, the totality of Shoji's web-like decoration on a three-dimensional form can only be sensed and partially glimpsed. Its lustred triangular sections shift in and out of reflectiveness as one handles or moves around the object, engendering a sense of close involvement with the object and its structure, function and materiality.

1 See Eugenie Keefer Bell, *The Japan Inspiration: Influence in crafts and design*, Perth: Art Gallery of Western Australia, 1997, for a discussion of Shoji's work in relation to Japanese influences in Australian crafts.

Alan **Watt**

Tanja, New South Wales

Born Melbourne, Victoria 1941

Training

Diploma of Art (Ceramics), 1966, and
Post Graduate Fellowship 1974, Royal
Melbourne Institute of Technology,
Melbourne, Vic.

Related professional experience

Lecturer Ceramics, State College of
Victoria, Melbourne, Vic. 1964–78.
Head of Ceramics, Canberra School of Art,
Australian National University, Canberra,
ACT, 1979–98.

Selected solo exhibitions

The Craft Centre, Melbourne, Vic., 1976;
Clive Parry Galleries, Melbourne, Vic.,
1977; Narek Gallery, Canberra, ACT, 1977;
Cooks Hill Gallery, Newcastle, NSW, 1983;
Devise Gallery, Melbourne, Vic., 1985;
Meridian Gallery, Melbourne, Vic., 1991;
Ceramic Art Gallery, Sydney, NSW, 1994;
Dick Bett Gallery, Hobart, Tas., 1995;
Narek Gallery, Canberra, ACT, 1995; Craft
Council of Northern Territory Gallery,
Darwin, NT, 1996; Artworks Gallery,
Nungurner, Vic., 1996; Distelfink Gallery,
Melbourne, Vic., 1997; Atrium Gallery,
Glasgow School of Art, Scotland, 1997;
Gallery Maronie, Kyoto, Japan, 1997;
Narek Gallery, Canberra, ACT, 1998;
European Ceramics Gallery,
Knaresborough, UK, 1998. *Composite of
Opposites*, Drill Hall Gallery, The Australian
National University, Canberra, ACT, 2001
(with Janet De Boos).

Selected group exhibitions

*Concorso Internazionale della Ceramica
d'Arte*, Palazzo delle Esposizione, Faenza,
Italy, 1979, 1983, 1988; *Contemporary
Australian Ceramics*, touring exhibition in
USA, Canada and SE Asia, 1983–85;
*Impulse and Form: Object makers and the
Australian experience*, Art Gallery of
Western Australia, Perth, WA, 1985;
3rd International Ceramic Competition,
Sopot, Poland, 1992; Mornington
Peninsula Arts Centre, Mornington, Vic.,
1996; *5th Triennial Exhibition of Small
Ceramics*, Zagreb, Croatia, 1997; *Nature as
Object: Craft and design from Japan,
Finland and Australia: The Third Australian
International Crafts Triennial*; Art Gallery of
Western Australia, Perth, WA, 1998; *The
Language of Clay*, Art Gallery of Western
Australia, Perth, WA, 1999; *Arts Scotland*,
Scottish Royal Academy, Edinburgh, UK,
1999; *Contemporary International
Ceramics*, Cordoba, Spain, 2000;
Contemporary Australian Ceramics, Hong
Kong, PRC, 2000; *International Academy
of Ceramics Exhibition*, Chosun Royal Kiln
Museum, Korea, 2001; *SOFA* (Narek
Gallery), Navy Pier, Chicago, Il, USA, 2001.

Public collections (Australia)

Art Gallery of South Australia, Adelaide,
SA; Art Gallery of Western Australia, Perth,
WA; Australian National University,
Canberra, ACT; Box Hill Town Hall
Collection, Melbourne, Vic.; Canberra
Museum and Art Gallery, Canberra, ACT;
Castlemaine Art Gallery, Castlemaine, Vic.;
City of Caulfield Art Centre, Melbourne,
Vic.; City of Fremantle, Fremantle, WA;
Devonport Gallery, Devonport, Tas.;
Geelong Art Gallery, Geelong, Vic.;
La Trobe University, Melbourne, Vic.;
La Trobe Valley Regional Art Gallery
Morwell, Vic.; Manly Art Gallery, Sydney,
NSW; McClelland Art Gallery and
Sculpture Park, Langwarrin, Vic.;
Melbourne University, Melbourne, Vic.;
Monash University, Melbourne, Vic.;
National Gallery of Australia, Canberra,
ACT; National Gallery of Victoria,
Melbourne, Vic.; Parliament House,
Canberra, ACT; Newcastle Region Art
Gallery, Newcastle, NSW; Orange Regional
Gallery, Orange, NSW; Powerhouse
Museum, Sydney, NSW; Queen Victoria
Museum and Art Gallery, Launceston, Tas.;
Queensland Art Gallery, Brisbane, Qld;
Shepparton Art Gallery, Shepparton, Vic.;
Tasmanian Museum and Art Gallery,
Hobart, Tas.; University of Canberra,
Canberra, ACT; University of Tasmania,
Hobart, Tas.; Victorian State Craft
Collection, Melbourne, Vic.

Public collections (international)

Auckland Museum, Auckland, New
Zealand; Keramion Ceramics Museum,
Frechen, Germany; Robert McDougall Art
Gallery, Christchurch, New Zealand;
Shigaraki Ceramic Cultural Park Museum,
Shigaraki, Japan; World Ceramic Centre,
Ichon, Korea.

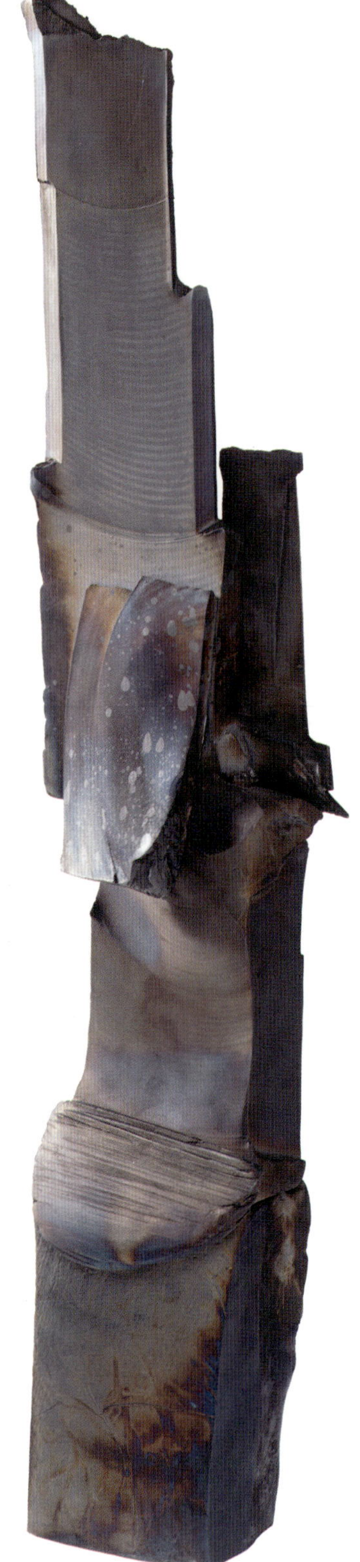

Alan **Watt**
Speckled pinnacle
black-fired earthenware with terra sigillata

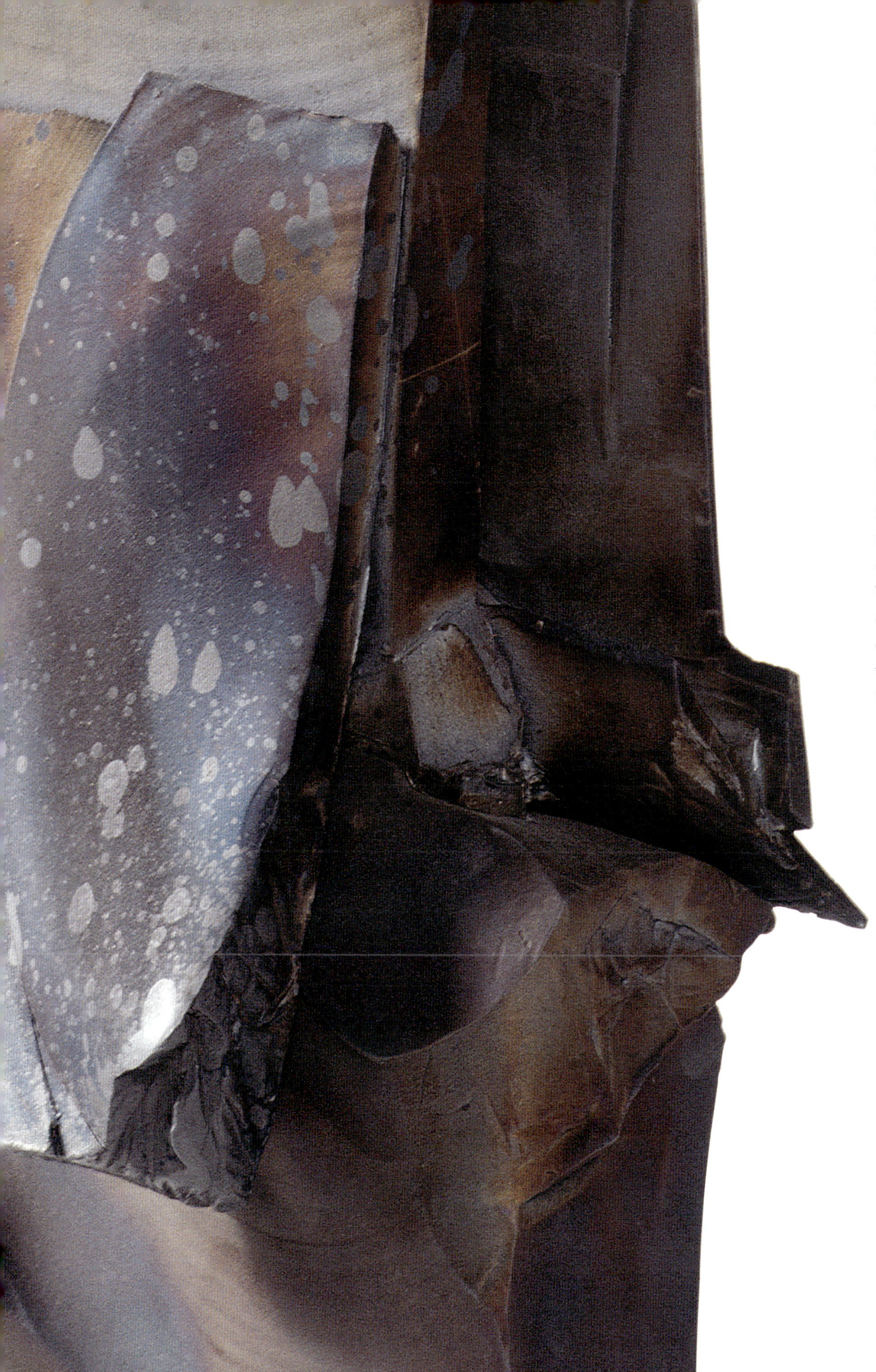

Alan **Watt**

Alan Watt has drawn upon violent human interventions into the landscape such as clearing, mining, road construction and erosion and expresses in his ceramics the raw beauty of the earth as it is revealed through these processes. His abstractions of these interventions and transformations have assumed sentinel-like proportions, with sharply cut surfaces reflecting light through rich and elusive iridescent surfaces. This commanding work is a development of these themes and illustrates Watt's innate understanding of the processes that transform clay to ceramic and that are in turn metaphors for the industrialisation of nature.

Margaret **West**
Blackheath, New South Wales
Born Melbourne, Victoria 1936

Training
Certificate of Art, 1955, Diploma of Art,
1975, Graduate Diploma of Art, 1976,
Royal Melbourne Institute of Technology,
Melbourne, Vic.; Diploma of Education,
Melbourne State College, Melbourne,
Vic., 1977.

Related professional experience
Lecturer from1979 and Head of Studio,
Jewellery and Object Design from
1989–99, Sydney College of the Arts,
University of New South Wales, Sydney,
NSW

Selected solo exhibitions
The Craft Centre, Melbourne, Vic., 1978;
Macquarie Galleries, Sydney, NSW, 1981,
1982; Makers Mark, Melbourne, Vic.,
1982,1987; Queen Victoria Museum and
Art Gallery, Launceston, touring to Crafts
Council of Tasmania, Hobart and Burnie
Art Gallery, Burnie, Tas., 1984;
Contemporary Jewellery Gallery, Sydney,
NSW, 1985; *Interstices: Works by Margaret
West from 1981–1992*, Canberra School
of Art Gallery, 1992 and Australian tour to
1994; *Notes: Jewellery and other objects*,
Crawford Gallery, Sydney, NSW, 1997;
Notes II: The sky is a garden, Gallery
Funaki, Melbourne, Vic., 1998, Kotelna
Gallery, Prague, Czech Republic, 1999,
Fisher Gallery, Auckland, New Zealand,
1999 and Galerie Ra, Amsterdam, The
Netherlands, 2000; Helen Drutt Gallery,
Philadelphia, PA, USA, 1999; *Double
Damask*, Mori Gallery, Sydney, NSW, 2001.

Selected group exhibitions since 1992
National Craft Award, 1992 and *VicHealth
National Craft Award*, 1995, National
Gallery of Victoria, Melbourne, Vic.;
Four Elements, Blaxland Gallery, Sydney,
NSW, 1993; *The River Styx/Sticks: Australia
and New Zealand artists' book project*,

National Library of Australia, Canberra,
ACT, 1995; *Nature as Object: Craft and
design from Japan, Finland and Australia:
The Third Australian International Crafts
Triennial*, Art Gallery of Western Australia,
Perth, WA, 1998; *Ra-expositie: New
jewellery by Australian artists*,
Galerie Ra, Amsterdam, The Netherlands,
1998; *Romanticism and Reason: Australian
jewellery 1957-1997*, Art Gallery of
Western Australia touring exhibition,
1998–99; *Brooching it Diplomatically:
A tribute to Madeleine K. Albright*,
Helen Drutt Gallery, Philadelphia, PA, USA
and European tour, 1998–2000;
Imagining: Art of the twentieth century,
Art Gallery of Western Australia, Perth,
WA, 1999; *Commemorative Medals and
Trophies: the politics of history*, Helen
Drutt Gallery, Philadelphia, PA, USA, 2000;
Be Jewelled, Monash Art Gallery,
Melbourne, Vic., 2000; *Craft from Scratch:
8. Trienniale – Form and Matters -
Australia and Germany*, Museum für
Angewandte Kunst, Frankfurt, Germany,
travelling exhibition, 2000; *Micromegas*,
Galerie für Angewande Kunst, Bayerischer
Kunstgewerbe-Verein, Munich, Germany;
Auriferous: The gold project,
Bathurst Regional Art Gallery, Bathurst,
NSW, 2001.

Public collections (Australia)
Art Gallery of Western Australia, Perth,
WA; Art Gallery of South Australia,
Adelaide, SA; National Gallery of Australia,
Canberra, ACT; National Gallery of
Victoria, Melbourne, Vic.; Powerhouse
Museum, Sydney, NSW; Queensland Art
Gallery, Brisbane, Qld; Queen Victoria
Museum and Art Gallery, Launceston, Tas.;
RMIT University, Melbourne, Vic.; Victorian
State Craft Collection, Melbourne, Vic.

Public collections (international)
Cooper-Hewitt Museum, Smithsonian
Institution, New York, USA.

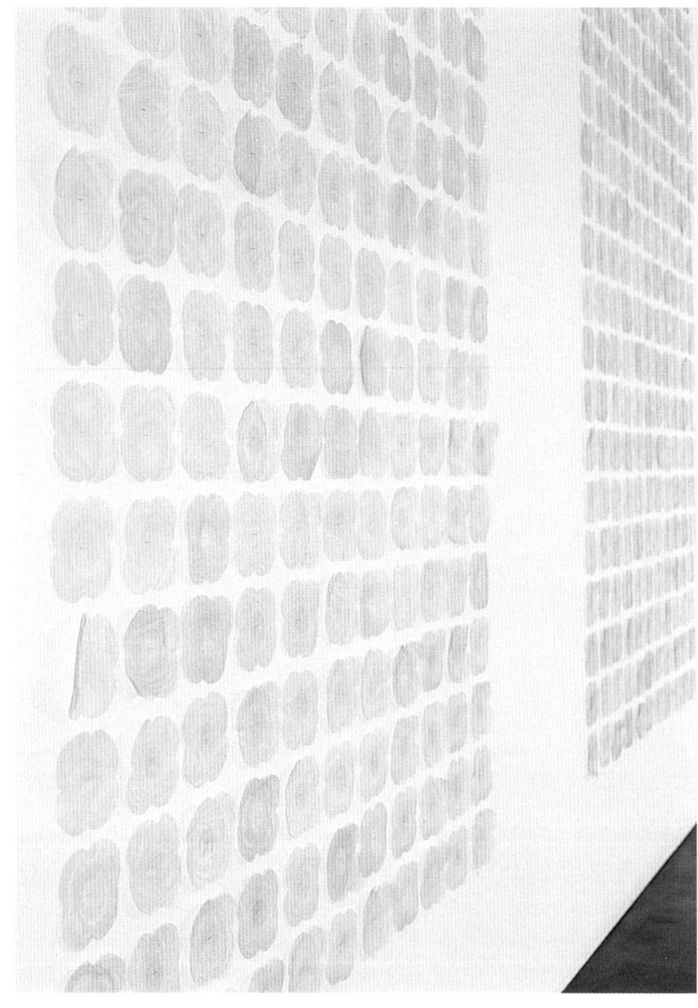

Margaret **West**
Double damask
506 phosphor bronze mesh units and paint

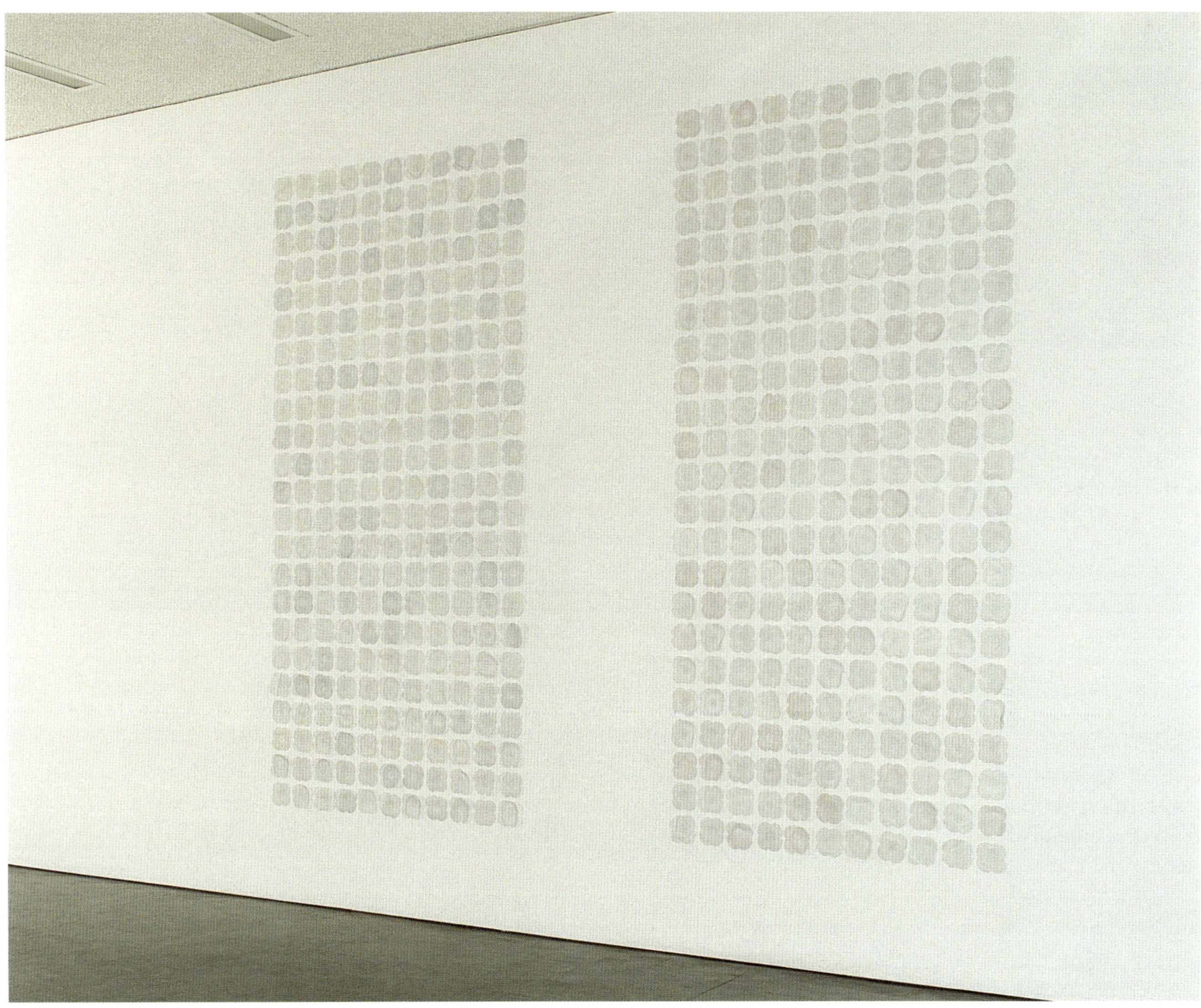

Margaret **West**

The boundaries between the traditional Australian domestic interior and the outside world have become marked by the use of codified materials and conventions, such as the metal mesh insect screen. The insect screen allows openness and security, modifying and softening the view beyond, yet obscuring the interior from outside. Margaret West exploits the dichotomies of this ubiquitous material in this screen-like work, cutting it into shapes of the four-petalled damask rose and painting each to emphasise the moiré effects of light and shadow.[1] The grid-like repetition of these abstracted forms suggests the symbolism of the cultivated rose garden, as a mediating element to the undomesticated natural environment beyond the home. It also alludes to the woven structure of that most cherished of domestic textiles, the formal white damask tablecloth, with its double-sided and subtle white-on-white reflective pattern, often based on roses. West's wall of roses is permeable and elusive, a metaphor for continuity and tradition in the face of change.[2]

1 See Julie Ewington, 'Wide (true) blue yonder' in *Object*, no 28, Sydney: Object – Australian Centre for Craft and Design, 2000, for an account of the development West's rose imagery in relation to her jewellery.

2 West developed this work during a 2000–01 Fellowship from the Australia Council.

73

Maureen **Williams**

Melbourne, Victoria

Born Port Pirie, South Australia 1952

Training

Bachelor of Arts, Chisholm Institute
of Technology, 1986.

Selected solo exhibitions

Qdos Arts, Lorne, Vic., 1992, 1996; Glass
Artists' Gallery, Sydney, NSW, 1996;
George Gallery, Melbourne, Vic., 1996,
1997, 1999; Galerie L, Hamburg,
Germany, 1997; Beaver Galleries,
Canberra, ACT, 2000

Selected group exhibitions since 1992

Australian Glass Triennial, Wagga Wagga
Regional Art Gallery, Wagga Wagga, NSW.
1992; *Australian Crafts 1990*, Meat
Market Craft Centre, Melbourne, Vic.,
1992; *Melbourne Makers*, Glass Artists'
Gallery, Sydney, NSW, 1992; *Australia
Revisited: celebrating 20 years of studio
glass*, Meat Market Craft Centre,
Melbourne, Vic., 1994; *Symmetry: crafts
meet kindred trades and professions*, Craft
Victoria, Melbourne, Vic., 1994; *Unique*,
State Craft Collection Gallery, Meat
Market Craft Centre, Vic., 1996; *Drawn in
Form*, Brisbane City Gallery, Brisbane, Qld;
Object Galleries, Sydney, NSW, 1999,
Exchanging Places, George Gallery at Ray
Hughes Gallery, Sydney, NSW, 1999;
G.A.S. International Expo 99, Tampa, FL,
USA, 1999; *Glass, Art & Science*
(Australian studio glass exhibition), Museu
do Vidro da Marinha Grande, Marinha
Grande, Portugal, 1999; *Luminous: Glass
from the Queensland Art Gallery
collection*, Queensland Art Gallery,
Brisbane, QLD, 1999; *Skill*, Mornington
Peninsula Arts Centre, Mornington, Vic.;
Craft Victoria travelling exhibition, 1999;
Space and Time, Monash University
Gallery, Melbourne, Vic 1999; *At the
Edge: Australian glass art*, Brisbane City
Gallery, Brisbane, Qld; Object Galleries,
Sydney, NSW; Galerie Handwerk, Munich,
Germany; National Glass Centre,
Sunderland, UK, 2000; *Australian Glass at
Masterworks*, Masterworks Gallery,
Auckland, NZ, 2000; *Craft from Scratch: 8.
Trienniale - Form and Matters -
Australia and Germany*, Museum für
Angewandte Kunst, Frankfurt, Germany,
travelling exhibition, 2000; *Image and
Imagination*, Quay School of the Arts
Gallery, Wanganui, NZ, 2000; *Hsinchu
International Glass Festival*, Hsinchu,
Taiwan, 2000; *Ranamok Glass Prize*, Volvo
Gallery, Sydney, NSW; travelling exhibition,
2001; *Transparent Things: Expressions in
glass*, National Gallery of Australia
Travelling Exhibition, Wagga Wagga
Regional Art Gallery, Wagga Wagga,
NSW, 2001; *Ecstasy*, Quadrivium, Sydney,
NSW, 2002.

Public collections (Australia)

Art Gallery of South Australia, Adelaide,
SA; Art Gallery of Western Australia, Perth,
WA; Artbank, Sydney, NSW; Monash
University, Melbourne, Vic.; National
Gallery of Australia, Canberra, ACT;
National Gallery of Victoria, Melbourne,
Vic.; Queensland Art Gallery, Brisbane,
Qld; Wagga Wagga Regional Art Gallery,
Wagga Wagga, NSW.

Public collections (international)

Die Neue Sammlung Museum, Munich,
Germany; Museu do Vidro da Marinha
Grande, Marinha Grande, Portugal.

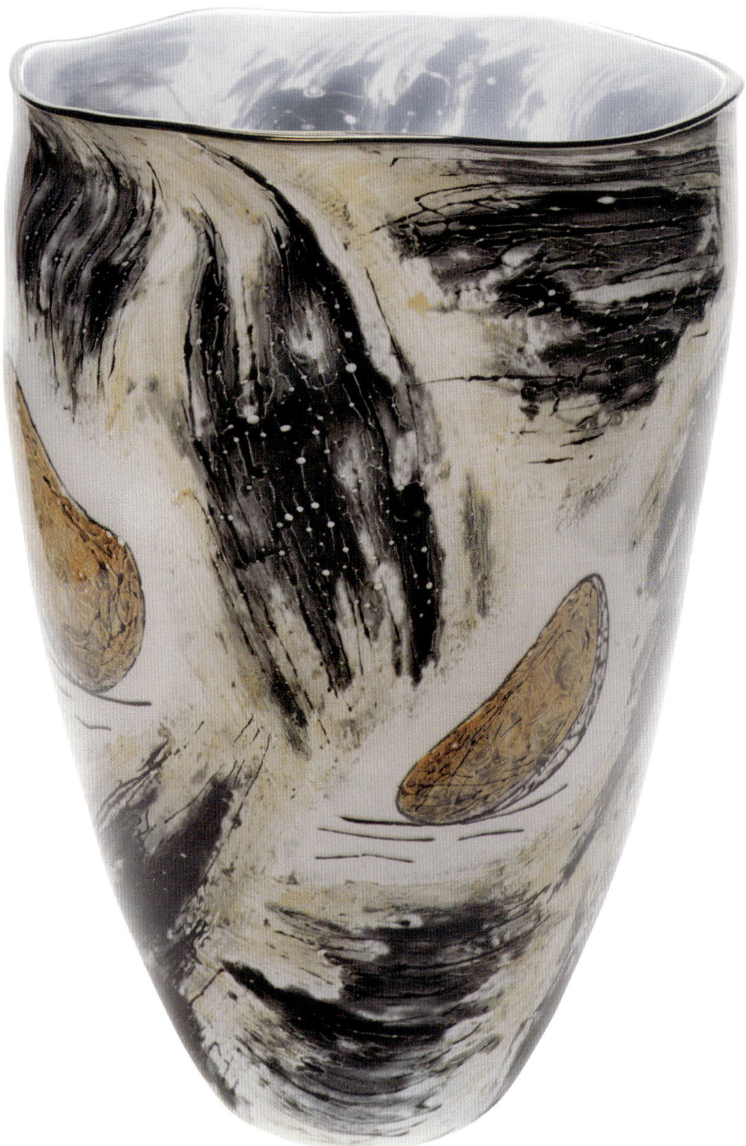

Maureen **Williams**
Clouded interaction, blown and
painted glass

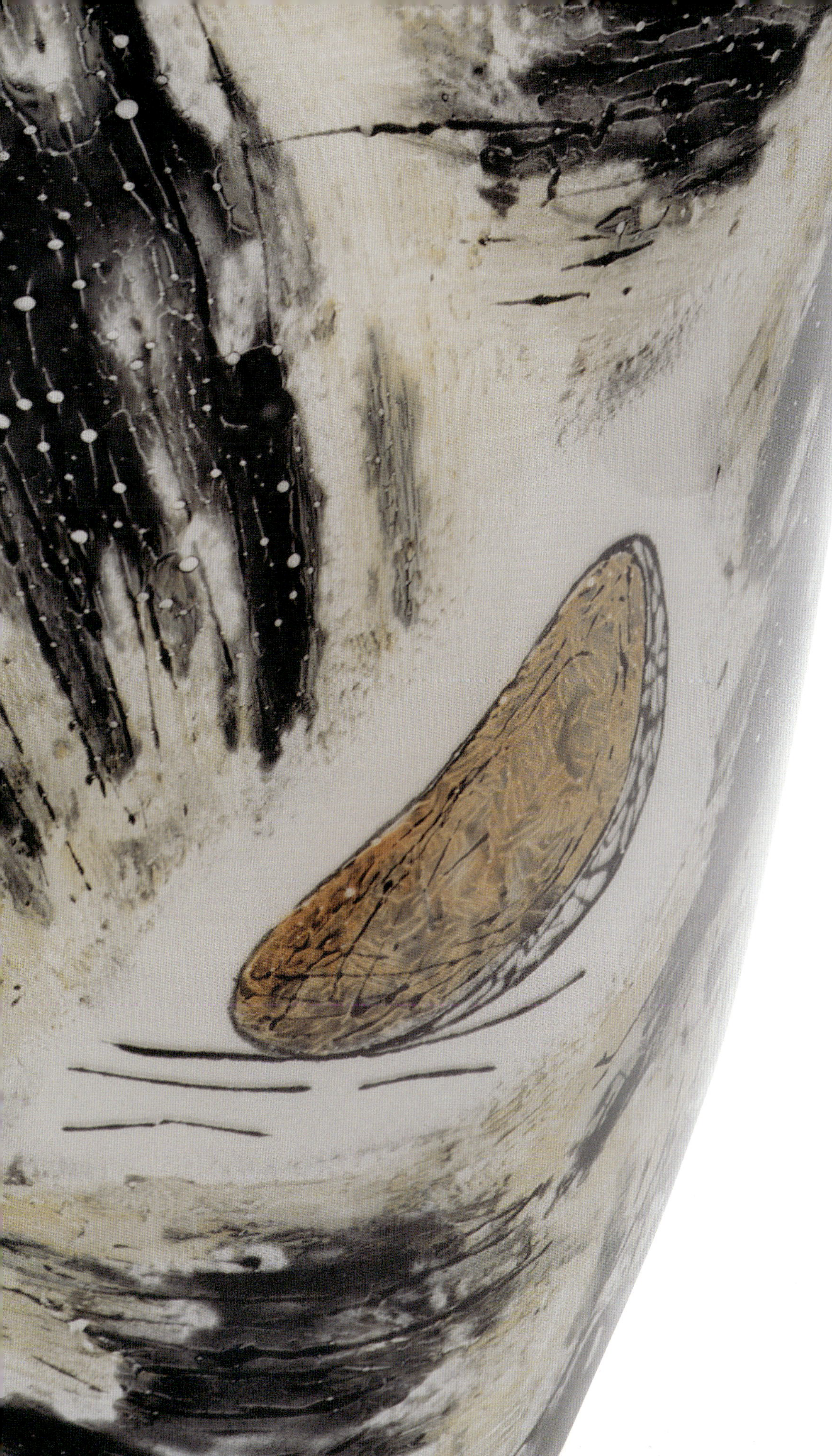

Maureen **Williams**

Maureen Williams uses one of the most archetypical forms in glass, the vessel, as a vehicle for painterly surface effects. Starting with blown, vortex-like forms, she animates their translucent white surfaces with vigorous gestural marks in vitreous paint. Using the constant action and fluidity inherent in the process of hot-working glass, she creates through her painted surfaces dreamlike abstract imagery, suggesting stormy skies, swirling dust and the shimmer of the dry Australian landscape. Williams' glass sweeps us into its narrative but, like a mirage, remains tantalisingly beyond our visual grasp.

75

Liz **Williamson**
Sydney, New South Wales
Born Sydney, New South Wales 1952

Training
Bachelor of Education and Commerce, Melbourne University, Melbourne, Vic., 1967–70; Handloom weaving course, Melbourne College of Textiles, Melbourne, Vic., 1978–80; Tapestry weaving course, Victorian Tapestry Workshop, Melbourne, Vic., 1980; Bachelor of Art (Textile Design), Royal Melbourne Institute of Technology, Melbourne, Vic., 1981–83.

Related professional experience
Lecturer, Textiles Workshop, Canberra School of Art, Australian National University, Canberra, ACT, 1991–96; 1997– present: Lecturer, Textiles and Honours Co-ordinator, School of Design Studies, College of Fine Arts, University of New South Wales, Sydney, NSW.

Selected solo exhibitions
Wraps and Scarves, Brown Paper Gallery, Lawson, NSW, 1992; *Pieces of Colour*, Jam Factory Craft and Design Centre, Adelaide, SA, 1993; *New Colour*, Craftspace, Sydney, NSW, 1994; *Undulations*, Beaver Galleries, Canberra, ACT, 1995; *Wraps*, Beaver Galleries, Canberra, ACT, 1998; *Surface*, Crawford Gallery, Sydney, NSW, 1999.

Selected group exhibitions since 1992
VicHealth National Craft Award, National Gallery of Victoria, Melbourne, Vic., 1992, 1995; *Design Visions: Australian International Crafts Triennial*, Art Gallery of Western Australia, Perth, WA, 1992; *Textiles and Praxis*, Craftwest Gallery, Perth, WA, 1992, *National Craft Acquisition Award*, Northern Territory Museum of Arts and Sciences, Darwin, NT, 1992; *Jahresmesse Kunsthandwerk*, Museum für Kunst und Gewerbe and Galerie L, Hamburg, Germany, 1992; *Discerning Textiles*, Goulburn Regional Art Gallery, Goulburn, NSW, 1993 and national tour 1993–95; *Decoration and Diversity: New textiles*, Craftspace, Sydney, NSW, 1993; *Scarf: Social fabric of a nation*, Greenway Gallery, Hyde Park Barracks, Sydney, NSW, 1993; *Crossing Borders: Contemporary Australian textile art*, University of Wollongong for ExhibitsUSA, travelling exhibition to USA, 1995–97; *The Art of the Object*, Craft Australia travelling exhibition, Salon Municipal de Exposiciones, Montevideo, Uruguay and Instituto Cultural de Las Condes, Santiago, Chile, 1994; *Interior*, National Museum of Indonesia, Jakarta, Indonesia, 1994; *Crucible: Materials of invention*, Craft Victoria Gallery, Melbourne, Vic., 1994; *11th Tamworth Fibre Textile Biennial*, Tamworth City Gallery, Tamworth, NSW, 1994; *Wool in the Australian Imagination*, Greenway Gallery, Hyde Park Barracks, Sydney, NSW, 1994; *Below the Surface*, project, Goulburn Regional Art Gallery, Goulburn, NSW, 1994–96; *8th International Triennial of Tapestry*, Central Museum of Textiles, Lodz, Poland, 1995; *The Language of Thread*, Art Gallery of Western Australia, Perth, WA, 1996; *Second Look: Prospect Textile Biennial*, Prospect Gallery, Nailsworth, SA, 1996; *Made to Matter*, Craft ACT Gallery, Canberra, ACT, 1996; *12th Tamworth Fibre Textile Biennial*, Tamworth City Gallery, Tamworth, NSW, 1996; *Tracing Purpose*, Leedy Voulkos Gallery, Kansas City, Missouri, USA, 1997; *Australian Korean Textile Design*, RMIT Gallery, Melbourne, Vic., 1997; *Origins and New Perspectives: Contemporary Australian textiles*, Queen Victoria Museum and Art Gallery, Launceston, Tas. for *9th International Triennial of Tapestry* Lodz, Poland, 1998; *2nd Biennale du Lin Contemporain*, Linen Museum, Normandy, France, 1998; *Scintilla*, Craft ACT Gallery, Canberra, ACT, 1998; *Seppelt Contemporary Art Awards*, Museum of Contemporary Art, Sydney, NSW, 1998; *Mapping Identity*, Centre for Contemporary Craft, Sydney, NSW, 1998; *Skill*, Craft Victoria Gallery, Melbourne, Vic., 1998; *Contemporary Australian Craft*, Hokkaido Museum of Modern Art, Sapporo, Japan, 1999; *Kimono as Canvas*, Gallery East, Perth, WA and national tour 1999–2000; *Water Medicine*, John Curtin Gallery, Curtin University, Perth, WA, 1999 and national tour 1999–2000; *Textiles and the Body*, Kudos Gallery, Sydney, NSW, 2000; *Colonial to Contemporary*, Powerhouse Museum, Sydney, NSW, 2000; *e-textiles: Ventures – Jacquard weaving*, Le Centre des Textiles Contemporains de Montréal, Montreal, Canada, 2000 and North American and Australian tour 2000–01; *Frisson: 12th Tamworth Fibre Textile Biennial*, Tamworth City Gallery, Tamworth, NSW, 2000; *From Lausanne to Beijing – Beijing 2000 International Tapestry Art Exhibition*, Academy of Art and Design, Tsinghua University, Beijing, China, 2000; *Histories in the Making*, Ivan Dougherty Gallery, Sydney, NSW, 2001; *Possibilities of Cloth*, Sheehan Gallery, Walla Walla, WA, USA, 2001.

Public collections
Art Gallery of South Australia, Adelaide, SA; Art Gallery of Western Australia, Perth, WA; National Gallery of Australia, Canberra, ACT; National Gallery of Victoria, Melbourne, Vic.; Museum and Art Gallery of the Northern Territory, Darwin, NT; Powerhouse Museum, Sydney, NSW; Tamworth City Gallery, Tamworth, NSW; Victorian State Craft Collection, Melbourne, Vic.

Liz **Williamson**
Flower 2 (from Repair series)
Jacquard-woven cotton and linen

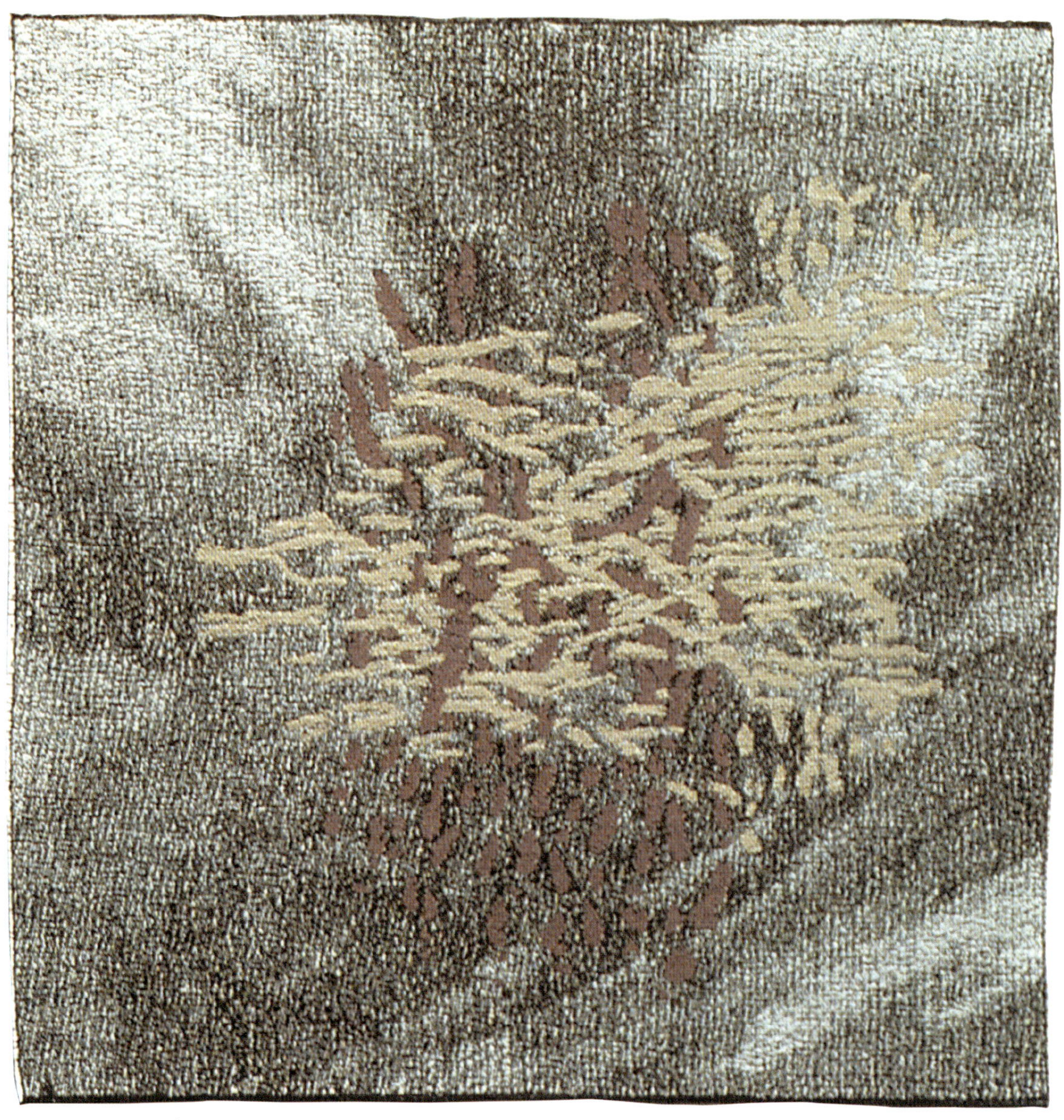

Liz **Williamson**

Liz Williamson's intensely coloured and textured woven textiles – shawls, scarves and wraps – envelop and transform the wearer, allowing intimate encounters with the fabric's lush tactility. Her recent works investigate the life of less elegant, but equally personal, domestic fabrics and the physical effects of wear and tear – disintegration, fraying and fading – and the subsequent transformation of these materials through repairs such as patching and darning. This work is part of a series of textiles, handwoven on a computerised Jacquard loom from digitised, close-up images of such repairs.[1] As the individual stitches of darning build new texture and prolong the life of a fabric, their digital images form the building blocks of these new textiles. Through this process, the craft of necessity becomes an abstracted shadow of experience, celebrating continuity and change.

1 Williamson's Jacquard Project was undertaken during 1999–2001 at Le Centre des Textiles Contemporains de Montréal in Montreal, Canada, with assistance from the Commonwealth Government through the Australia Council, its arts funding and advisory body, and the University of New South Wales.

Checklist of works

Measurements are in order of height, width and depth. All works are in the collection of the National Gallery of Australia, unless noted otherwise. Photography of works by the National Gallery of Australia unless noted otherwise. Page numbers in parentheses following artists' names refer to catalogue illustrations.

Robert **Baines** (p. 11)
born Melbourne, Australia 1949
La Columbella tea and coffee set
1992–1994 Melbourne, Victoria
6-piece tea and coffee service, comprising teapot, coffeepot, hot water jug, milk jug, sugar bowl and tray.
titanium and sterling silver
23.0 x 45.0 x 45.0 cm
Acquired 2001   2001.132.1–6

Frank **Bauer** (pp. 12,13)
born Hannover, Germany 1942,
arrived Australia 1971
Light sculpture 2001
Adelaide, South Australia
wall/suspension lighting units
aluminium: perforated and anodised;
21 x 12-volt Xenon lamps
135.0 x 185.0 x 20.0 cm
Acquired 2002   2002.3

Les **Blakebrough** (pp. 60,61)
born Kingston, Surrey, Great Britain 1930,
arrived Australia 1948
Forest Floor 2000
Hobart, Tasmania
carved 'Southern Ice' porcelain
26.1 x 26.7 x 26.7 cm
Acquired 2001   2001.142
Southern Ice bowl 2000
Hobart, Tasmania
'Southern Ice' porcelain with metal salts decoration
14.0 x 42.0 x 42.0 cm
Acquired 2001   2001.143

Matthew **Curtis** (pp. 14,15)
born Luton, Great Britain 1964,
arrived Australia 1981
Constructed bowl (Ruby) 2001
Sydney, New South Wales
glass: blown and constructed, with stainless steel rim
32.0 x 48.0 x 48.0 cm
Acquired 2001   2001.44

Janet **DeBoos** (pp. 34,35)
born Melbourne, Victoria 1948
Large vase 2001
Wee Jasper, New South Wales
glazed porcelain
29.0 x 30.0 x 30.0 cm
Acquired 2001   2001.196.A–O

Pippin **Drysdale** (pp. 62,63)
born Melbourne, Victoria 1943
Koh-E-Nida 2000
Fremantle, Western Australia
glazed porcelain
48.5 x 23.5 x 23.5 cm
Acquired 2001   2001.189

Anne **Dybka** (pp. 36,37)
born Portsmouth, Great Britain 1921,
arrived Australia 1956
The shoal 2001 Sydney, New South Wales
cased glass: engraved
29.0 x 18.0 x 18.0 cm
Acquired 2001   2001.191

Mark **Edgoose** (pp. 16,17)
born Warragul, Victoria 1960
Circle 2001
Sydney, New South Wales
titanium, aluminium and nylon brush
9.5 x 62.0 x 62.0 cm
Acquired 2002   2002.5
Photographer: Peter Clarke

Viliama **Grakalic** (pp. 8,18,19)
born Zagreb, Yugoslavia 1942,
arrived Australia 1963
Noughts and crosses 2000
Melbourne, Victoria
925 silver, bone, mother-of-pearl, 18 carat gold, magnet and epoxy
50.0 x 32.0 x 0.4 cm
Acquired 2002   2002.6

Tony **Hanning** (pp. 38,39)
born Traralgon, Victoria 1950
Mr and Mrs Anon 2000
Yinnar, Victoria
glass: sandblasted and engraved
22.0 x 24.5 x 24.5 cm
Acquired 2001   2001.50

Brian **Hirst** (pp. 32,40,41)
born Yallourn, Victoria 1956
Flat form – Teal 2001 2001
Sydney, New South Wales
glass: blown, with gold, silver and copper foil
52.0 x 39.0 x 12.0 cm

Marian **Hosking** (pp. 64,65)
born Melbourne, Victoria 1948
Vessel with four brooches: Leptospermum, Casaurina, Banksia, Angophora 2001
Melbourne, Victoria
sterling silver, pierced and cast; stainless steel bead rivets
33.5 x 8.0 x 5.0; 7.0 x 7.0 x 1.0;
8.5 x 5.5 x 1.5; 7.0 x 7.0 x 1.0;
6.5 x 7.7 x 1.0 cm
Acquired 2002   2002.7.1–5

Johannes **Kuhnen** (p. 21)
born Essen, Germany 1952,
arrived Australia 1981
Centrepiece/Tray 1998
Michelago, New South Wales
anodised aluminium, silver and monel
5.0 x 32.0 x 48.5 cm
Acquired 2002   2002.8
Photographer: Johannes Kuhnen

Helge **Larsen** (pp. 66,67)
born Copenhagen, Denmark 1929,
arrived Australia 1961
Darani **Lewers**
born Sydney, New South Wales 1936
Traces neck ring 2000
Sydney, New South Wales
sterling silver, stone, iron and glazed ceramic shard
10.9 x 17.0 cm
Acquired 2001   2001.148
La Macarena brooch 2000
Sydney, New South Wales
sterling silver, wood and lapis lazuli

6.5 x 5.5 cm
Acquired 2001   2001.149
Bermagui Series ring 2000
Sydney, New South Wales
sterling silver, bone and pebble
4.0 x 5.0 cm
Acquired 2001   2001.150

Kay **Lawrence** (pp. 4,42,43)
born Canberra, ACT 1947
Translation 1999–2000
Uraidla, South Australia
woven tapestry: wool, cotton and linen
45.0 x 312.0 cm
Acquired 2001   2001.192

Sue **Lorraine** (pp. 22,23)
born Melbourne, Victoria 1955
Continuous model 2001
Adelaide, South Australia
mild steel sheet and tube, heat-coloured
47.0 x 13.0 x 3.0 cm
Acquired 2002   2002.9
Bronchial model 2001
Adelaide, South Australia
mild steel sheet and tube, heat-coloured
56.5 x 17.0 x 5.0 cm
Acquired 2002   2002.10
Elongated model 2001
Adelaide, South Australia
mild steel sheet and tube, heat-coloured
67.5 x 10.5 x 1.5 cm
Acquired 2002   2002.11

Jessica **Loughlin** (pp. 44,45)
born Melbourne, Victoria 1975
Interval between two horizons 1999
glass: kiln-formed, wheel-cut, enamelled and engraved.
5.5 x 85.0 x 17.0 cm
Acquired 2001   2001.194
Photographer: Andrew Dunbar

Helmut **Lueckenhausen** (p. 47)
born Cologne, Germany 1950,
arrived Australia 1954
Wunderkabinet pair (Wunderkabinets 2 & 3) 1999 Melbourne, Victoria
silky oak, silky oak veneer, silver ash, silver ash veneer, glass and sterling silver keys.
125 x 53.0 x 119.0 cm each
Acquired 2002   2002.2.1–2

Jeff **Mincham** (pp. 50,51)
born Milang, South Australia 1950
Highland journey 2000
Cherryville, South Australia
earthenware with patinated copper-matt
and alkaline glaze
36.0 x 53.0 x 13.5 cm
Acquired 2001   2001.190

Klaus **Moje** (cover, p. 25)
born Hamburg, Germany 1936,
arrived Australia 1982
Fragments 1–2001 2001
Canberra, Australian Capital Territory
glass: fused and ground mosaic glass
7.5 x 53.2 cm
Acquired 2002   2002.12
Photographer: Klaus Moje

Milton **Moon** (pp. 50,51)
born Melbourne, Victoria 1926
Yandicoogina platter 1998
Adelaide, South Australia
glazed stoneware
7.0 x 62.0 x 59.0 cm
Acquired 2000   2000.217
Bimba floor pot from *Olary Uplands series*
1997   Adelaide, South Australia
glazed stoneware
63.4 x 45.0 x 45.0 cm
Acquired 2000   2000.216

Nick **Mount** (pp. 52,53)
born Adelaide, South Australia 1952
Scent bottle 2001
Adelaide, South Australia
glass: blown double-overlay, fabricated,
ground and polished
127.0 x 30.0 x 30.0 cm
Acquired 2001   2001.193

Kevin **Perkins** (p. 55)
born Launceston, Tasmania 1945
Cape Barren Goose cabinet 1995
Franklin, Tasmania
Huon pine, crossfire and birdseye
Huon pine veneers, satin sycamore,
Ceylon ebony, purpleheart, bevelled glass
and silver
224.0 x 140.0 x 90.0 cm
Acquired 2001   2001.182

Mitsuo **Shoji** (pp. 68,69)
born Osaka, Japan 1946,
arrived Australia 1973
Gaman I – Tattoo 2000
Sydney, New South Wales
stoneware with gold and silver leaf foil
and coloured inlays
85.0 x 40.0 x 40.0 cm
Acquired 2000   2000.594

S!X (pp. 56,57)
established Melbourne, Victoria 1994 by:
Denise **Sprynskyj**
born Melbourne, Victoria 1960
Peter **Boyd**
born Melbourne, Victoria 1971
*Percy Grainger jacket 'Remixed Movement
No 6'* 1999 Melbourne, Victoria
wool, silk, cotton, paper, Mylar and
heat-transfer print
79.0 x 50.0 cm (variable)
Acquired 2001 with funds from the
Australian Costume and Textile Society
2001.151
*Outfit: Upside down trouser skirt, Victorian
women shirt, Denim corset and Denim
handbag/backpack* 1996
Melbourne, Victoria
skirt: wool, viscose and cotton; shirt:
cotton, polyester, plastic and paper;
corset: cotton, wool, plastic and paper;
handbag: cotton, plastic and metal chain
134.0 x 103.0 cm (variable)
Acquired 2001 with funds from the
Australian Costume and Textile Society
2001.153.A–D

Catherine **Truman** (p. 27)
born Glenelg, South Australia 1957
Interior under scrutiny no 13 2001
Adelaide, South Australia
carved English lime wood and shu-niku ink
6.0 x 3.5 cm
Acquired 2002   2002.15
Interior under scrutiny no 12 2001
Adelaide, South Australia
carved English lime wood and paint
7.0 x 7.0 x 5.0 cm
Acquired 2002   2002.13

Interior under scrutiny no 2 2001
Adelaide, South Australia
carved English lime wood and paint
70.0 x 5.0 x 5.0 cm
Acquired 2002   2002.14

Jenny **Turner** (pp. 28,29)
born Wollongong, New South Wales 1939
Shawl 2000
Hobart, Tasmania
woven superfine wool and silk
213.0 x 78.0 cm
Acquired 2001   2001.145
Shawl 2000
woven superfine wool and silk
213.0 x 78.0 cm
Acquired 2001   2001.146

Alan **Watt** (pp. 70,71)
born Melbourne, Victoria 1941
Speckled pinnacle 2001
Tanja, New South Wales
blackfired earthenware with terra sigillata
103.0 x 22.0 x 13.0 cm
Acquired 2001   2001.195

Margaret **West** (pp. 58,72,73)
born Melbourne, Victoria 1936
Double damask 2001
Blackheath, New South Wales
506 phosphor bronze mesh units
and paint, stapled to wall
332.0 x 385.0 x 1.0 cm
Acquired 2002   2002.16
Photographer: Sue Blackburn
Margaret West's project has been assisted
by the Commonwealth Government
through the Australia Council, its arts
funding and advisory body.

Richard **Whiteley** (pp. 30,31)
born Great Britain 1963,
arrived Australia 1963
Event horizon 2000
Sydney, New South Wales
glass (45% lead crystal): cast, and polished
75.0 x 62.0 x 11.0 cm
Acquired 2001   2001.47

Maureen **Williams** (pp. 74,75)
born Port Pirie, South Australia 1952
Clouded interaction 2000
Melbourne, Victoria
glass: blown and painted
53.8 x 37.0 x 37.0 cm
Acquired 2000   2000.2

Liz **Williamson** (p. 77)
born Sydney, New South Wales 1949
Repair series: 2001
Sydney, New South Wales
Singlet 1
Jacquard-woven cotton and wool
51.0 x 53.5 cm
Pink repair
Jacquard-woven cotton and linen
52.0 x 71.0 cm
Jacquard-woven cotton and linen
52.0 x 99.0 cm
Flower 2
Jacquard-woven cotton and linen
52.0 x 52.0 cm
Acquired 2002   2002.17.1–4
Darned series:
Sydney, New South Wales
Brown
Jacquard-woven cotton and linen
51.0 x 56.0 cm
Towel
Jacquard-woven cotton and linen
51.0 x 56.0 cm
Singlet 2
Jacquard-woven cotton and wool
51.5 x 54.0 cm
Damask
Jacquard-woven cotton and linen brocade
49.0 x 56.0 cm
Collection of the artist
Liz Williamson's Jacquard project has been
assisted by the Commonwealth
Government through the Australia
Council, its arts funding and advisory body,
and the University of New South Wales.

Select bibliography

Anderson, Patricia, *Contemporary Jewellery: The Australian experience 1977–1987*, Sydney: Millennium, 1988.

Anderson, Patricia, *Contemporary Jewellery in Australia and New Zealand*, Singapore: Craftsman House, 1998.

At the Edge: Australische glaskunst, Australian glass art, Brisbane: Brisbane City Council, 2000.

Bell, Eugenie Keefer, *The Japan Inspiration: Influence in crafts and design*, Perth: Art Gallery of Western Australia, 1997.

Bell, Robert, *Design Visions: Australian International Crafts Triennial*, Perth: Art Gallery of Western Australia, 1992.

Bell, Robert, *Perth International Crafts Triennial*, Perth: Art Gallery of Western Australia, 1989.

Bell, Robert, Stenros, Anne and Hida, Toyojiro, *Nature As Object: Craft and design from Japan, Finland and Australia: The Third Australian International Crafts Triennial*, Perth: Art Gallery of Western Australia, 1998.

Bogle, Michael and Landman, Peta, *Modern Australian Furniture: Profiles of contemporary designer-makers*, Singapore: Craftsman House, 1989.

Cochrane, Grace *The Crafts Movement in Australia: A history*, Sydney: New South Wales University Press, 1992.

Contemporary Australian Craft, Sapporo: Hokkaido Museum of Modern Art with the Powerhouse Museum, The Yomiuri Shimbun and the Japanese Association of Art Museums, 1999.

Crocker, Robert (ed.), *Designing Minds – Contemporary issues in craft, design and industry (Proceedings of the Designing Minds Symposium)*, Adelaide: University of South Australia, 2000.

DeBoos, Janet, *Handbook for Australian Potters*, Melbourne: Methuen LBC, 1999.

Edwards, Geoffrey, *Art of Glass: Glass in the collection of the National Gallery of Victoria*, Melbourne: National Gallery of Victoria, 1998.

Edwards, Geoffrey, *Klaus Moje Glass: A retrospective exhibition*, Melbourne: National Gallery of Victoria, 1995.

Ewington, Julie, *Interstices: Works by Margaret West 1981–1992*, Canberra: Canberra School of Art, 1992.

Fitzpatrick, Kirsten, *Against the Grain: Australian sculptural furniture*, Brisbane: Brisbane City Council, 2000.

Frank Bauer, Adelaide: Frank Bauer, 2000.

Gray Street Workshop – Celebrating 15 years: An anthology, Sydney: Object, Australian Centre for Craft and Design, with Gray Street Workshop, 2000.

Holmes, Jonathan, *Les Blakebrough – Potter*, Sydney: Bay Books, 1988.

Ioannou, Noris, *Australian Studio Glass: The movement, its makers and their art*, Sydney: Craftsman House, 1995.

Ioannou, Noris, *Masters of Their Craft: Tradition and innovation in the Australian contemporary decorative arts*, Singapore: Craftsman House, 1997.

Ioannou, Noris, *The Culture Brokers: Towards a redefinition of Australian contemporary craft*, Adelaide: State Publishing, South Australia, 1989.

King, Glenda, *Art of Adornment – Australian contemporary jewellery*, Launceston: Queen Victoria Museum and Art Gallery, 1993.

King, Glenda, *Origins and New Perspectives – Contemporary Australian textiles*, Launceston: Queen Victoria Museum and Art Gallery, 1998.

Lane, Terence, *Cicely and Colin Rigg Craft Award 1997* Melbourne: National Gallery of Victoria, 1997.

Mansfield, Janet, *Contemporary Ceramic Art in Australia and New Zealand*, Singapore: Craftsman House, 1995.

McCracken, Gillian, *Frisson:14th Tamworth Textile Biennial*, Tamworth: Tamworth City Gallery, 2000.

McDonald, John et al., *Federation: Australian art and society 1901–2001*, Canberra: National Gallery of Australia, 2000.

McPhee, John, *Australian Decorative Arts in the Australian National Gallery*, Canberra: Australian National Gallery, 1982.

Menz, Christopher, *Australian Decorative Arts 1820s–1990s: Art Gallery of South Australia*, Adelaide: Art Gallery Board of South Australia, 1996.

Menz, Christopher, *Milton Moon Retrospective*, Adelaide: Art Gallery Board of South Australia, 1991.

O'Callaghan, Judith, *Helge Larsen & Darani Lewers – A retrospective*, Melbourne, National Gallery of Victoria, 1986.

Osborne, Margot (ed.) et al., *The Return of Beauty*, Adelaide: JamFactory Contemporary Craft and Design, 2000.

Pascoe, Joe (ed.), *Delinquent Angel: Australian historical, Aboriginal and contemporary ceramics*, Florence: Centro Di, 1995.

Rowley, Sue, *Craft and Contemporary Theory*, Sydney: Allen & Unwin, 1997.

Rowley, Sue and Leitch, C., *Crossing Borders: Contemporary Australian textile art*, Wollongong: The University of Wollongong, 1995.

Rowley, Sue, *The Somatic Object*, Sydney: The University of New South Wales College of Fine Arts, 1997.

Runde, Sabine; Soltek, Stefan and Menz, Christopher, *Craft from Scratch: 8. Triennale – Form and Matters – Australia and Germany*, Frankfurt am Main: Dezernates für Kultur and Freizeit vom Museum für Angewandte Kunst Frankfurt , 2000.

The Art of the Object: Contemporary craft from Australia, Sydney: Craft Australia, 1994.

The Glass World of Klaus Moje, Hsin Chu, South Korea: Hsin Chu Municipal Glass Museum, 2001.

Were, Ian; Bearman, Nicole and Champion, Paul (eds), *Designing Minds*, Sydney: Object – Australian Centre for Craft and Design, 2000.

1995 VicHealth National Craft Award, Melbourne: Craft Victoria, 1995